KANT: A GUIDE FOR THE PERPLEXED

KANT: A GUIDE FOR THE PERPLEXED

T. K. SEUNG

continuum

CONTINUUM
Continuum International Publishing Group
The Tower Building   80 Maiden Lane
11 York Road   Suite 704
London SE1 7NX   New York NY 10038

www.continuumbooks.com

First published 2007
Reprinted 2008, 2009

British Library Cataloguing-in-Publication Data
A catalogue record for this book is available from the British Library.

ISBN-10: HB: 0-8264-8579-0
          PB: 0-8264-8580-4
ISBN-13: HB: 978-0-8264-8579-3
          PB: 978-0-8264-8580-9

Library of Congress Cataloging-in-Publication Data
A catalog record for this book is available from the Library of Congress.

Typeset by Acorn Bookwork Ltd, Salisbury, Wiltshire
Printed in Great Britain by the MPG Books Group,
Bodmin and King's Lynn

CONTENTS

PREFACE

There are few philosophical texts so confusing and so perplexing as Kant's works. Their complexity may seem to display the grandeur of his vaunted architectonic. But his prose contains an endless series of opaque expositions and oracular repetitions. Hence it is the most common fate of his readers to get lost in his texts well before they can get perplexed with his ideas. I have designed this volume to help those readers find their way and sort out his tangled arguments. In this endeavour, I follow one common thread that runs through his entire philosophy, namely, the relation between the a priori and the a posteriori elements of human experience. The a posteriori elements are empirical; we share them with other animals. The a priori elements are the special endowment for human beings. In Kant's view, we can elevate our existence beyond the brute animal condition by transforming the a posteriori elements into rational experience through the a priori elements. He calls those a priori elements the transcendental conditions because they enable us to transcend the empirical condition. Hence his philosophy is called transcendental philosophy, and the common thread running through all his works is the transcendental thread for weaving his philosophical works. So I invite my readers to follow this winding and twisting thread and unravel his textual tangles.

Kant divides his philosophy into two domains, theoretical and practical. His theoretical philosophy is his theory of knowledge and science; his practical philosophy is his theory of ethics and politics. The first chapter of this book is a study of his theoretical philosophy, whose principal text is the *Critique of Pure Reason*, usually known as the first *Critique*. The second chapter is a study of his practical philosophy, which is presented in four major texts: the *Groundwork for the Metaphysics of Morals*, the *Metaphysics of Morals, Religion within the Boundaries of Mere Reason,* and the *Critique of Practical Reason*. The last of these four is usually known as the second *Critique*. These two chapters are followed by the third and last chapter, which is an inquiry into his theory of aesthetics and teleology. Kant could not assign either of these two topics to the two domains of theory and practice. So he wrote the *Critique of Judgement* after the first two *Critiques*. But the third *Critique* is really two critiques in one. It contains the Critique of Aesthetic Judgement and the Critique of Teleological Judgement. The latter is close to theoretical philosophy because it is concerned with the problem of biological sciences. The former is close to practical philosophy because it involves the problem of normative standards. But Kant bundles them together under the label of reflective judgement and consigns them to the third domain of his philosophy, which lies beyond the two domains of theory and practice. I will briefly sketch the content of these three chapters in this book.

In the first *Critique*, Kant deploys the a priori/a posteriori relation as the form/matter duality for the reconciliation between continental rationalism and British empiricism. On the empirical level, Kant endorses Hume's phenomenalism: Empirical intuitions are totally subjective and every empirical subject is trapped in a world of subjective impressions. He holds that these subjective impressions can be converted into an objective perceptual world only by a priori concepts and intuitions. This is their transcendental function, and his explanation of these functions is his transcendental account. It consists of three steps. The first step is to prove the existence of a priori elements. This is the proof of their genetic apriority, that is, they are prior in their origin to empirical elements. The second step is not a proof, but an assumption. Kant assumes that their genetic apriority guarantees their epistemic apriority, that is, they are known to be necessarily true. This assumption is based on his belief that knowledge of necessary truths can be derived only from a priori sources because empirical intuitions are always contingent. The third step is another assumption. He now assumes that only their epistemic apriority and necessity can provide the objective framework for converting subjective empirical intuitions into objective entities. He reduces objectivity to epistemic apriority and necessity. In his transcendental philosophy, objectivity cannot be admitted as a primitive property of objects because all objects are subject-dependent. Nothing can be objective unless it is necessary (epistemic apriority), and nothing can be necessary unless it is a priori (genetic apriority). In Kant's transcendental account, objectivity is grounded in epistemic apriority, which is in turn grounded in genetic apriority. Hence the ultimate foundation of his transcendental argument is the genetic apriority of pure intuitions and the categories.

The first two of these three steps take place in the Metaphysical Deduction and the last step in the Transcendental Deduction. In §26 of the B Deduction, Kant says, 'In the *metaphysical deduction* the a priori origin of the categories has been proved through their complete agreement with the general logical functions of thought; in the *transcendental deduction* we have shown their possibility as a priori modes of knowledge of objects of intuition in general' (B159, tr. Kemp Smith). This long sentence describes the logical relation between the two Deductions. The Metaphysical Deduction is supposed to have proved the genetic apriority of categories (their a priori origin) by their logical derivation. This is the first step of Kant's transcendental account. The Transcendental Deduction is supposed to have demonstrated the 'a priori modes of knowledge of objects of intuition in general'. This is the proof for the objective knowledge of empirical intuitions because 'the a priori modes of knowledge' means objective knowledge and because 'objects of intuition in general' means all intuitions including empirical intuitions. This proof is the third step of his transcendental account. The second step is missing, but it is Kant's a priori assumption that the genetic apriority of categories establishes their epistemic apriority. Therefore, the second step is the logical consequence of the first step and serves as the premise for the Transcendental Deduction. Thus I have linked together the Metaphysical Deduction and the Transcendental Deduction against the prevailing convention of treating them as separate and independent.

It is often complained that the Transcendental Deduction does not prove the causal principle. This complaint arises from the misunderstanding of Kant's procedure. The epistemic apriority (necessary truth) of all categories is not meant to be proven in the

Transcendental Deduction. The categories and their epistemic necessity are not Kant's explanandum, but his explanans in the Transcendental Deduction. They are presupposed as the premise for his transcendental argument, and this premise has been prepared by the Metaphysical Deduction, which has supposedly proven the genetic apriority of the categories, which in turn guarantees their epistemic apriority and necessity. Hence the Metaphysical Deduction is meant to be the logical basis for the Transcendental Deduction. But this logical relation of the two Deductions has never been clearly recognized in Kant scholarship. The Metaphysical Deduction has largely been dismissed because it is based on a series of flimsy arguments. But the Transcendental Argument has been taken seriously as an independent argument. It has been assumed that the genetic apriority of categories can be readily proven by showing that they cannot be traced back to empirical intuitions. But this simple empirical test is only a negative proof that cannot fully guarantee their genetic apriority. Even if they cannot be derived from impressions, they need not be a priori because they can be the products of construction. This is why Kant tried to provide the positive proof for the genetic apriority of categories by his logical derivation although he was fully aware of the negative proof. So I stress the logical link of the Metaphysical Deduction to the Transcendental Deduction.

In chapter 1 of this book, I subject the three steps of Kant's transcendental account to a rigorous scrutiny and expose their weakness. But I do not stop there. I try to see it as the central vehicle for his Copernican revolution in philosophy. Just as Copernicus shifted the centre of the world from the earth to the sun, Kant relocates the centre of cognition from the object to the subject. His new model requires the conformity of objects to concepts, whereas the old model required the conformity of concepts to objects. In the old model, the concepts were applied to the independently existing objects. But the new model does not recognize the independent existence of objects. They are constructed by the synthetic function of categories. This is Kant's constructivism. His new model is the construction model; his old model was the application model. His constructivism should be concluded by the end of the Analytic of Concepts. But he continues his exposition in the Analytic of Principles by raising the new question of how to apply the categories to empirical intuitions. This problem of categorial application cannot arise in the construction model. It is carried over from the *Inaugural Dissertation*, whose central problem was the application of categories. It predates Kant's Copernican revolution, which has produced the construction model. The Transcendental Deduction should be sufficient for Transcendental Analytic; there is no point in reinstating the application model. But old habits die hard. Instead of jettisoning the application model, Kant tries to retain and assimilate it into the construction model. In some passages, he talks as though the application of categories were inseparably connected with their synthetic function. He is trying to fuse the two models into one, thereby producing a systematic confusion in the Transcendental Analytic. This is my thesis of two models for the composition and complication of the first *Critique*.

Kant's central problem in practical philosophy is how to find normative standards. In the Transcendental Dialectic of the first *Critique*, he settles on Platonic Ideas as the universal normative principles and describes them as the archetypes that transcend the world of senses. They are the ideals of perfection that can never be fully realized in the world of phenomena. They fulfil a much higher need than the categories, so argues Kant. The latter is for knowing the world of appearances; the former is for the practical task of governing our life. He names two Platonic Ideas: the Idea of Virtue and the Idea of Republic. The former is the ideal of a perfect individual; the latter is the ideal of a perfect community. He stresses that these ideals of pure reason can never be derived from experience. While the rationalists illegitimately extend their speculation beyond the domain of sensibility, he says, the empiricists are guilty of dogmatically denying supersensible normative Ideas. But those Ideas provide the ultimate principles of morality, legislation, and religion. Hence the transcendent Ideas are the necessary conditions for the possibility of practical life, just as the categories of the understanding are the necessary conditions for the possibility of experience in the phenomenal world. The necessary conditions are the transcendental conditions, and Kant identifies them as the transcendent Ideas for his practical philosophy. Thus he has given two transcendental arguments for two sets of transcendental conditions: one for the categories and the other for the transcendent Ideas. He then explains in the Canon of Pure Reason of the first *Critique* how these Ideas can provide the foundation for all moral laws. This is his espousal of ethical Platonism.

In the *Groundwork for the Metaphysics of Morals*, Kant abandons his ethical Platonism and seeks a new foundation for his moral theory in the radical concept of rational autonomy: Practical reason prescribes moral laws without depending on any external authority. This has been called his Copernican revolution in ethics. When the will is determined by its object, it becomes heteronomous. But it is autonomous when it determines its own object. Kant's ethical Platonism followed the pre-Copernican tradition of seeking the conformity of moral laws to objects, namely, Platonic Ideas. In his new Copernican model of ethics, practical reason prescribes moral laws on its own authority just as the understanding prescribes a priori laws to nature. Just as the a priori laws of nature are dictated by the forms of understanding, so the moral laws are dictated by the form of practical reason, the principle of logical consistency. This formal principle can satisfy the requirement for his radical concept of rational autonomy because pure practical reason relies only on its own form and nothing else. There are two types of rational principle: substantive and formal. Platonic Ideas are the normative principles of substantive rationality. But practical reason can operate on its own principle of formal rationality when it frees itself from the constraint of transcendent Ideas and makes moral laws through its own pure form without any substantive content. This is his ethical formalism to replace his ethical Platonism.

In the *Groundwork*, Kant states the formal rational principle as the first formula of the categorical imperative and uses it as the universal principle for generating and selecting moral maxims. Its only criterion is claimed to be the formal requirement of logical consistency. But this minimal criterion cannot discriminate moral from immoral maxims because no maxim can harbour an outright contradiction. So Kant stretches and twists his formal criterion to cover all rational and prudential choices, thereby illicitly endowing his formal principle with substantive content. By this illicit traffic, he also transforms the categorical imperative to the hypothetical one and reduces rational autonomy to heteronomy. In the second formulation of the categorical imperative, he openly endorses the substantive principle of treating human beings as ends in themselves and never as mere means. But he abuses the concept of an end in itself. When he introduces this concept, he claims only human beings as objective ends. But he extends the concept to include their subjective ends such as desires and purposes. Since the subjective ends are empirically contingent, they can turn the categorical imperative into a hypothetical command if they are adopted as its end.

Incredibly, Kant tries to show that the substantive principle of the second formula yields the same results in the selection of moral maxims as the formal principle of the first formula. But that is impossible because the substantive principle lays down a far stiffer ethical requirement than the minimal formal principle. He then joins the two principles as the form and matter of moral law: The formal principle is its form and the substantive principle is its matter. In spite of their form/matter relation, he insists that they are two independent principles, each of which can operate without the other. But this goes against his own notion of form and matter: They can never be independent of each other because they are two complementary components of a single object. These anomalies and absurdities completely spoil the theoretical integrity of the categorical imperative. Kant tries to clean up this theoretical mess in the second *Critique* by jettisoning the categorical imperative and its multiple formulations.

In the second *Critique*, Kant does not even mention the categorical imperative. At most, he refers to the categorical command, which can be associated with any moral laws because all moral laws are categorical commands. He retains only the first formula of the categorical imperative and calls it the fundamental law of a supersensible nature, which he equates with the archetypal nature (*natura archetypa*). 'Archetypes' is his favourite icon for Platonic Ideas. When he explains the application of his fundamental law, he relies not on the formal criterion of self-consistency but on the substantive criterion of evaluating moral maxims in reference to the ideal natural order of archetypes (*natura archetypa*), which he emphatically distinguishes from the empirical natural order of ectypes (*natura ectypa*). Thus he transforms the formal principle into a substantive one and reinstates his ethical Platonism. The rational autonomy of ethical formalism is like a king without a kingdom because it is vacuous. Kant saves it from its vacuity by giving it the entire natural order of archetypes for its kingdom. But this manoeuvre has been executed so ingeniously and so surreptitiously that it has never been detected to the best of my knowledge. It was Kant's secret restoration of normative Platonism that nullified his open Copernican revolution in ethics. In chapter 2 of this book, I detail and discuss all the insurmountable problems that are unavoidable for his Copernican revolution in ethics. They may explain his eventual return to ethical Platonism. His ethical formalism was only a flicker of his fatally ill-conceived theory, which was categorically abandoned shortly after the *Groundwork*. But its magnification as the heart of his moral philosophy has totally blinded our eyes to the recurrent Platonic themes in his ethical writings.

In the aesthetic domain, Kant again has to cope with the problem of normative standards because he wants to maintain that aesthetic judgements are not subjective but objective. He has to give his transcendental account of their universality and necessity. It is doubly difficult to do this for aesthetic judgements because they are supposedly made by aesthetic feelings. He tries out two ways of doing it: aesthetic formalism and aesthetic Platonism. In the Analytic of the Beautiful, he presents his aesthetic formalism. This is the formalism of pure feeling. The pleasurable feeling of beauty is supposed to arise from the free interplay between the imagination and the understanding. But Kant stresses that the feeling itself is free of all concepts and forms. His aesthetic formalism is full of content but devoid of forms, whereas his ethical formalism was all forms without any content. In the Analytic of the Sublime, he abandons aesthetic formalism and begins to espouse aesthetic Platonism, which becomes full-blown in his theory of fine arts. He redefines beauty in terms of aesthetic Ideas, which are described as the sensible renditions of invisible rational Ideas. He stresses their indispensability for the production and appreciation of beauty.

There is a tension between aesthetic formalism and Platonism, which is analogous to the tension between ethical formalism and Platonism. Ethical formalism is absolutely autonomous but totally vacuous, whereas ethical Platonism is constrained by Platonic Ideas. Aesthetic formalism gives absolute freedom to aesthetic feeling. Hence its judgements can go wild because there is no way to constrain them. Kant says that aesthetic feeling must be not only free, but also lawful. He eventually secures its lawfulness by accepting the constraint of Platonic Ideas for aesthetic judgements. Thus he accepts Platonic Ideas as the transcendental condition for aesthetic judgements as firmly as for ethical judgements. But his aesthetic Platonism has never been recognized any better than his ethical Platonism. His extended discussion of aesthetic Ideas is usually treated as a strange digression from his aesthetic formalism, but I take it as his appropriation of aesthetic Platonism. I propose that aesthetic Ideas are constructed by articulating the Platonic Idea of Beauty for the phenomenal world. But it has been taken for granted that aesthetic formalism prevails over Kant's entire aesthetic theory. When the commentators face the aesthetic antinomy at the end of the Critique of Aesthetic Judgement, they automatically read it within the framework of aesthetic formalism. But the antinomy cannot even be stated in the language of aesthetic formalism. Both its thesis ('A judgement of taste is not based on concepts') and its antithesis ('A judgement of taste is based on concepts') involve concepts, which are completely exorcised from aesthetic formalism. The aesthetic antinomy can be stated only in the language of aesthetic Platonism. Kant resolves the antinomy by using indeterminate concepts, which cannot be found in the language of aesthetic formalism, either. But they are readily available in aesthetic Platonism; they are none other than aesthetic Ideas. In chapter 3 of this book, I fully discuss why and how Kant has replaced his aesthetic formalism with his aesthetic Platonism.

Aesthetic Ideas are not transcendent, but immanent because they belong to the aesthetic imagination and sensibility. They are created by articulating the transcendent Idea of Beauty for the phenomenal world. Seven years after the third *Critique*, Kant extends the construction of immanent Ideas to the ethical domain in the *Metaphysics of Morals*, where he parades a battery of immanent ethical Ideas ranging from the Idea of social contract and the Idea of a republican constitution to the Ideas of natural and moral perfection. Those immanent Ideas are created by articulating the transcendent Ideas of Justice and Virtue for the phenomenal world. Kant deploys the immanent Ideas of Justice in Part I of the *Metaphysics of Morals* (Theory of Justice) and the immanent Ideas of Virtue in its Part II (Theory of Virtue). Hence his ethical Platonism in this work is different from his old ethical Platonism. The latter was based on the transcendent Ideas, which he called the archetypes. In the *Groundwork*, he complained against the indeterminacy of transcendent Ideas. He overcomes their indeterminacy by constructing immanent Ideas that are more determinate than the transcendent Ideas. This is the descent of Platonic Ideas to the phenomenal world for their realization. These immanent Ideas became the fountainhead for the German Idealism of Hegel and Schelling. Even John Rawls's theory of justice was inspired by Kant's immanent Ideas of social contract and the republican constitution as articulated in the *Metaphysics of Morals*. His ethical Platonism has been a fruitful and influential legacy. But the three versions (epistemic, ethical, and aesthetic) of his formalist programme, which was launched under the banner of his Copernican revolution in philosophy, have borne no fruitful results. This is my careful appraisal of Kant's lifelong struggle and his eventual achievement.

I have reached this overall appraisal by working out a systematic interconnection of the three *Critiques*. Although those three volumes belong to Kant's overarching architectonic, their connection is so elusive that most scholars have studied them in isolation. The field of Kant scholarship has thus become like a strange castle divided into three tightly segregated fortresses, each of which wants to conduct its business without knowing what is happening in the other two. I have tried to see the interconnection of the three *Critiques* by following the transcendental thread I proposed for our guide at the beginning of this preface. But this thread is not a simple string; it is woven of two uneven strands. One of them is a formalist strand; the other is a substantive one. The formalist strand is Kant's formalism that pervades his three *Critiques*, but his formalism is not uniform. In the first *Critique*, it is composed of the forms of intuition (space and time) and the forms of understanding (the categories). Since these forms have substantive content, the formalism of the first *Critique* can be given the paradoxical label of substantive formalism. The formalism of the categorical imperative is truly formal; it is governed by the logical principle of formal consistency. It can be called the logical formalism in distinction from the substantive formalism. The formalism of the third *Critique* is different again from these two versions. It is the formalism of aesthetic feelings that stands neither on pure concepts nor on a logical principle. Hence it can be called emotive formalism, which sounds like a contradiction in terms because feelings are generally assumed to be the content of

experience rather than its form. Although these three versions of
Kantian formalism share a common label, they provide altogether
different forms of organizing human experience. Hence their difference has been the chief obstacle to unraveling the formalist connection of the three *Critiques*.

The historical origin of Kant's formalism is the principle of
formal rationality that he has inherited from Leibniz and Hume.
For Leibniz, this principle is the principle of identity; for Hume, it
is the principle governing the relation of ideas. In both cases, it is
an analytical principle that cannot handle synthetic judgements. It
governs the logical forms that have no substantive content.
Deeply dissatisfied with this traditional concept of empty formal
rationality, Kant tries to enrich his formalism with substantive
content and empower it with synthetic functions. This radical
novelty of his formalism is his transcendental magic. It may be
called his doctrine of transubstantivation because its operation is
as magical as the medieval doctrine of transubstantiation. In the
first *Critique*, Kant claims that the formal categories are transformed into the substantive ones. In the *Groundwork*, he claims to
generate substantive moral laws by using only the formal principle
of self-consistency. In the third *Critique*, he claims to transmute
the subjective feeling of pleasure into the formal mechanism of
aesthetic judgement. In all of these ventures, I will show, Kant's
program of transubstantivation turns out to be abortive because it
is a logically impossible operation. But he does not always rely on
the magic of transubstantivation; sometimes he directly appeals to
the principles of substantive rationality such as Platonic Ideas.
This constitutes the substantive strand of our transcendental
thread. But the Platonic connection of the three *Critiques* is even
more difficult to detect than their formalist connection because it
is largely hidden. It is played out like a deep base tune submerged
under the sonorous tune of formalism. In the last two *Critiques*,
Kant deploys Platonic Ideas without openly acknowledging them.
In the first *Critique*, he even tries to dispense with them on the
ground that they are unnecessary for the knowledge of phenomena. Hence the Platonic connection is neither overt nor inclusive
of all three *Critiques*. But even the first *Critique* is not totally left
out of the Platonic connection. Kant introduces Platonic Ideas
and then acknowledges them as the foundation of normative philosophy in the Transcendental Dialectic and the Canon of Pure

Reason. He deploys two versions of Platonism: immanent and transcendent. The immanent Ideas are constructed by articulating transcendent Platonic Ideas for the natural world. Hence his Platonism is not much simpler than his formalism.

Kant produced the different versions of formalism and Platonism because he never came to be fully satisfied with his own philosophical position. Like Procrustes, he kept revising his intellectual framework for his own satisfaction throughout his protracted career. He wrote the first *Critique* because he wanted to overhaul the philosophical edifice he had built in the *Inaugural Dissertation*. When he was writing the first *Critique* he had never intended it to be one member of a three-volume set. On the contrary, it had been designed as the only Critique of entire Pure Reason. He had to write two more *Critiques* because he made two more radical revisions of his philosophy. Thus the three *Critiques* stand as the milestones for marking the three successive philosophical revisions. Therefore, it is a grievous error to regard them as three segments of a single unified architecture, as is conventionally understood in Kant scholarship. These three pieces can never be joined together in a single edifice because they are structurally incompatible with each other. Their connection can be understood only thematically because they mark the thematic development of Kant's transcendental philosophy. In this book, I have tried to explore his transcendental thematics by following our transcendental thread. I will show that the thematic connection of three *Critiques* is not statically frozen, but develops dynamically. By grasping this dynamic development, I hope, my readers can gain a synoptic understanding of Kant's entire philosophy.

.

ABBREVIATIONS

(KANT'S WORKS AND TRANSLATIONS)

A and B   *A* for the first edition of *Critique of Pure Reason*, and *B* for the second edition. The numbers that follow these two letters refer to the page numbers of the Prussian Academy edition. Available translations: Paul Guyer and Allen Wood, Cambridge: Cambridge University Press, 1998; Werner Pluhar, Indianapolis: Hackett, 1996; Norman Kemp Smith, New York: St. Martin's Press, 1965.

C_2 *Critique of Practical Reason.* The numbers that follow this letter refer to the page numbers of the Prussian Academy edition. Available translations: Lewis White Beck, New York: Macmillan, 1956; Mary Gregor, Cambridge: Cambridge University Press, 1997.

C_3 *Critique of Judgement.* The numbers that follow this letter refer to the page numbers of the Prussian Academy edition. Available translations: Paul Guyer, Cambridge: Cambridge University Press, 2000; Werner Pluhar, Indianapolis: Hackett, 1987.

GMM   *Groundwork for the Metaphysics of Morals.* The numbers that follow these letters refer to the page numbers of the Prussian Academy edition. Available translations: James Ellington, Indianapolis: Hackett, 1981; Mary Gregor, Cambridge: Cambridge University Press, 1997.

KGS   *Kants gesammelte Schrifter* (Kant's Complete Writings). The Prussian Academy Edition. (Berlin: G. Reimer, 1902–).

MM   *The Metaphysics of Morals.* The numbers that follow these two letters refer to the page numbers of the Prussian Academy edition. Available translations: Mary Gregor, Cambridge: Cambridge University Press, 1996; James Ellington, *The Metaphysical Elements of Justice* (Part I of *MM*), Indianapolis: Hackett, 1999, and *The Metaphysical Principles of Virtue* (Part II of *MM*), Indianapolis: Bobbs-Merrill, 1965.

P   *Prolegomena to Any Future Metaphysics.* Available translations: James Ellington, Indianapolis: Hackett, 1977; Peter Lucas and Günter Zöller, Oxford: Oxford University Press, 2004.

R   *Religion within the Boundaries of Mere Reason.* The numbers that follow this letter refer to the page numbers of the Prussian Academy edition. Available translation: Allen Wood and George di Giovanni, Cambridge: Cambridge University Press, 1998.

THREE ESSAYS WITHOUT ABBREVIATIONS

Idea for a Universal History with a Cosmopolitan Intent. Included in Ted Humphrey, tr., *Perpetual Peace and Other Essays on Politics, History, and Morals.* Indianapolis: Hackett, 1983.

Perpetual Peace. Included in Ted Humphrey, tr., *Perpetual Peace and Other Essays on Politics, History, and Morals.*

The End of All Things. Included in Ted Humphrey, tr., *Perpetual Peace and Other Essays on Politics, History, and Morals.*

CHAPTER I

THEORETICAL REASON

(KNOWLEDGE, EXPERIENCE, AND SCIENCE)

Kant's technical terminology is the first obstacle for understanding his *Critique of Pure Reason*. So let us start by clarifying his basic terms and distinctions. Some of his basic terms do not even sound technical, for example, 'sensation' and 'experience', but they have technical meanings, which are quite different from their ordinary meanings. All his basic terms belong to the language of perception because the *Critique* is a grand theory of perception. The theories of perception can be divided into three classes: (1) direct realism, (2) representationalism, and (3) phenomenalism. Direct realism is the commonsense view that we directly perceive the physical objects whose existence is independent of our perception. This naïve belief was shattered by Cartesian doubt. According to Descartes, the perceived object is not a physical object but a collection of sensations. A physical object may lie hidden behind those sensations and even cause their production. But we have no direct access to physical objects as the common sense believes. This Cartesian view is called representationalism because the perceptual world is assumed to represent the physical world. If we have no access to physical objects, we have no empirical evidence for their existence. By 'empirical evidence' is meant evidence based on sensation. For this reason, David Hume rejects the existence of physical objects and their connection to perception. A perceived object is nothing more than a collection of sense impressions. They do not represent anything. This empiricist view of perception is called phenomenalism because sense impressions are phenomena. It is also called subjective idealism. This is derived from Bishop Berkeley's theory of ideas. He uses one word 'idea' to refer to all objects of immediate awareness – perceptions, memories, emotions, etc. He further holds that there is no distinction between physical objects and ideas because every physical object is no more than a collection of ideas. So his motto is *esse est percipi* (To be is to be perceived). Nothing can exist outside perception, and every perception is subjective. This subjective idealism is his phenomenalism. There are two serious problems with phenomenalism. First, everyone is trapped in a subjective world of impressions. Your world is different from mine; there is no common world shared by all. This is the problem of solipsism. Second, there are no enduring perceptual objects because every perception is subject to perpetual changes. All objects of your visual perception cease to exist as soon as you close your eyes, but they regain their existence as soon as you open your eyes again. There is nothing enduring; everything is intermittent. This is as counter-intuitive as solipsism.

Kant rejects phenomenalism as well as direct realism and accepts representationalism. He uses the word 'sensibility' as a collective label for all organs and functions of sensation. Sensibility contains two elements, a priori and a posteriori. The a priori elements are space and time. They belong not to the physical world, but to human sensibility. This is one of the radical novelties in his theory of perception. The a posteriori elements of sensibility are sensations. Space and time are called the forms of intuition because they provide the framework for receiving sensations. Space and time are also called pure intuitions in contrast to the empirical (impure) intuitions of sensation. The two terms 'pure' and 'a priori' are interchangeable with each other and opposed to 'a posteriori' and 'empirical'. The a priori elements are genetically *prior to* the a posteriori elements. When Kant uses 'a priori' in its genetic sense, it has the same meaning as the Cartesian term 'innate' in the innate ideas. The a priori elements have their seats in the subject, Kant holds, whereas the subject receives the empirical data from outside. The empirical elements are alien to the cognitive subject, whereas the a priori elements are innate. The empirical elements are also called appearances. The pure intuitions of space and time are the framework or the screen for presenting the appearances of the objects that exist independently of our sensibility. Those objects are called the things in themselves, which are supposed to exist beyond space and time. They are also called noumena, while their appearances are called phenomena. The world of phenomena is the sensible world; it is accessible to our sensibility. The world of noumena is the super-sensible world; it transcends our sensibility.

Our sensibility is not a transparent but an opaque screen for presenting the appearances of things in themselves. This opaque screen shows nothing at all about the nature of noumena. Hence human knowledge is limited to the world of phenomena or appearances. The noumenal world is inaccessible and unknowable. When an appearance becomes an object of our awareness, we have a sensation or experience. But the word 'experience' in Kant's lexicon is highly ambiguous. It can mean either a mere subjective sensation or an objective perception, which in turn means the objective knowledge of a perceptual object. But knowledge requires intellect in addition to sensibility. Intellect is the faculty of thought that employs concepts such as the concept of dog, a general idea or a universal one. We can use concepts for describing and understanding an object, for example, 'This is a dog' or 'This dog is black'. These propositions express what Kant calls judgements. In his lexicon, the two words 'judgement' and 'proposition' are interchangeable. He takes judgement as the basic unit of knowledge. The two elements of judgement are concepts and objects. A judgement (proposition) describes an object by using concepts. Intellect can provide concepts, but not objects. It is the function of sensibility to provide objects.

The direct awareness of an object is called intuition. But the word 'intuition' can mean either the act of direct awareness or the object of this awareness. The object of intuition can be designated by a demonstrative such as 'this', which singles out a particular object. This function cannot be performed by concepts or univer-sals. The concept of dog cannot single out any particular dog. The discrimination of one particular object from another depends on sensibility, whereas their description in terms of concepts belongs to intellect. There lies the division of labour between intellect and sensibility. Only by their cooperation can they produce judge-ments, the basic units of knowledge. Kant's theory of knowledge is designed to explain their indispensable cooperation for the pro-duction of human knowledge. Neither intellect nor sensibility alone can produce knowledge. This is his epistemic dualism. This point is stressed in Kant's famous dictum, 'Thoughts without content are empty; intuitions without concepts are blind' (A51/B75).

Kant divides all elements of knowledge into two general classes: thoughts and intuitions (or concepts and percepts), whose demarcation follows the demarcation between intellect and sensibility. Kant uses the German word, *Vorstellung*, as the most general noun for any cognitive elements whether they are conceptual or perceptual. This word literally means whatever is set before you. In Kant's lexicon, it means whatever is present in consciousness. There are two English translations for *Vorstellung*. Werner Pluhar renders it as presentation. This translation is relatively literal. The other translators have used the word 'representation'. This nonliteral translation has been encouraged by Kant's occasional practice of placing the Latin word *repraesentatio* in parentheses right after the German word *Vorstellung*, probably because of his allegiance to representationalism. I will mostly use 'representation' rather than 'presentation'. There is a vast variety of representation: percepts and concepts, impressions and memories, judgements and inferences, etc: in short, whatever presents itself in consciousness.

The demarcation between the two worlds of phenomena and noumena leads to Kant's recognition of two levels of human intellect: the understanding and reason. The understanding is concerned with the world of phenomena, and reason with the world of noumena. Both rational faculties are equipped with pure concepts, which are a priori in their origin, that is, they are not derived from empirical sources. The pure concepts of the understanding are called the categories. They are the concepts of an object in general; their function is to describe an object. The understanding employs them for making judgements about the perceptual objects, thereby producing the knowledge of phenomena. The pure concepts of reason are called the Ideas of reason. They are the concepts of noumena. But those concepts cannot be used to gain the knowledge of noumena because they are inaccessible to human intuition. They are only Ideas that can never be developed to knowledge. At most, they can provide the epistemic ground for theoretical conjectures and practical beliefs. The functional difference between the categories of understanding and the Ideas of reason roughly corresponds to the difference between the Aristotelian categories and the Platonic Ideas or Forms.

The distinction between a priori and a posteriori elements concerns the subjectivity and objectivity of experience. The a posteriori elements are subjective; my sensation is mine and your sensation is yours. The a priori elements are objective because they are common to all cognitive subjects. My pure intuitions of sense of space and time are the same as yours. Our perception begins with subjective sensations, but they are converted into objective knowledge in the framework of a priori concepts and intuitions, according to Kant. He calls those a priori elements the transcendental conditions for converting subjective empirical data into objective experience or knowledge. To explain this conversion is the central task in the *Critique of Pure Reason*. The term 'transcendental' is uniquely Kantian. It should not be confused with the more traditional term 'transcendent'. Both words are derived from 'transcend'. The things in themselves (noumena) are transcendent; they transcend the world of appearances (phenomena). But the transcendental conditions transcend the subjectivity of individual subjects. Those conditions have nothing to do with the transcendent world. On the contrary, they are the a priori elements that make possible the objective experience (knowledge) of phenomena. Kant's philosophy is called transcendental philosophy because it is an account of transcendental elements for human experience or knowledge.

The transcendental elements belong to the transcendental subject, just as the empirical elements belong to the empirical subject. The term 'subject' is correlative to the term 'object'. The transcendental object is the object for the transcendental subject; the empirical object is the object for the empirical subject. The transcendental object is objective because the transcendental subject is objective. The empirical object is subjective because the empirical subject is subjective. The transcendental object is the objective perceptual world, but it derives its objectivity from the objectivity of the transcendental subject. This is the basic difference between the objectivity of our common sense and the objectivity of Kant's transcendental sense. In our common sense, objectivity belongs to the objects that exist independently of all subjects. But there are no such objects in Kant's phenomenal world. They can exist only as the objects of the transcendental apperception or the empirical apperception. The latter is not only the consciousness of empirical objects, but also the self-consciousness of an empirical subject. This comes from Hume's theory of self-consciousness. Your empirical world is nothing more than the collection of your impressions, according to Hume. This is the object of your empirical consciousness. Hume also says that your empirical self is nothing more than the collection of your impressions. Therefore, your consciousness of the empirical world is your consciousness of your empirical self. Kant does not only adopt Hume's theory of the empirical subject and its identity with the empirical object, but extends it to the transcendental level. The transcendental subject is coextensive with the transcendental object. Therefore the consciousness of the transcendental object, the objective perceptual world, is the self-consciousness of the transcendental subject.

The transcendental subject and the empirical subject are not two separate entities. They are two components of every human being as a cognitive subject. There are many empirical subjects, but there is only one transcendental subject. The former are existential subjects; the latter is a logical subject. The empirical subjects are real entities, who are individuated from each other and exist in space and time. The transcendental subject is an ideal entity, which neither comes into being nor goes out of existence. It is common to all human beings. They share the same transcendental subject as they share the same space and time and the same understanding and reason. Transcendental subjects and objects should not be confused with transcendent subjects and objects, which belong to the world of noumena. To the confusion of his readers, Kant sometimes uses 'transcendental subject' and 'transcendental object' to refer to transcendent subjects and objects.

Kant's genetic distinction between the a priori and the a posteriori elements is convertible to their epistemic distinction. For example, he says that we have a priori knowledge of the pure intuitions of space and time because they are genetically a priori. A priori knowledge is the epistemic apriority; a priori origin is the genetic apriority. A priori knowledge is knowledge of necessary truths that cannot be false. Kant says that necessity and strict universality are the sure signs of a priori cognition (B4). A posteriori knowledge is knowledge of contingent truths that can be false. The conversion of genetic apriority to epistemic apriority can be reversed: epistemic apriority is convertible to genetic apriority. For example, space and time are genetically a priori because we have a priori knowledge of them. In short, genetic apriority and epistemic apriority are convertible to each other. So are genetic aposteriority and epistemic aposteriority. Because empirical intuitions are genetically a posteriori, we can have only a posteriori (contingent) knowledge of them. Conversely, we can say that they are genetically a posteriori because we can have only a posteriori knowledge of them. Which is primary, genetic apriority and aposteriority or epistemic apriority and aposteriority? This is the most baffling question in the whole *Critique* because Kant never faces this question squarely.

Kant uses the a priori/a posteriori distinction not only for the cognitive elements, but also for propositions (or judgements), which are composed of those elements. He recognizes two classes of propositions, a priori or a posteriori, just as he has recognized two classes of concepts and intuitions. He has two ways of distinguishing between a priori and a posteriori propositions, genetic and epistemic. The genetic way is to make the distinction in terms of their components. For example, he regards all mathematical propositions as a priori because they involve only pure intuitions. On the basis of this genetic definition, he claims that they are true a priori. Their a priori truths are the truths of absolute necessity and unrestricted universality because they do not depend on empirical evidence. Kant also gives a genetic definition of empirical propositions as those propositions composed of empirical elements. They are true only contingently, he says, because they depend on empirical elements. But the genetic definition does not work well for the propositions that are composed of both a priori and a posteriori elements. For example, Kant regards 'Every change has a cause' as an a priori proposition. But he says that this a priori position is not pure because it contains the empirical concept of change (B3). By the genetic definition, the causal principle is a priori and a posteriori at the same time because it also contains the pure concept of cause. But Kant classifies it as an a priori proposition on the ground that it is necessarily true. On the other hand, he would regard 'Smoking is the cause of lung cancer' as an a posteriori proposition because its empirical truth is contingent, although it contains the pure concept of cause. In these two cases, he is giving the epistemic distinction between a priori and a posteriori propositions, which is made not in terms of their genetic components, but in terms of their epistemic status. The necessity and contingency of their truths are the definien for the epistemic definitions. But they are the consequence of their genetic definition.

7

We finally come to Kant's distinction between analysis and synthesis. Analysis is the method of taking apart a complex whole to its constituent elements, for example, breaking down an atom to its constituent elements. It can also be regarded as the method of analysing the concept of atom. Synthesis is the converse method of analysis. Whereas analysis breaks up a complex whole to simple parts, synthesis assembles simple parts to build a complex whole. It is a synthetic operation to construct a triangle by joining three straight lines. By using the analysis/synthesis distinction, Kant divides all cognitions into analytic and synthetic judgements. Their distinction is based on the relation between the subject and the predicate in a judgement. In an analytic judgement, the predicate is contained in the concept of the subject. This is called the containment criterion. For example, 'A body is extended' is an analytic judgement (proposition). The property of being extended is an essential element of a body. Therefore, the concept of extension is contained in the concept of body. We can also say that the former concept is included in the latter concept. Hence the containment criterion is also called the inclusion criterion. The relation of containment (or inclusion) can be revealed by the method of analysis; that is, by analysing a complex concept to its simple elements. By the criterion of containment, 'Some bodies are heavy' is a synthetic judgement. The concept of being heavy is not contained in the concept of body. By the same criterion, 'All bachelors are unmarried' is an analytic judgement, while 'Some bachelors are happy' is synthetic. When the predicate is not contained in the subject, the former adds some new information that is not included in the latter. For that reason, Kant says that the synthetic judgement is ampliative; that is, it amplifies the information contained in the subject. The analytic judgement is not ampliative but only explicative, that is, it only explicates the information already contained in the subject. Hence it belongs to the method of analysis, while the synthetic judgement belongs to the method of synthesis.

Kant has given two ways of dividing all judgements (or propositions): (1) analytic vs. synthetic and (2) a priori vs. a posteriori. Let us now consider their cross-over relation. All analytic judgements are true a priori. They are necessarily true because they do not depend on empirical evidence, even when they contain empirical concepts. But the synthetic judgements can be either a priori or a posteriori. The a posteriori synthetic judgement is common-place. Most of our judgements about the perceptual world are synthetic and a posteriori. But Kant holds that there are synthetic judgements that are true a priori. This is the novelty of his theory. He claims to find a priori synthetic truths not only in mathematics and physics, but even in our common understanding, for example, the a priori truth of the causal principle (B3–6). He further holds that only a priori synthetic principles can provide the scientific basis for mathematics and physics. This is his theory of foundationalism. Without such a priori foundations, he says, the so-called scientific endeavour is no more than groping in the dark. But how can any synthetic propositions have a priori truths? This is one of the central questions in the *Critique of Pure Reason*. This question will be handled first in the Transcendental Aesthetic and then in the Transcendental Analytic.

THE TRANSCENDENTAL AESTHETIC (SPACE AND TIME)

Space and time are called pure intuitions because they are devoid of empirical content. They are also called the forms of intuition because they serve as the framework for receiving empirical intuitions. Kant first analyses the concept of space and then of time. Each inquiry is divided into a metaphysical and a transcendental exposition. By 'the exposition of a concept' is meant the analysis of a concept. In the Metaphysical Exposition of the Concept of Space, he lists four points. First, space is not an empirical concept that has been abstracted from outer experiences. This point is made against two well-known theories of space. One of them is Hume's theory of space: The idea of space is derived from empirical intuitions. The other is Leibniz's theory. He believed that space could not be an independently existing entity because it could not act on other objects. So he concluded that space was constituted by the relation of objects. But Leibniz recognizes two types of objects: the monads and the perceptual objects. Accordingly, he entertained two relational theories of space. In his younger days, he thought that space was constituted by the relation of monads. He also believed that every extended object was an aggregate of monads. But he later realized that there could be no spatial relation of monads because he defined them as non-spatial entities. So he revised his theory of space by locating it in the perceptual world of each monad. The extended objects are now said to be only phenomena, the appearances rather than the real things. In this later theory, space belongs to the subjective world of a monad, whereas it was supposed to lie outside the monads in the earlier theory.

In his later theory, Leibniz holds that each monad has its own space, which is constituted by the relation of its perceptual objects. But the relation of perceptual objects does not always produce space. One perceptual object may be similar to another, but their similarity relation has nothing to do with space. One perceptual object may appear earlier than another. Again their temporal relation has nothing to do with space. Space can be constituted by the relation of perceptual objects only if their relation is already spatial. But they can have spatial relations only if they are already located in space and separated from one another by space. Space is the fundamental condition for the individuation of perceptual objects and their spatial relation. That is why Kant calls space the outer or external intuition. It is the common medium that places the objects external to each other and even to the empirical subject. Apart from this spatial function of individuation, there can be no distinction of objects and their spatial relations. Therefore, Kant concludes, space cannot be obtained by the relations of outer appearances (A23/B38). On the contrary, space is prior to their spatial relations. This is Kant's objection to Leibniz. This criticism equally applies to Hume's empirical theory of space because it is hardly distinguishable from Leibniz's theory. Humean impressions are as subjective as Leibnizian monadic perceptions. Kant's theory of a priori space asserts its genetic priority to empirical intuitions. If the concept of space were derived from Humean impressions, the former would be genetically posterior to the latter. But Kant holds the opposite view. Because space is prior to sensations, the former cannot be infected by the contingency of the latter.

Kant's second point further elaborates on the genetic priority of space to empirical intuitions. We can never have a representation of there being no space though we can think of an empty space containing no empirical objects. This thought experiment is supposed to show that the sense of space is prior to the perception of empirical objects. The claim that pure intuitions are prior to empirical intuitions concerns their dependence/independence relation. Pure intuitions do not depend on empirical intuitions, whereas the latter depend on the former. The empirical objects may come and go because they are a posteriori and contingent. But space is always there because it is an a priori and necessary intuition, which is inseparable from the cognitive subject. You may object to this view on the ground that space was created in a big bang and will be destroyed altogether in a big crunch. But Kant does not recognize the existence of physical space. He has reduced it to the form of intuition. So he is talking about our sense of space. This is an important point to remember in understanding his theory. Kant's third point is that space is not a discursive concept, but a pure intuition. By 'a discursive concept' is meant a generic concept that can apply to many objects. If the concept of space is empirically derived as Hume says, it should apply to many spaces that are accessible to empirical intuitions. Each empirical intuition has its own space. But the connection of one empirical space to another is never made by another empirical intuition or impression. There is no overarching impression that includes all empirical spaces. But we never leave these empirical spaces as separate entities. On the contrary, we piece them together as parts of one space. When we speak of many spaces, Kant says, we mean many parts of one space. The whole of space is prior to its parts; the former is presupposed for the union of the latter. Because the whole space can never be given empirically, Kant says, it must be given as an object of pure intuition.

So space performs two functions. It serves as a framework for empirical perceptions and also as an object of pure intuition. In the latter capacity, it provides the basis for a priori synthetic propositions of geometry; for example, there is only one straight line between two points, or space has three dimensions. Kant says that such truths cannot be derived from geometric concepts such as the concepts of point and line. Like any other concepts, geometric concepts alone can produce only analytic propositions. Kant holds that concepts can produce synthetic propositions only when they are linked to objects. Hence the synthetic a priori propositions of geometry depend on the pure intuition of space. If our intuition of space were a posteriori, Kant says, the science of geometry could never have achieved apodeictic certainty. In that case, its truths would be empirical and contingent. Finally, the one space has an infinite magnitude. This is Kant's fourth and final point. In our sense of space, we cannot even imagine its limit or boundary. Space is an infinite whole. You may again object to this on the ground that physical space is limited, according to today's astrophysics. But Kant is again talking about our sense of space. Only after examining our sense of space and time will he consider what lies beyond space and time. This is the plan of his exploration.

These four points of the Metaphysical Exposition provide the basis for Kant's Transcendental Exposition of the Concept of Space, by which he means the explication of how a priori synthetic cognitions of geometry are possible. He has already done this in making the third point of the Metaphysical Exposition of Space. It is baffling why Kant restates it as the Transcendental Exposition of Space. Later we will consider his motive for this repetition. For the moment, let us examine the standard objections to his view that geometrical propositions are a priori synthetic. One way or another, these objections are based on the fact that Kant was writing before the development of non-Euclidean geometries. He was taking for granted that Euclid's *Elements* had firmly established the science of geometry as a system of a priori synthetic propositions. His favourite example is the proposition that the straight line between two points is the shortest. He says that it is a priori because it can never be false. He also says that it is synthetic for the following reason. The predicate of this proposition ('the shortest'), which is quantitative, cannot be contained in its subject ('the straight line between two points'), which is qualitative. He assumes that there is nothing in common between qualitative and quantitative terms. He further believes that the synthetic truth of this proposition can be secured not by concepts, but only by our intuition of space. That is, we can see its truth only by consulting our sense of space. Kant may say that Euclid's axioms only codify the commonsense understanding embedded in our sense of space.

Kant's critics have contested his account by offering a non-Euclidean definition of straight line. In geodesic terms, for example, a straight line can be defined as the shortest line between two points: a line between any two points is straight if it is shorter than any other lines between them. On this definition, the proposition that the straight line between two points is the shortest turns out to be analytic. But this is an unfair criticism because the proffered definition is unacceptable. For Kant, the concept of 'straight' is a primitive term, which cannot be defined in any other terms. He believes that we can tell whether or not a line is straight by an intuitive inspection, that is, without measuring its length and comparing it with that of other lines. Even if every straight line turns out to be the shortest, to define the former in terms of the latter can give only an extensional definition. Imagine a world where every blue object is circular. This universal fact can support the extensional definition of 'blue' as the class of all circular objects. But it cannot be taken as the intensional definition of blue. Likewise, the geodesic definition of straight line cannot be an intensional one. Kant assumes that it cannot be defined intensionally because it is a primitive concept.

Some critics have conceded that Kant's view of geometry is true for the Euclidean space, but not for the non-Euclidean spaces, where the Euclidean straight line need not be the shortest between two points. But non-Euclidean geometries can be considered from two perspectives, theoretical and physical. From the theoretical perspective, they are purely theoretical constructions that may have no relevance at all for physical space. The truth of their propositions is totally confined within their theoretical systems. A purely theoretical proposition is true if it can be proven within its system. Its truth is only conceptual; it lies in the relation of concepts. Therefore, it is analytic and a priori, but says nothing about physical space. But a geometrical system can be true not only theoretically but also physically, that is, it can truly describe physical space. When a geometrical system is physically true, it is a special branch of physical science, which is as empirical as physics. Although its propositions are not analytic but synthetic, they can never be true a priori. Kant takes geometry neither as a purely theoretical system nor as a physical science, but as the science of pure intuition. In this regard, he is true to the Euclidean tradition. His novelty is to provide the pure intuition of space as the matrix of objects for geometrical axioms and theorems. Without those objects, Euclidean geometry would be no more than a formal theoretical system.

Kant can meet the challenge of non-Euclidean geometries on three levels. On the first level, he can take them as purely theoretical constructions. They are only fictions, which can pose no threat to Kant's account of geometry. On the second level, he can take them as competing accounts of our sense of space. Do non-Euclidean geometries describe our intuition of space more accurately than Euclidian geometry? In answering this question, we have to distinguish our empirical intuition of space from our pure intuition. Kant can concede that our empirical sense of space is not Euclidean. Our empirical sense of space is finite, but our a priori sense of space is infinite, so Kant claims. When we look at railway tracks, the distance between them appears to become shorter and shorter and they appear to converge at a distant point although they are supposedly parallel to each other. This is non-Euclidean. But when we imagine two parallel lines in our pure intuition, they keep the same distance between them and never converge at any point. This is Euclidean. When we try to explain the straight lines and figures of a non-Euclidean space, we tend to draw them on a Euclidean surface. Evidently, the Euclidean space is much more readily in tune with our native sense of space. On this ground, Kant may say that Euclidean geometry truly describes our natural sense of space and that non-Euclidean geometries are deliberately contrived and enclosed within our natural sense of space. On the third level, Kant has to face the contention that physical space is non-Euclidean, especially the claim advanced by Einstein's general theory of relativity. This is the most serious challenge to his theory. The existence of physical space goes against his claim that space can exist only as the form of perceptions. This is his transcendental idealism, which we will examine later. Before taking up that topic, we have to consider Kant's theory of time.

There is one basic difference between space and time. Space is outer sense; time is inner sense. Space is the a priori form of external relations between perceptual objects; time is the a priori form of the subject's inner states. Kant stresses that the recognition of inner states is not a purely intellectual activity. One can perceive oneself only as an appearance in time like any other perceptual object. In spite of this difference between space and time, the Metaphysical Exposition of the Concept of Time roughly follows the same format as the Metaphysical Exposition of the Concept of Space. Kant makes five points on time, whose content is roughly the same as that of his four points on space. His third point on space is expanded to his third and fourth points on time. The first of those five points is that time is not an empirical concept, which corresponds to his view that space is not an empirical concept. He says that time is the a priori condition for the two temporal relations of simultaneity and succession, that is, these two relations are impossible without presupposing time as the framework of perceptions. Therefore, the concept of time cannot be empirically derived from the impressions of simultaneous and successive events, as the empiricists may claim. Kant's second point is the genetic priority of time over appearances, which is analogous to the genetic priority of space over appearances. We can imagine an empty time as we can imagine an empty space, but we cannot imagine empirical objects without placing them in time. He says appearances may come and go, but time itself cannot be removed. His third point is that the a priori necessity of time is the basis for the axioms about time. But he lists only one such axiom: Time has one dimension. Strangely, he does not count the irreversibility of time as another axiom. His fourth point is that time is not a discursive concept, but a pure form of sensible intuition. There is only one time just as there is only one space. He says that different times are parts of one and the same time. His fifth and final point is the infinitude of time. There is no boundary to time. Just like space, time is given as an infinite whole. At this point, the symmetry between space and time breaks down.

Unlike space, time is never given as an infinite whole. It is impossible to intuit the totality of time like that of space. Our intuition of time is always limited to a single moment. We may anticipate the future time or remember the past time, but these objects of remembrance and anticipation cannot be called the objects of our intuition. Kant is mixing up the intuition of time with the concept of time. We indeed conceive time as infinite, although we cannot intuit its infinity. In that case, we cannot be certain whether Kant is talking about our intuition or our concept of time. This uncertainty may be reflected in the title of this section, the Metaphysical Exposition of the Concept of Time. If he is talking about the nature of time, he should have entitled it the Metaphysical Exposition of Time. The injection of the phrase 'the concept of' is inexplicable. The same charge of confusion can be made against the Metaphysical Exposition of the Concept of Space. I have defended Kant's theory of space on the ground that the object of his analysis is our sense of space rather than physical space. But our sense of space is our intuition of space, which should be distinguished from our concept of space. I have no idea what is meant by Kant's assertion that we intuit the infinitude of space. At most, he can say that we can conceive its infinitude. For these reasons, I am inclined to believe that his Metaphysical Expositions of the Concept of Space and the Concept of Time are his analyses of the concepts of space and time, not their intuitions. In fact, he surely talks about the concepts of space and time when he says that space and time are neither empirical concepts nor discursive concepts.

The distinction between the concept and the intuition of space corresponds to Malbranche's distinction between the intelligible space and the sensible space. As a Platonist, he believes that the science of geometry is true only in the intelligible space, but not in the sensible space. The sensible space is an object of intuition; the intelligible space is an object of thought. But this Platonic difference has been erased by Kant's theory of space. With its erasure, it becomes almost impossible to recognize the difference between the concept and the intuition of space. The concept of space empty of its empirical content becomes indistinguishable from the intuition of space empty of its empirical content. Because both of them are blank, it is hard to tell them apart. The one space, in which many fragmentary spatial perceptions are supposedly put together, may well be one conceptual space rather than one intuition of space as Kant claims. The conceptual space can be as a priori as the pure intuition of space. But the a priori intuition of infinite space is as questionable as that of infinite time. So I propose that Kant has mistaken his Euclidean concept of space for the intuition of Euclidean space just as he has mistaken his concept of infinite time for the intuition of infinite time. This mistake has led him to another mistake: that of believing that the intuition of space can explain the synthetic a priori truths of geometry. This is the chain of mistakes in the Transcendental Aesthetic.

The axioms of Euclidean geometry are analytically derivable from the Euclidean concept of space. There is no need to give the transcendental account of Euclidean geometry if Kant is operating with the Euclidean concept of space. He should give the transcendental account of the Euclidean concept of space. In the Transcendental Deduction, to our surprise, he claims to have given it, presumably in the Transcendental Aesthetic. He says, 'We have above traced the concepts of space and time to their sources by means of a transcendental deduction, and explained and determined their *a priori* objective validity' (A87/B119, tr. Guyer and Wood). But he has not even tried to give a transcendental deduction of the concepts of space and time by tracing them to their sources. Because space and time are proven to be pure intuitions, he may think, they can be taken as the original sources for the concepts of space and time. But he has done the exact opposite. By mistaking his concepts of space and time for pure intuitions, he has derived his theory of pure intuitions from his concepts of space and time. This is his transcendental illusion.

In the Analytic of Principles, we will find him saying that time cannot be perceived by itself, but only through empirical intuitions (A182/B225). If time cannot be perceived, it cannot be intuited, either. It is phenomenologically impossible for us ever to get to the pure intuition of space and time. At most, we can think of space and time as pure intuitions by removing their empirical content in our thought. That is the conceptual operation that Kant performs in the Metaphysical Expositions. He has mistaken this conceptual operation for an a priori intuition, the intuitive feel of directly inspecting space and time devoid of all empirical content. Thus he has never substantiated his claim for the pure intuitions of space and time. He banks it on the a priori knowledge of geometry. But this alleged a priori knowledge belongs not to the pure intuition of space, but to his Euclidean concept of space. Because Kant's theory of pure intuitions stands on this confusion between concepts and intuitions, it may be called his transcendental illusion.

In the Transcendental Exposition of the Concept of Time, Kant concedes that he is going to restate what he has already said as the third point in the Metaphysical Exposition. This is exactly what he did in the Transcendental Expositions of the Concept of Space. The first edition of the *Critique* did not have the Transcendental Expositions of Space and Time. They were added to the second edition. By the time he was writing the second edition, it appears, he realized that he had mixed up two topics in his Metaphysical Expositions of Space and Time, namely, (1) their a priori origin and independence of empirical intuitions and (2) our a priori knowledge of their properties. The same term 'a priori' has the genetic sense in (1) and the epistemic sense in (2). By using it for these two senses in the Metaphysical Expositions of the first edition, he was discussing two different issues without noticing their difference. The genetic apriority is different from the epistemic apriority. Their difference can be made manifest by using the word 'pure'. A priori intuitions are sometime called pure intuitions, but a priori knowledge is rarely called pure knowledge. The word 'pure' in 'pure intuitions' and 'pure concepts' has only the genetic sense, never the epistemic one. In the first edition of the *Critique*, he probably did not clearly see the distinction between the genetic apriority of pure intuitions and their epistemic apriority. So he presented them together as the a priori character of space and time. Though he decided to separate the two topics for the second edition, he did not bother to reorganize his expositions. Instead he left the Metaphysical Expositions intact and only restated their epistemic apriority in the newly added Transcendental Expositions.

Let us now consider the logical relation between the Metaphysical and the Transcendental Exposition. The thesis of the latter can be stated as: A priori synthetic cognitions of space (the axioms of geometry) are possible because space is an a priori intuition. The subordinate clause of this thesis contains the thesis of the Metaphysical Exposition. Therefore the Metaphysical Exposition is the premise for the Transcendental Exposition. The former is supposed to prove the genetic apriority of pure intuitions (they are prior to empirical intuitions), which is taken to be equivalent to their epistemic apriority because genetic apriority is convertible to epistemic apriority. Thus the a priori knowledge of space secured by the Metaphysical Exposition serves as the basis for the Transcendental Exposition of a priori synthetic propositions in geometry. We have already noted that the Metaphysical Expositions contains Kant's questionable theory of pure intuitions. But this is not the only questionable feature of the proof. Equally questionable is the assumption that the genetic apriority of pure intuitions is convertible to their epistemic apriority. This assumption is based on the further assumption that whatever is innate to the subject is knowable a priori. That is, genetic apriority guarantees epistemic apriority. Let us examine this uncontested assumption in Kant's philosophy. How do we ever get to know the properties of space and time? When our knowledge of space is described as the a priori knowledge of a priori intuition, it may sound like a tautological truth. But when it is redescribed as the a priori knowledge of pure intuition, it no longer sounds tautological. Genetic apriority can never guarantee epistemic apriority. Even if space and time may be innate to my nature as Kant claims, that cannot guarantee my a priori knowledge of them because there is no guarantee for the a priori knowledge of my own nature.

Kant's dogma on the a priori knowledge of a priori cognitive elements is similar to the Cartesian dogma on the innate knowledge of innate ideas. Descartes defines innate ideas genetically and claims that they are clear and distinct. He takes it for granted that their genetic condition secures their epistemic condition of being clear and distinct. Therefore he never feels the need to explain how their genetic condition guarantees their epistemic condition. This is his royal road of innate ideas, which is now converted to Kant's royal road of a priori cognitive elements. But this royal road is blocked by some innate ideas that are far from clear and distinct. For example, the idea of God which Descartes regards as innate is one of the most confusing ideas. He defines God as the most perfect being. But what counts as perfection is highly indeterminate. Does the most perfect being have arms, legs, and wings? If it does, how many of them? Many theologians have said that the divine perfection should exclude having arms, legs, and wings. By my standards, however, not to have them is a clear imperfection. Because the most perfect being cannot miss even one attribute, whether it be spiritual or material, Spinoza holds that God must have an infinite number of attributes. But it is impossible to have a clear and distinct idea of God with countless attributes, each of which can have no limit of perfection. In *Groundwork for the Metaphysics of Morals*, Kant notes that the ontological concept of perfection is empty and indeterminate (GMM 443). Just as the innateness of an idea cannot guarantee that it is clear and distinct, the genetic apriority of space and time cannot guarantee their epistemic apriority. Therefore, the Metaphysical Exposition cannot provide the basis for the Transcendental Exposition.

Kant is not the only one to be impressed with the apriority of geometry. It has been known for a long time that the basic axioms and theorems of geometry belong to our common sense. Plato takes note of this point in *Meno*, where Socrates elicits geometrical propositions from a slave boy, who has never been tutored in geometry. The anthropologists of our day have found that the children of an Amazonian tribe can readily solve simple geometrical puzzles without any mathematical training. Plato has given his own transcendental account of geometry, which involves two doctrines: (1) the existence of eternal Ideas and (2) the recollection of the vision of those Ideas. According to him, the slave boy can solve simple geometrical problems by recalling his forgotten vision of Ideas in a previous existence. Not many people will take this as a more plausible account than Kant's. But the anthropologists offer a more credible one: our Euclidean sense of space is inscribed in our brain. Therefore it can be called a priori. Of course, it is anti-Kantian to house our a priori sense of space and time in an empirical object, namely, the brain. But where is Kant going to house his a priori sense of space and time, if not in an empirical object? He never takes up this question. This is the most serious objection to his theory of pure intuitions.

TRANSCENDENTAL IDEALISM

Kant's theory of space and time as formal intuitions leads him to reject the existence of physical space and time. This goes against the commonsense belief that our sense of space and time reflects physical space and time. Though Kant pays no attention to the commonsense view, he considers two theories of space and time prevailing in his day: (1) space and time exist as properties of substances and (2) they exist independently like substances. The former view leads to Liebniz's relational theory of space and time, and the latter to Newton's theory of absolute space and time. On Leibniz's theory, Kant claims, mathematical propositions would be contingent. He takes it as the most serious objection because he never questions the apriority of mathematical science. But he concedes that his Leibnizian opponents can say that mathematical propositions are only creatures of imagination (A40/B57). In fact, there is no clear demarcation between our sense of space and our spatial imagination in Kant's theory. The imagined space may be as fictitious as the imaginary unicorn. There can be no real intuition of an empty space, as we noted earlier. Likewise, the infinite space cannot be an object of intuition, but only a product of spatial imagination. Euclid's parallel postulate may be true a priori only in an imaginary space. In that case, Kant's opponents have the right to claim that mathematical propositions are creatures of imagination. That is another way of saying that they are theoretical fictions. This view of mathematics is unacceptable for Kant because he firmly believes it is an a priori science.

Kant holds that the absolute certainty of mathematics cannot be explained, either, by Newton's theory of absolute space and time, which exist like the infinite container of all objects. In Kant's view, the existence of such an infinite entity is a sheer absurdity. This view is based on the long-revered metaphysical thesis that no actual infinities can exist, which goes back to Aristotle. We may think that there exist a great number of stars or an infinite number of them. But the latter cannot really exist. All actual objects must be definite and countable. If space and time are infinite as Newton claims, Kant argues, they cannot be actual entities, but only the forms of perception. This shows that his theory of space as an infinite object of pure intuition is largely influenced by Newton's theory of infinite space. Newton himself was puzzled over the infinite space and looked upon it as a sort of sensorium for God, through which the omnipresent being intuitively sees all things (*Optics*, bk 3. pt 1. q 28). Kant has converted Newton's idea of divine sensorium into his idea of human sensorium for the transcendental subject. For Newton, however, the infinite space was not an object of a priori intuition, but only a conceptual hypothesis for his scientific theory.

If space and time are only the forms of perception, the entire world of appearances should be subjective. This is Bishop Berkeley's subjective idealism or phenomenalism, as we noted at the beginning of this chapter. But Kant insists that his idealism is fundamentally different from Berkeley's. To explain their difference, he introduces two technical distinctions: (1) empirical reality vs. ideality and (2) transcendental reality vs. ideality. 'Empirically ideal' means to exist only for an empirical subject; 'empirically real' means to exist in independence of any empirical subjects. The former means to be empirically subjective; the latter means to be empirically objective. If I say that the tree is empirically ideal, I mean to say that it exists only for my empirical perception. If I say that the tree is empirically real, I mean to say that its existence is independent of any empirical subjects. For Berkeley, the trees are not empirically real, but empirically ideal. Kant rejects his empirical or subjective idealism. He distinguishes 'empirically ideal' from his 'transcendentally ideal', which means to exist for the transcendental subject, and 'empirically real' from 'transcendentally real', which means to exist in independence of the transcendental subject. He calls his theory of perception transcendental idealism in distinction from Berkeley's empirical idealism.

According to Kant's transcendental idealism, physical objects are empirically real, that is, their existence is independent of empirical subjects and their perceptions. This is the commonsense view. But Kant also rejects this view because it assumes physical objects to be transcendentally real, that is, their existence is independent of even the transcendental subject. This goes against his transcendental idealism. Physical objects can exist only for the transcendental subject because they can exist only in space and time, the forms of intuition for the transcendental subject. Physical objects are empirically real but not transcendentally real; they are transcendentally ideal but not empirically ideal. The same distinctions apply to space and time. They are transcendentally ideal, but empirically real. Their existence does not depend on any empirical subjects. On the contrary, the existence of the latter depends on space and time. But space and time are not transcendentally real; their existence depends on the transcendental subject.

The transcendentally ideal objects are phenomena. They are the appearances of the transcendentally real objects, the things in themselves or noumena. Thus Kant's transcendental idealism leads to his demarcation between the world of phenomena in space and time and the world of noumena beyond space and time. The former is accessible to human cognition, but the latter is inaccessible and unknowable. This is Kant's two-world view, which has been a controversial topic. If noumena are unknowable, how can Kant say that they are neither spatial nor temporal? This has been the natural response. In Kant's lexicon, 'knowledge' and 'knowable' are technical terms: something can be known or knowable only if it is an object of perception. If it is not, it can still be an object of opinion or belief. Kant's statements about noumena are meant to express his opinions or beliefs. But this defence is not good enough for his transcendental idealism because it stands on his theory of pure intuitions. We have already seen that he has never demonstrated its truth, especially his claim that our intuitions of space and time are infinite. He further assumes that the infinite space is a sheer absurdity that can exist only in the phenomenal world, but not in the noumenal world. But if it is a sheer absurdity, it cannot exist in the phenomenal world, either. On the other hand, it is impossible to tell whether such a sheer absurdity can or cannot exist in the noumenal world because we can know nothing about it. It is highly possible for all absurdities to exist in the noumenal world. When Goethe appropriates the Kantian noumena as the ultimate ground of the universe in his *Faust*, he calls it the Abyss. He further characterizes it as Chaos and Nothing, both of which defy distinction and description because it is situated beyond space and time, the essential media for individuation and recognition in the phenomenal world. It stands beyond reason and unreason where even the basic laws of logic do not hold.

Some commentators have rejected the standard two-world interpretation of Kant's transcendental idealism and championed the one-world interpretation, which is also called the dual aspect theory. The two-world interpretation is an old tradition. The one-world interpretation is a revisionary attempt to salvage Kant's transcendental idealism for our age, which cannot accept a two-world view. According to this new interpretation, phenomena constitute the aspect of physical objects as they are known to human beings, whereas noumena are the aspect of the same objects as they exist in their own right. But the language of aspects does not fit Kant's notion of appearance: A phenomenon is an appearance of a noumenon. If Jane is intelligent, her intelligence is one of her aspects. It is one of her attributes. On the other hand, if she appears intelligent to me, her intelligent appearance is not one of her aspects or attributes. The appearance belongs to me, whereas the attribute belongs to her. Therefore, the Kantian appearance cannot be an aspect of the thing in itself. The dual aspect theory is also called the dual perspective theory. Phenomena are the way physical objects are seen from the human perspective; noumena are the way they are apart from any perspective. But the language of perspectivism does fit Kant's notion of noumena, either, because noumena do not depend on any perspective. The dual perspectivism gives the misleading impression that even the thing in itself is relative to some point of view. To be sure, Kant sometimes says that the thing itself is known to divine intellect. But that does not mean that its nature depends on the divine perspective.

Although, some of Kant's statements are open for the one-world interpretation, but they are equally compatible with the two-world view. On the other hand, there are many passages of Kant's text that are patently incompatible with the one-world view. Moreover, the one-world view involves a contradiction. Phenomena are spatial and temporal, but nomenena are neither spatial nor temporal. If phenomena and noumena are two aspects of the same objects, their properties are contradictory, as James Van Cleve points out.[1] The problem of contradiction becomes even more glaring if it is stated in terms of existence. The existence of phenomena is temporal; they are subject to generation and destruction in time. But the existence of noumena is timeless; they are immune to generation and destruction. These two modes of existence cannot belong to the same objects. The one-world view may be plausible if it is contained within the domain of physical objects. But Kant's domain of noumena covers many other entities than physical objects; for example, God and Platonic Ideas. There is no way to give a dual aspect account of these transcendent entities. This is the decisive objection to the one-world view.

Kant's conception of noumena or things in themselves is eclectic. It is drawn from two sources: (1) the Cartesian–Lockean tradition and (2) the Platonic–Leibnizian tradition. Kant's concept of thing in itself came from the Cartesian notion of material substance as the cause of our perception. It first became Locke's notion of material substance as the substrate of perceptual properties, which he called 'nothing but the supposed, but unknown, support'. It is unknown because it is perceptually inaccessible. Likewise, Kant assumes that there must be a substratum for the support of appearances because they cannot support themselves. This substratum is the thing in itself, which is as unknowable as the Lockean material substance. But the Kantian thing in itself is different from the Cartesian–Lockean material substance in one respect. The latter is in space and time; the former is beyond space and time. In that regard, the thing in itself is more like a Platonic Idea, which is situated beyond space and time and which is called noumenon by Leibniz.

In his *Inaugural Dissertation*, Kant had already used the terms 'noumena' and 'phenomena', which he had inherited from Leibniz. The Leibnizian distinction goes back to Plato, who looked upon phenomena as the copies or appearances of Ideas. The phenomena are the objects of sense; the Ideas are the objects of intellect. Leibniz calls these intellectual objects the noumena because they are the objects of *nous*, the Greek word for intellect. Noumena are intelligible; phenomena are sensible. This also comes from Plato, according to whom only the Ideas are fully intelligible and knowable while the phenomena are never fully intelligible and knowable. We can have only opinions and conjectures about the latter because they lie somewhere between the fully intelligible and the totally unintelligible. Kant also calls the world of noumena the intelligible world. This is paradoxical because he also holds that the things in themselves are unknowable. How can the intelligible world be unknowable or how can the unknowable world be intelligible? This paradox is produced by Kant's conflation of the Platonic–Leibnizian tradition with the Cartesian–Lockean tradition. According to Plato and Leibniz, noumena are intelligible; according to Descartes and Locke, the material substances are unknowable. Kant has produced a paradox by fusing these two incompatible ideas into one. But he manages to avoid the paradox by saying that noumenal substrate is intelligible only to divine intellect, but unknowable to human intellect. In his lexicon, the same word 'substrate' can mean a Lockean substance and/or a Platonic Idea. Into this mixed bag of supersensible entities, Kant also throws in the Christian God as the substrate of the entire natural world.

Kant's demarcation between the thing in itself and appearance may look mysterious, but it is his version of the traditional metaphysical distinction between reality and appearance. 'The thing in itself' is Kant's term for reality. The aura of mystery descends on his distinction between reality and appearance when he places all reality beyond space and time, even physical reality. This peculiarity is the drastic divergence of his transcendental idealism from the ontological tradition of the West. His transcendental idealism is dictated by his theory of space and time, namely, they are only the forms of our intuitions. But we have noted that his a priori theory of space and time is his transcendental illusion induced by his confusion between the concepts of space and time and their intuitions. Therefore, it is far more sensible to reject his transcendental idealism together with his theory of space and time than to engage in any revisionary interpretation for its reformulation and salvation.

THE CATEGORIES

In the Transcendental Aesthetic, Kant has explained how sensibility provides the objects of perception. But those objects can be known only when they become the objects of judgement. To make a judgement is to describe an object in a proposition by using concepts, and its most basic concepts are the pure concepts of the understanding. Kant calls them the categories because they play the same role as the Aristotelian categories. These a priori concepts present two transcendental problems: (1) their discovery and (2) their validation. I will treat (1) in this section and (2) in the next one. Kant does not want to use an empirical method of discovering the pure concepts. If they are a priori, he believes, they must be collected and systematized by an a priori method. For this reason, he chides Aristotle for his empirical way of picking up his categories one after another and gathering them into a haphazard list. Kant's a priori method is to use the table of judgement as the key to the discovery of all pure concepts of the understanding, and this method is claimed to be a priori and systematic because the table of judgement expresses the form of the understanding (A70/B95). He first presents the table of judgement:

1. Quantity – universal, particular, singular
2. Quality – affirmative, negative, infinite
3. Relation – categorical, hypothetical, disjunctive
4. Modality – problematic, assertoric, apodeictic

This table lists twelve logical forms for stating a judgement, which are divided into four triplets, whose headings are Quantity, Quality, Relation, and Modality. The quantity of judgement can take one of the three forms: universal (All men are mortal), particular (Some men are mortal), and singular (This man is mortal). The same is true with the other three headings. Kant then presents the table of categories:

1. Quantity – unity, plurality, totality
2. Quality – reality, negation, limitation
3. Relation – substance and attribute, cause and effect, community
4. Modality – possibility–impossibility, existence–nonexistence, necessity–contingency

This table lists twelve categories, which are also divided into four triplets, whose headings are again Quantity, Quality, Relation, and Modality. There are three categories of quantity: unity, plurality, and totality. The same is true of the other triplets. The two tables are meant to show the one-to-one correspondence between the categories and the forms of judgement. By virtue of this relation, the forms of judgement can lead to a systematic discovery of the categories. Kant says that this list of categories is a complete system of all categories because it is generated systematically from one common principle, namely, the forms of judgement ingrained in the understanding (A81/B106). The system of categories is the basic framework for his Transcendental Logic. He says, 'This system of categories makes all treatment of every object of pure reason itself systematic' (P §39). This is the foundation for his dream of building up metaphysics as a secure science, which he has avowed to accomplish in the Preface to the *Critique* (Bxiv–xxiv).

Kant takes enormous pride in having discovered the one-to-one mapping relation between the categories and the forms of judgement. Amazingly, he has made this historical discovery by using logic alone. But how has it escaped the attention of logicians for so long? This is a baffling historical question. Why does the mapping relation obtain between the categories and the forms of judgement? This logical question is even more baffling. Here is Kant's explanation for the logical question:

The same function which gives unity to the various representations *in a judgement* also gives unity to the mere synthesis of various representations *in an intuition*; and this unity, in its most general expression, we entitle the pure concepts of understanding. The same understanding, through the same operations by which in concepts, by means of analytical unity, it produces the logical form of a judgement, also introduces a transcendental content into its representations, by means of synthetic unity of manifold in intuition in general. (A79/B102–3, tr. Kemp Smith)

This may be called Kant's double function theory of categories, that is, the pure concepts of understanding perform two functions. One is to provide synthetic unity; the other is to provide analytic unity. The former is performed in the domain of intuitions, the latter in the domain of concepts. The forms of judgement are the various ways of expressing analytic unity. These forms of analytic unity belong to general (or formal) logic, which abstracts from all content of judgements, namely, their objects (A54/B78). On the other hand, the forms of synthetic unity belong to his transcendental logic, which studies the function of the categories in the domain of intuitions and their objects. The forms of judgement and the categories are conceptually identical and only functionally different. Kant's double function theory is at the same time his identity theory of the categories and the forms of judgement. The pure concepts of understanding provide the common basis for general logic (the logic of analysis) and transcendental logic (the logic of synthesis). Kant calls the function of analytic unity the logical function because it belongs to general logic. Because this logical function is expressed by the forms of judgement, he calls the latter the logical functions of the understanding. The function of synthetic unity is called the real function of the understanding because it deals with real objects. This is the extralogical function; it goes beyond logic. If the same concepts perform these two types of function, the forms of judgement can indeed be used as the logical clue for a systematic tabulation of all categories.

Kant's double function theory of categories, however, is highly suspect. Let us consider the relation of the categories to the forms of judgement by consulting Aristotle's logical works, the *Categoriae* and *De Interpretatione*. In the *Categoriae*, he divides linguistic expressions into two groups: simple and complex. The complex expressions are sentences or propositions such as 'An ox runs' or 'The man wins'; the simple expressions are words such as 'man', 'ox', 'run', and 'win'. Words are the basic elements for constructing propositions, whose truth can be asserted or denied. But words can be neither true nor false. The *Categoriae* is the examination of words, which Aristotle classifies into the expressions for substance, quantity, quality, relation, place, time, position, state, action, or affection. There is nothing logical in this classification of words. Hence the *Categoriae* has never been accepted as a logical treatise. But *De Interpretatione* is definitely a logical treatise. After showing the composition of propositions by the use of words, Aristotle talks about the logical operation of their assertion and denial and examines their logical relation to one another. He makes the fourfold distinction of propositional forms (*De Int.* 17a8–21a34): (1) Affirmation vs. Negation, (2) Universal vs. Particular, (3) Simple vs. Composite, and (4) Possible vs. Necessary. This may be called Aristotle's table of judgement, which Kant modifies into his table of judgement as we will see later.

Let us first notice the basic difference between Aristotle's categories and his forms of judgement. Their difference can be captured by the distinction between logical and descriptive terms. The descriptive terms describe extralogical objects such as individuals, properties, and relations. They are what Kant calls the concepts of an object. But the logical terms do not describe any objects because their function is not descriptive but logical. The logical particle 'and' performs the logical or grammatical function of joining one proposition to another. The affirmation of a proposition is the logical operation of asserting its truth. The logical function is generically different from the descriptive function. Since logical functions are based on logical terms and descriptive functions on descriptive terms, there is a generic difference between logical and descriptive terms. But Kant claims the identity of logical and descriptive terms on the ground that they are based on the same pure concepts of understanding. According to his double function theory of categories, the same pure concepts perform the logical functions in the domain of concepts and the synthetic functions in the domain of intuitions. His double function theory of categories reflects his fundamental confusion between logical and descriptive functions. This confusion is as serious and as fatal for his transcendental idealism as his confusion between the concepts of space and time and their a priori intuitions. But he counts his theory of categories as an additional support for his transcendental idealism. Together with the pure intuitions, he holds, the pure concepts restrict the human understanding to the knowledge of appearances and block out the knowledge of the things in themselves.

Let us now note a systematic difference between Kant's and Aristotle's tables of judgement. The latter consists of four couplets, but Kant has converted them into four triplets by adding a third member to each couplet. He explains this addition as follows. In the quality of judgement, he adds the infinite judgement ('The soul is non-mortal') as the third form in addition to affirmative and negative judgements. The affirmative judgement assigns a predicate to the subject; the negative judgement denies it. In its logical form, he admits, the infinite judgement is the same as the affirmative judgement ('The soul is mortal'). But they take on different predicates. The predicate 'non-mortal' refers to an infinite (unlimited) extension excluded from the domain of 'mortal'. The former is an infinite predicate; the latter is a finite one. In that case, Kant is dividing the affirmative judgement into the finite and the infinite judgement. This is a subdivision of affirmative judgement, which is based on the nature of predicates. But the original distinction between affirmative and negative judgements is not based on the nature of predicates because it is a purely logical distinction between affirmation and denial. We can affirm or deny a proposition whether it contains a positive or negative predicate. The nature of predicates is the nature of descriptive terms, which has nothing to do with the logical functions of affirmation and denial. These logical functions are performed by logical terms. Since the forms of judgement only express the logical functions, they have nothing to do with descriptive terms. Kant cannot revise and expand the table of judgement on the basis of predicates because they are descriptive terms. But he has his own excuse: 'General logic abstracts from all content of the predicate (even though it be negative); it enquires only whether the predicate be ascribed to the subject or opposed to it' (A72/B97, tr. Kemp Smith). But transcendental logic considers the content of judgement. This is the excuse for the modification of the table of judgement.

So there are two types of judgement-forms. One is based on the purely logical forms of judgement totally abstracted from its content; the other is based on the semantic content of descriptive terms. The latter should be called the transcendental table of judgement because it belongs to transcendental logic. The former should be called the formal table of judgement because it belongs to formal logic, which Kant calls general logic. These two types of judgement-forms are completely different. The formal judgement-forms are formal and logical; the transcendental judgement-forms are material and extralogical. Kant makes his table of judgement by converting the formal table to the transcendental table. He does not openly admit the conversion, but only claims to add one member to each of the four groups in the formal table of judgement on the basis of content. This may give the impression that the original two members are left intact by the addition. But affirmative and negative judgements are also redefined by the nature of their predicates just like infinite judgement. They no longer serve their old logical function of affirmation and denial. That is why Kant can derive the categories of reality and negation from affirmative and negative judgements. The category of reality is a descriptive concept embedded in an affirmative predicate. The category of negation is a descriptive concept embedded in a negative predicate. The categories of reality and negative reality can never be derived from the logical forms of affirmation and denial. But Kant can derive them from the forms of affirmative and negative judgements because he has redefined them in terms of descriptive terms. Therefore, his derivation is circular. He first revises the table of judgement in terms of the categories, and then derives the categories from the table of judgement.

Kant again appeals to the content or rather quantity of knowledge in adding the singular judgement as the third member of the quantity of judgement. Although logicians are justified in treating singular judgements as equivalent to universal judgements, he says, they should be discriminated with respect to the quantity of knowledge because the singular judgement stands to the universal judgement as unity to infinity (A71/B96). In that case, he should derive the concept of unity from singular judgement and the concept of infinity from universal judgement. Instead, he derives the concept of unity from universal judgement and the concept of totality from singular judgement. This looks like a careless mistake of confusion. But he has simply added 'totality' as the third category to the traditional pair of unity and plurality as he has added singular judgement to the traditional pair of universal and particular judgements. His additions are simply mechanical. But it is a serious mistake to place singular judgement on the same level with universal and particular judgements because they belong to different orders of predicate logic. Universal and particular judgements belong to the first order, and singular judgement to the zero order. Instead of distinguishing singular from universal and particular judgements, Kant should have distinguished it from plural judgement because these two belong to the same zero order. The singular judgement takes a single subject; the plural judgement takes a plural subject. Though both of them belong to the same order of predicate logic, they indeed differ with respect to the quantity of knowledge.

Compare two propositions, 'Three men committed this crime' and 'Only one man committed this crime'. The first proposition is a plural judgement, which conveys a greater quantity of knowledge (three men) than the second proposition, which is a singular judgement (only one man). These two propositions employ quantitative predicates ('one' and 'three'). It is easy to derive the quantitative category of unity from the singular judgement and the quantitative category of plurality from the plural judgement, because the two quantitative categories are embedded in the two forms of quantitative judgement. But no quantitative categories can be derived from universal and particular judgements because their quantifiers contain no quantitative predicates. The universal proposition, 'Every man in this room smokes', does not indicate whether it involves one man or many men. There may be only one man or five men in this room. Likewise, the particular proposition, 'some gods are immortal', does not indicate how many gods are involved in this assertion. It is true even if there is only one immortal god. The category of plurality can be derived from plural judgement, but not from particular judgement. But Kant can derive the quantitative categories from universal and particular judgements if he has transformed the quantity of judgement into quantitative judgements. Since quantitative judgements contain quantitative terms, the derivation of quantitative categories from those judgements is again circular.

Kant's handling of the relation of judgement is unsystematic. He describes categorical judgement as the relation of two concepts and hypothetical and disjunctive judgement as the relation of two judgements. They are two different kinds of relation. But Kant gives no reason why they are grouped together. Nor does he explain why he lumps disjunctive judgement together with categorical and hypothetical judgements. The latter two have long been paired in general logic because 'categorical' and 'hypothetical' are opposite terms. But neither of them is related to the term of 'disjunctive'. Disjunctive judgement can be paired with conjunctive judgement. But Kant does not even acknowledge conjunctive judgement in his table of judgement. Although he derives the category of community from disjunctive judgement, it would be more natural to derive it from conjunctive judgement. Kant derives the category of cause and effect from the hypothetical judgement. To be sure, this judgement-form can express a causal relation, but it can express many other relations. The logical relation of ground and consequence is different from the relation of cause and effect. The former is logical; the latter is descriptive. Only by converting the logical relation to the descriptive relation can Kant derive the causal category from the hypothetical judgement. Then his derivation again becomes circular. Kant derives the category of substance and accident from the categorical judgement, the logical relation of subject and predicate. Here again his derivation works if the logical relation is converted into the descriptive relation of substance and accident. The logical function of a subject is to refer to anything in the world; for example, 'This fiction is bad' or 'Courage is a virtue'. Neither courage nor a fiction is a substance. Because the categorical judgement states the relation between two concepts as Kant says, all relational categories can be derived from it, for example, the causal category. In fact, the causal relation is usually stated in a categorical judgement, for example, 'Smoking is a cause of lung cancer'. The relation of substance and accident is only one of the countless relations that can be derived from the categorical judgement.

Kant's modal categories are different from other categories because the former do not belong to the content of judgement. But his list of three modal categories deviates from the traditional fourfold distinction of possible–impossible and necessary–contingent. Though the assertoric judgement may have been in the logic books of his day, it is no different from the affirmative judgement in the quality of judgement. In fact, the category of existence derived from assertoric judgement is equivalent to the category of reality derived from affirmative judgement. Since neither of these two judgements contains a modal term, they should not be admitted in the modality of judgement. Kant derives the category of possibility from problematic judgement, thereby confusing the concept of possibility with that of probability. There is nothing problematic in his derivation of necessity from apodeictic judgement. In general, the modal categories constitute the forms of modal judgement. In this case alone, Kant can claim the identity between the pure concepts of the understanding and the forms of judgement. But his double function theory of categories is not true even in this case because the modal categories do not perform synthetic functions.

Outside the modal categories, the categories of understanding cannot be identical with the forms of judgement because they are generically different. The forms of judgement are logical; the categories are descriptive. Kant creates a semblance of their identity by converting the judgement-forms of general logic to those of his transcendental logic. Even this conversion cannot be the conversion of logical concepts to descriptive ones because such a conversion is impossible. This impossible conversion should be called Kant's transubstantivation because it is claimed to transform formal concepts into substantive ones. Its contention sounds as mysterious as the medieval doctrine of transubstantiation. The conversion of judgement-forms is really his substitution of logical concepts with descriptive concepts. But Kant never recognizes his own substitution and still believes in his double function theory of categories: the same pure concepts perform the logical functions as the forms of judgement and the synthetic functions as the categories. Because of this belief, he refers to the pure concepts by two labels, 'the categories' and 'the logical functions'. He even uses the expression 'the categories' to refer to the forms of judgement as well as to pure concepts. Thus the four expressions of 'pure concepts', 'the forms of judgement', 'the logical functions', and 'the categories' are used interchangeably throughout the *Critique of Pure Reason*. This creates a terminological confusion. For example, when he talks about the logical functions of understanding, he may be talking about the forms of judgement or the categories. Likewise, when he talks about the categories, he may be talking about the forms of judgement or the pure concepts. Because the double function theory of categories is Kant's illusion, there can be no systematic correlation between the table of judgement and the categories. Instead of finding the categories by using the forms of judgement, he makes up the forms of judgement by using the categories. As we noted earlier, his table of judgements is incomplete and unsystematic. He refuses to admit plural judgement along with singular judgement and conjunctive judgement along with disjunctive judgement. Nor does he admit finite judgement along with infinite judgement.

Kant's list of categories is equally incomplete and unsystematic because he has never found a systematic method for collecting them. Hence there is no guarantee that Kant has assembled all the categories. In fact, he betrays his own qualm about this in the Amphiboly of Concepts of Reflection. He examines four pairs of concepts, which look like pure concepts. One of those pairs is the concepts of identity and difference, two basic categories for Plato and Leibniz. In the Transcendental Deduction, Kant will say that the concepts of identity and difference play an important role in deciding whether different perceptions belong to one and the same object or different ones (A103). Nevertheless, he wilfully dismisses the concepts of identity and difference as mere concepts of comparison (A262/B318). This is his excuse for excluding them from his table of categories. He could not derive those two categories from his table of judgement because the logic of his day did not recognize the judgements of identity and difference as forms of judgement. An even more serious omission involves the headings for the four triplets in his table of categories: Quantity, Quality, Relation, and Modality. Because they are only four headings, they are not treated as pure concepts of the understanding. But they are the most basic of all Aristotelian categories. Even Kant himself will use them as his four basic categories in formulating the four antinomies of pure reason in the Transcendental Dialectic. He will again use them in his metaphysical discussion on the nature of matter in the *Metaphysical Foundations of Natural Science*. In the *Critique of Judgement*, he will use them again in defining the four modes of aesthetic judgement. If these four basic categories are added to his table of categories, their number will be increased from twelve to sixteen. But those four categories cannot be derived from his table of judgement because there are no judgement-forms corresponding to them.

The most serious omission is the concept of an object, the hub of all Kantian categories. Just as the Aristotelian categories are the predicates of a substance, so the Kantian categories are the predicates of an object in general. Therefore the concept of an object is as central in Kant's categorial scheme as the concept of substance is in Aristotle's categorial scheme. Kant even gives a transcendental schema for the concept of an object in the Schematism (A142/B182). This is his informal recognition of its categorial status. But it is not listed on his table of categories because it cannot be embedded in any form of judgement. So we can fully confirm our earlier view that there is no connection whatsoever between the categories and the forms of judgement. Thus Kant's vaunted project of discovering and systematizing all categories turns out to be a logical sleight of hand, which has been covered up by his systematic confusion between logical and descriptive terms. Kant has fostered this project on his belief that there must be an a priori way of discovering all the categories if they are pure concepts. This belief in turns stands on the assumption that the genetic apriority guarantees the epistemic apriority, that is, we can have a priori knowledge of all a priori elements. In our examination of the Transcendental Aesthetic, we have already seen that this is Kant's transcendental illusion because genetic apriority can never guarantee epistemic apriority.

In the logical derivation of categories, Kant's motive is not limited to proving their a priori origin. He also wants to resolve one big mystery in the doctrine of innate ideas, the origin of their meanings. How do the innate ideas get their meanings if they are not derived from empirical objects? The rationalists have tried to explain this mystery by saying that the innate ideas have their meanings as their innate properties endowed by God. Kant cannot accept this *deus ex machina*. Nor can he endorse the empiricist account because it endangers the apriority of the categories. He tries to find his *tertium quid* by dividing the form of a concept from its content. Prior to its application to experience, he says, a pure concept is only 'the logical form of a concept, not the concept itself through which something is thought' (A95, tr. Kemp Smith). But what is the logical form of a concept? Here is Kant's explanation of this strange expression:

> We demand in every concept, first, the logical form of a concept (of thought) in general, and secondly, the possibility of giving it an object to which it may be applied. In the absence of such object, it has no meaning and is completely lacking in content, though it may still contain the logical function which is required for making a concept out of any data that may be presented. (A239/B293, tr. Kemp Smith)

This is Kant's general distinction regarding all concepts: Every concept consists of two components. One of them is its logical form; the other is the possibility of its application to an object. He takes the latter as its meaning. Since the meaning of a concept is its content, he is distinguishing the form of a concept from its content. But this distinction is hard to understand because it is unconventional. Let us try to understand it by applying it to the concept of horse. Kant would say that the meaning of this concept is the objects, namely horses, to which it can apply. What is the logical form of this concept? Kant identifies it as 'the logical function which is required for making a concept out of any data that may be presented'. But there is no logical form or function which is required for making the concept of horse. Hence Kant's distinction between the form of concepts and their content makes no sense if it is taken a universal distinction regarding all concepts. But we can treat it as a special distinction concerning the pure concepts of understanding. Kant assigns not one but two logical functions to those a priori concepts. One of them is to provide the forms of judgement; the other is to provide the forms of concepts. Evidently, Kant assumes that these two logical functions are performed by pure concepts. He already talked of these two functions in his double function theory of categories. He said that the categories performed the analytic function as the forms of judgement and the synthetic function in the domain of intuitions. We have seen that this double function theory involves the conversion of pure concepts from formal (logical) to material (extralogical) concepts, namely, Kant's mystery operation of transubstantiation. The mystery expression 'the logical form of a concept' only means a formal concept, which in turn is the same as a form of judgement. By this complicated theory, Kant reduces an innate idea to the form of a concept, but endows it with the power to be converted to a material concept. This is his compromise between the rationalist theory of innate ideas and the empiricist theory of all ideas. But this compromise cannot work because the categorial conversion from formal to material concepts is only his logical trickery, as we noted earlier.

I have taken great pains in exposing this trickery for one special reason. As we will see, Kant's logical derivation of categories is meant to be the vital premise for the Transcendental Deduction, which will be discussed in the next section. But the importance of the Metaphysical Deduction is not limited to this role. Kant says that the table of categories provides the complete plan for his philosophy as a science (A83/B109). In §39 of the *Prolegomena*, he says, 'This system of categories makes all treatment of any object of pure reason itself systematic ... for it exhausts all the moments of the understanding, under which every other concept must be brought.' The table of categories is designed to be the ultimate foundation of his grand architectonic, but it has been almost universally neglected in Kant scholarship.

THE TRANSCENDENTAL DEDUCTION

Kant recognizes two ways to validate concepts, empirical and transcendental. The empirical way is Hume's method: Ideas are invalid and false unless they can be traced back to impressions. By this method, Kant says, the pure concepts of understanding would be shown to be invalid and empty because they can find no object among appearances (A90/B122). So he proposes the transcendental method of validation for the categories. The two methods of validation concern the relation between concepts and objects. Their relation can take two forms: (1) concepts conform to objects and (2) objects conform to concepts. The former is the priority of objects over concepts; the latter is the priority of concepts over objects. Empiricism subscribes to the priority of objects over concepts; the validity of concepts depends on objects. The traditional metaphysics has also subscribed to the priority of objects over concepts. Kant breaks this long tradition and advocates the priority of concepts over objects as far as the pure concepts are concerned (A92/B125). He calls it his Copernican revolution in philosophy (Bxvi). Just as Copernicus shifted the centre of the world from the earth to the sun, Kant is relocating the centre of cognition from the object to the subject. There are no empirical intuitions, to which the pure concepts and the pure intuitions must conform. On the contrary, the former must conform to the latter before they can be converted into objective objects for empirical knowledge. The categories are necessary for this conversion as much as the pure intuitions of space and time are. This conversion may be called Kant's transcendental magic. It is the backbone of the Transcendental Deduction.

The outline of Kant's transcendental argument is to claim that the categories are valid because they are necessary for the possibility of experience. Since 'experience' means empirical knowledge or the knowledge of objects, the outline can also be stated as: The categories make empirical knowledge possible. Since empirical knowledge is the knowledge of the objective perceptual world, the outline can also be stated as: The categories make possible the objective perceptual world by combining subjective sensations into perceptual objects. They are different ways of expressing the role of categories in Kant's transcendental magic of converting subjective impressions into objective knowledge. He deploys two methods for implementing the Transcendental Deduction, progressive and regressive. In the progressive approach, he shows how subjective sensations are assembled into objective perceptual objects and what role the categories play in this construction process. In the regressive approach, he reverses this procedure. He begins with objective experience and analyses it to disclose the categories as its essential constituents. The regressive approach is the analytic method; the progressive approach is the synthetic method. The latter is called the subjective deduction of categories because it is based on the function of subjective cognitive elements. The former is called the objective deduction because it is based on the analysis of objective knowledge. The subjective and the objective deductions are two parts of the Transcendental Deduction of the first edition, which has been known as the A Deduction. But Kant revised it for the second edition of the *Critique*, which has been known as the B Deduction. I will first discuss the A Deduction and then the B Deduction.

The A Deduction begins with the subjective deduction. It is the story of threefold synthesis: (1) the synthesis of apprehension in intuition, (2) the synthesis of reproduction in imagination, and (3) the synthesis of recognition in a concept. They are the three levels of perception. Because synthesis is the act of combining the manifold of intuition into one object, it is also called the act of combination. On Kant's theory, perception is a continuous process of combining sensory impressions as they are continuously given to the subject. This is the basic difference of his theory from Hume's, according to which perception is a simple process of imprint. On the most basic level, Kant holds, perception begins with the synthesis of apprehension. For example, the sensory image of a horse contains a manifold; it is composed of many parts. To perceive the relation of those parts to one another is the synthesis of apprehension, by which you can see that the horse's eyes are located in its head or that its tail is attached to its rear end. But one perceptual image, which is limited to a single moment, is not sufficient for the perception of a horse, because every moment generates a new image of the horse. You have to put together a series of sensory images for a rounded picture. By the time you get a new image, your old images will be gone. You have to recall the old images to join them with the new image. Kant calls this process the synthesis of reproduction in imagination because the imagination is the faculty of storing and recalling images. The synthesis of imagination extends the synthesis of apprehension beyond the present moment. The understanding finally recognizes this product by using concepts. This is the synthesis of recognition in a concept.

In this scheme of threefold synthesis, sense provides sensory materials, imagination puts them together to build a perceptual object, and the understanding recognizes it. This recognition can be stated as a judgement. This is the way concepts and intuitions come together to produce experience or knowledge. Each of these three syntheses has two features, empirical and transcendental. The empirical synthesis operates on the manifold of empirical intuition, and the transcendental synthesis on the manifold of pure intuitions of space and time. They are the transcendental content for the transcendental synthesis. The example of perceiving a horse requires an empirical synthesis, that is, the synthesis of empirical sensations such as the colours and sounds that come from the horse. By the time you place those impressions in the objective space and time, you are making a transcendental synthesis of the same data because space and time are the pure intuitions that belong to the transcendental subject. On the other hand, the empirical data belong to the empirical subject. So does the empirical synthesis. The imagination that handles the empirical synthesis is called the reproductive imagination; the imagination that handles the transcendental synthesis is called the productive imagination. The pure images of time and space are not reproduced but produced because they are a priori. The product of empirical synthesis is a subjective object because it belongs to an empirical subject. It can become an objective object by being placed in the framework of transcendental synthesis, which belongs to the transcendental subject.

On Kant's theory, objectivity can be secured only by necessity, which in turn can be secured only by a priori elements. In short, what is objective is what is necessary. But nothing can be necessary except for the a priori elements because all a posteriori elements are contingent. This is the most important premise that runs through the entire *Critique of Pure Reason*. In the Transcendental Aesthetic, Kant holds that space and time are objective because they are a priori intuitions whereas all empirical intuitions are subjective. Space and time provide the a priori framework for the transcendental synthesis for combining all subjective empirical intuitions into one unified objective world. This is the transcendental object. Kant says, 'The pure concept of this transcendental object (which in all of our cognitions is really always one and the same = X) is that which in all of our empirical concepts in general can provide relation to an object, i.e., objective reality' (A109, tr. Guyer and Wood). He goes on to say that this concept contains no determinate intuition and that its function is to provide the objective unity of all appearances in consciousness. Since objectivity is always based on the necessity of a priori elements, he holds, the objective unity of the transcendental object must be derived from the necessary unity of transcendental apperception. The transcendental object is the object of transcendental apperception, the consciousness of the transcendental subject. The transcendental subject and the transcendental object are correlative to each other (A123).

Although the objective perceptual world appears to exist independently, Kant holds, it exists only as an object of the transcendental subject. Some commentators have read the Transcendental Deduction as the proof of objectivity just on the basis of any consciousness. But that cannot be Kant's argument because he repeatedly says that the object of empirical consciousness is only subjective. It takes not *any* consciousness but transcendental consciousness to convert subjective empirical intuitions into objective objects. What role do the categories play in this magic process? They provide the rules of synthesis for the synthesis of recognition. It appears that all the synthetic work of combining intuitions into objects is performed by the transcendental imagination, which projects subjective empirical intuitions into the objective frame of space and time. If the synthesis of recognition is to recognize this objective world, the understanding can do it simply by exercising its logical functions, namely, the forms of judgement. But those logical functions are not sufficient, Kant says, because the perceptual world is governed by synthetic necessity whereas the logical functions can provide only analytic necessity (A104). The combination of empirical intuitions in the framework of space and time cannot be objective unless their combination is a priori and necessary. Kant holds that their necessary combination is secured by the synthetic function of the categories. For example, the temporal succession of one impression after another is contingent, but it can become a necessary relation when those impressions are synthesized or organized under the category of causation (A112). Thus the understanding prescribes the causal law to nature. This is what is meant by Kant's Copernican revolution, that is, subjective impressions are converted into objective objects by their conformity to the pure concepts. Their conformity establishes the objective validity of categories. This is the subjective deduction.

This argument is reversed in the objective deduction, which begins with the unity of transcendental apperception. Paul Guyer recognizes two premises: the deduction from knowledge of objects and the deduction from apperception.[2] But the transcendental apperception is correlative to the transcendental object, as we noted earlier. Hence to use the transcendental apperception as a premise is the same as to use the transcendental object as a premise. The unity of transcendental apperception is a synthetic unity, which combines all perceptions into one experience, that is, the experience of one objective perceptual world, which is none other than the transcendental object. Kant says, 'There is only **one** experience, in which all perceptions are presented as in thoroughgoing and lawlike connection, just as there is only one space and time, in which all forms of appearance and all relation of being or non-being take place' (A110, tr. Guyer and Wood). He again stresses the necessity governing the synthetic unity of transcendental apperception in contrast to the contingent unity of empirical synthesis and consciousness (A111–13). This is followed by his familiar argument that the necessary unity of transcendental consciousness can be secured only by the categories because those a priori concepts alone can make the necessary synthesis of appearances. Thus they provide the coherent connection of appearances, which Kant calls their affinity or association. Without this a priori categorial framework, he holds, the association of empirical intuitions would be wild and chaotic. So he concludes, 'Thus the order and regularity in the appearances, which we entitle *nature*, we ourselves introduce' (A125, tr. Kemp Smith). He then restates the necessary unity of transcendental apperception as the necessary unity of nature and attributes it to the a priori rules of synthesis. He concludes the objective deduction by calling the understanding the law-giver of nature because it prescribes the a priori rules of synthesis as the laws of nature. This is the same outcome as that of the subjective deduction.

By 'prescribing a priori laws for nature', Kant means the imposition of the categories on appearances for the construction of what is called the world of natural phenomena. This is Kantian constructivism, the central point in his Copernican revolution and for both the subjective and the objective deduction. Their difference lies only in the procedure of exposition. The subjective deduction is from the bottom up; it begins with the most basic elements of perception and builds them up to reach the transcendental unity of apperception, the highest level of experience. The objective deduction is from the top down; it reverses the procedure of the subjective deduction. The bottom-up procedure is the synthetic or progressive method; the top-down procedure is the analytic or regressive method. But Kant does not really prove the validity of the causal or any other categories. This has been a huge disappointment for most commentators. They are naturally induced to expect him to prove the validity of the categories because Kant opens the Transcendental Deduction by expressing his intention to tackle the question of right (*quid juris*) for the categories. But he does not even try to prove the validity of the categories. Instead of proving their validity, he presupposes it. The aim of the Transcendental Deduction is to explain their synthetic function in producing objective knowledge by presupposing their validity. Karl Ameriks clarifies this point by comparing the Transcendental Deduction to the Transcendental Expositions in the Transcendental Aesthetic.[3] The Transcendental Exposition of Space is not meant to prove the a priori synthetic truths of geometry. In fact, Kant never questions them, but takes them for granted. The Transcendental Exposition is to explain how they are possible, by using his a priori theory of space. This procedure of explanation is Kant's transcendental account.

Ameriks contends that the Transcendental Deduction should be understood as a transcendental account in a regressive sense. Kant's aim is not to prove but to explain the validity of the categories. Ameriks says that the misunderstanding of this critical point has been the basis for the prevailing interpretation of the Transcendental Deduction, which he calls the received interpretation. It has been championed by such prominent scholars as Peter Strawson, Jonathan Bennett, and Robert Paul Wolff. One way or another, Ameriks says, all of them have tried to read the Transcendental Deduction as a progressive argument, which leads logically from a premise to a conclusion. For example, the Transcendental Deduction is often taken as the deductive argument from the transcendental apperception to the a priori synthetic principles. Because Kant never gives such a deductive proof, his transcendental argument has been branded as faulty or deficient by the champions of the prevailing interpretation. But this is a wrong way of reading it, according to Ameriks; the right way is to take it as a regressive argument. Ameriks's distinction between progressive and regressive arguments is not exactly the same as my own account of these as the distinction between the bottom-up argument in the subjective deduction and the top-down argument in the objective deduction. Ameriks believes that both the subjective and the objective deductions should be read as a regressive argument whereas they have been read as a progressive one. This plunges us into a big terminological confusion of 'progressive' and 'regressive'. Perhaps we can avoid it by using Charles Peirce's distinction between deduction and abduction. The Peircean deduction is the logical deduction of a conclusion from a premise. The Peircean abduction is the opposite process of finding an explanation for any given fact or proposition. Ameriks's contention can be restated as: The Transcendental Deduction is meant to be an abductive argument, but it has been taken for a deductive one by many Kant scholars.

This is the most critical point for understanding Kant's tortuous manoeuvre in the Transcendental Deduction, whether it is successful or not. But Ameriks's crucial thesis cannot become complete until Kant's transcendental explanandum is clearly spelled out. What is to be explained by his transcendental account? Ameriks calls it 'empirical knowledge' and 'some empirical knowledge'. But that can make the Deduction too easy. Empirical knowledge can be explained even by Hume's theory of knowledge. But Kant's requirement for empirical knowledge is far stiffer than Hume's. The former includes objectivity and necessity. Kant's transcendental explanandum is neither the Humean empirical knowledge nor the empirical knowledge of common sense, but the knowledge of pure natural science. In §15 of the *Prolegomena*, he says, 'We nevertheless actually possess a pure natural science in which are propounded, *a priori* and with all the necessity requisite to apodeictic propositions, laws to which nature is subject' (tr. Ellington). These a priori laws are the same as those Kant says the understanding prescribes to nature in the Transcendental Deduction of the first *Critique*. Pure natural science is the study of these a priori laws of nature. In the second edition Introduction, Kant claims to find a priori synthetic truths not only in mathematics and physics, but even in our common understanding, for example, the a priori truth of the causal principle (B3–6). He further holds that only a priori synthetic principles can provide the secure basis for a science in mathematics and physics. This establishes a parallel between his transcendental account of geometry and his transcendental account of empirical knowledge. Just as he tries to explain the synthetic necessity of geometry, so he tries to explain the synthetic necessity of pure natural science and the common understanding. If the transcendental explanandum for the Transcendental Deduction is defined in this stiff manner, the requirement for the regressive deduction cannot be any weaker than the requirement for the progressive deduction. These two forms of deduction have to cover exactly the same points. Therefore they are substantively identical and only procedurally different, as I said earlier.

Before we can fully understand Ameriks's crucial thesis, we also have to clarify Kant's transcendental explanans, which is required for explaining his transcendental explanandum. Unfortunately, Ameriks says nothing about it. In fact, the transcendental explanans is as elusive as the transcendental explanandum. For example, does the causal principle belong to the explanans or explanandum? Most commentators do not even consider this question in their critical evaluation of the Transcendental Deduction. But their critical evaluation cannot have a clear target until Kant's explanans and explanandum are clearly identified. Before taking on this elusive question, we had better consider the B Deduction. In the first edition preface to the *Critique*, Kant has expressed his uneasiness over the A Deduction. There he says that the subjective deduction is not essential for proving the objective validity of the categories, that is, only the objective deduction is essential for his purpose. He admits that the subjective deduction is somewhat hypothetical. But he claims that it cannot affect the full force of the objective deduction. He makes this point largely to forestall adverse criticism. But the A Deduction was unfavourably received by his critics. So he reorganized it as the B Deduction, which eliminates the subjective deduction and begins with the transcendental apperception. Hence the B Deduction appears to be a restatement of the objective deduction of the A Deduction. But the B Deduction contains one textual enigma. In §26, Kant says that the transcendental deduction has been given in §20 and §21. In fact, §20 gives the appearance of summing up his transcendental argument. §21 is labelled as an Observation. He often uses this label for incidental remarks following an important proof. Hence §21 may appear to be an appendage to §20, but what he says in it is totally contrary to this expectation. He says that he is only making a beginning for the deduction. How can he make a beginning for the transcendental deduction in §21, if he has finished it in §20? This has been the enigma for the B Deduction.

Dieter Henrich presented his solution of this enigma in the famous paper, 'The Proof Structure of Kant's Transcendental Deduction'. According to this paper, the Transcendental Deduction is a two-step argument. In the first step, the categories apply only to the representations united in a single intuition. But this restriction is lifted in the second step; the categories now apply to all representations. The scope of validation widens from one intuition to all intuitions. But this procedure of validation makes little sense because the problem of categorial validation cannot change from a smaller to a large scope of intuitions. The categorial function of synthesis is the same procedure whether it operates on one or many intuitions. Henrich's account of the two-step argument was so artificial that Henry Allison was prompted to revise it as follows. He uses the distinction between objective validity and objective reality to mark the two steps in the B Deduction. Although he cannot make the distinction with precision, he says, objective validity concerns all types of object, whereas objective reality concerns only what Strawson calls the object in the weighty sense. He then argues that the objective validity of categories is proved in the first stage of the B Deduction and their objective reality in the second stage.[4] But the objective reality of categories is inseparable from their objective validity because the former stands on the latter (A95). Hence Allison's account of the two steps is as artificial as Henrich's. But I have not found any better account of the textual enigma than these two. So I venture to offer my own.

The function of categories is differently described in A and B Deductions. In the A Deduction, Kant considers only their synthetic function as the rules of synthesis. In the B Deduction, he first considers their logical function as the forms of judgement and then their synthetic function. Hence the B Deduction goes through two stages. The first stage is completed by §20, and the second stage begins in §21. I will try to substantiate this point. At the beginning of the B Deduction, Kant stresses the logical function of the categories. He says that all categories are grounded in logical functions of judgement (B131). In the next three sections, he restates his theory of the transcendental apperception as the basic premise for his proof. He again stresses the objective unity of the transcendental consciousness in contrast to the subjective unity of the empirical consciousness as he did in the A Deduction. But his next move is surprising. In §19, he invokes the logical function of judgement to explain the objectivity of the transcendental consciousness. He says that a judgement states the objective relation between its subject and predicate by its copula 'is'. The judgement 'The body is heavy' states the objective relation of two representations. Hence it is different from their subjective association of empirical intuitions. Their objective relation can be derived only from their necessary relation in the transcendental apperception (B142). Thus, every judgement states an objective fact, which is independent of subjective feelings, because it secures the objective relation of subject and predicate. Kant says that this objective function is performed by the categories. This is a strange assertion because he has just assigned the objective function not to the categories, but to the forms of judgement. But the categories in their logical function are none other than the forms of judgement as we noted earlier. This is his account of categorial function on the logical level. When he states a summary of this account in §20, he stresses the logical function of judgement twice and then says, 'Now the *categories* are just these [logical] functions of judgement' (B143).

This is the first stage of the B Deduction that does not go beyond the logical function of pure concepts. But their synthetic functions, which are required for the unity of transcendental apperception, are discussed in the second stage of the B Deduction. In §21, Kant talks about the synthetic function of the understanding. This is the beginning of the second stage of the B Deduction. Whereas the first stage is limited to the logical function of the categories, the second stage extends to their role as the rules of synthesis (B145). The relation of these two stages is the relation of form and matter. When Kant says that a judgement is objective in §19, he is talking about its objectivity only in its form. It is a further question whether it is objective in its matter or content. If his statement is taken without this qualification, every judgement should be objective in both form and matter. That would contradict his own distinction between the judgement of perception and the judgement of experience in the *Prolegomena*, where he assigns subjectivity to the judgement of perception and objectivity to the judgement of experience. This contradiction can be avoided by the distinction between the form and matter of judgement. The judgement of experience is objective both in its form and matter, whereas the judgement of perception is objective only in its form, but not in its matter. The matter or content of judgement will be provided by the transcendental synthesis of imagination, which is performed by the synthetic function of the categories. This theory of synthetic function was presented in the subjective deduction of the first edition. Thus Kant reinstates the subjective deduction in §24 of the B Deduction and then reaffirms the conclusion of the A Deduction: The categories prescribe laws a priori to appearances and the understanding is the law-giver of nature. Therefore, the B Deduction yields the same result as the A Deduction. But the two stages of the B Deduction fully mirror the double function theory of categories. Their function of analytic unity is described in the first stage, and their function of synthetic unity in the second stage. On these two stages, the categories provide two levels of unity in the transcendental apperception. Kant ignored the first stage in the A Deduction because he was chiefly concerned with the synthetic function.

Now we have to take on the elusive question: What are Kant's transcendental explanandum and explanans? At the beginning of our discussion on the Transcendental Deduction, I variously described the outline of his transcendental argument: (1) to explain the possibility of experience, (2) to explain the possibility of empirical knowledge because 'experience' means empirical knowledge, and (3) to explain the possibility of the objective perceptual world because knowledge of such a perceptual world is empirical knowledge. Any of these can be used for the description of Kant's transcendental explanandum. Let us settle on the objective perceptual world. There is no need to give a transcendental account of it in the commonsense understanding, because there is nothing extraordinary about the objective perceptual world. But we should remember that Kant rejects this commonsense view of perception. Instead he accepts the subjectivist view of perception and repeatedly states that empirical intuitions are always subjective. Kant has inherited this view not only from Descartes and Leibniz, but also from Berkeley and Hume. On the subjectivist view, the objective perceptual world is impossible because everyone is trapped in an egocentric circle of subjective impressions. Humean phenomenalism is well known for its problem of scepticism. But its more serious problem is its solipsism. On that score, the Cartesians and the Leibnizians are not any better off than the Humeans because all of them subscribe to the subjectivist theory of perception. This theory has transformed the objective perceptual world from a commonplace to a miracle. This miracle is Kant's transcendental explanandum. He has to explain how this objective miracle arises from the subjective chaos of impressions. This is what I have called Kant's transcendental magic.

To explain the objective perceptual world is the objective deduction, and its explanandum is the objective world. But Kant's transcendental explanans is not so simple because it is not given as a single shot, but in a series of complicated moves. The first move is to explain the objectivity of the perceptual world. Kant cannot take objectivity as a primitive attribute of perceptual objects because they are made of subjective impressions. He explains objectivity in terms of necessity: Whatever is necessary is objective. This makes the necessity of the perceptual world the next transcendental explanandum. But perceptual objects can contain nothing necessary because they are the contingent aggregates of empirical intuitions. Kant divides all epistemic elements into the two domains of contingency and necessity. The domain of contingency is empirical; the domain of necessity is a priori. Given this demarcation, the necessity of the perceptual world can be explained only in terms of a priori elements. Those a priori elements are the categories or their synthetic function in the construction of perceptual objects. The categories explain the necessity of the perceptual world, which in turn explains its objectivity, the original transcendental explanandum. Therefore, the categories are the ultimate explanans.

The synthetic function of categories belongs to the transcendental subject or the understanding, and the object constructed by this synthetic function is the transcendental object. This process of construction is performed by the threefold synthesis, and it is explained in the subjective deduction. Thus the subjective deduction also explains the transcendental object, the objective unity of the perceptual world. Therefore its explanandum is the same as the explanandum of the objective deduction. But the subjective and the objective deductions appear to differ in their ultimate explanans. The threefold synthesis of the subjective deduction involves not only the categories, but also imagination and apprehension. But these additional elements are also involved in the synthetic function of categories for the objective deduction. Therefore the same elements are deployed as explanans in both the subjective and the objective deductions. If there is any difference between the two, the subjective deduction more clearly lays out Kant's a priori constructivism in terms of the threefold synthesis than the objective synthesis. This important point is often overlooked by many because it is overshadowed by their obsession with the objective validity of the categories. But their objective validity is proven by showing their function in Kant's a priori construction and his Copernican revolution.

Many commentators have complained that the Transcendental Deduction fails to prove the validity of the categories. This complaint is usually based on their assumption that the categories are Kant's explanandum. But the categories are his explanans. They play the same role for the Transcendental Deduction as the one played by the pure intuitions for the Transcendental Exposition. Just as the pure intuitions explain the synthetic necessity of geometry, so the pure concepts explain the synthetic necessity of pure natural science, that is, the synthetic necessity of its a priori laws. Those laws are generated by the synthetic function of the categories. Kant says, 'Categories are concepts which prescribe laws *a priori* to appearances, and hence to nature, the sum of all appearances' (B163, tr. Pluhar). Pure natural science is the science of those a priori laws of nature, and it is enshrined in our commonsense understanding, according to Kant. Hence he recognizes a clear parallel between the pure concepts and the pure intuitions. He says that the a priori laws of appearances must agree with the pure concepts of understanding for the same reason that appearances must agree with the forms of intuition (B164). Those a priori laws of nature establish the objectivity and necessity of the perceptual world. Since they are constructed by the synthetic function of categories, the former are the explananda to be explained by the latter as their explanans. The causal principle is one of these a priori laws. It is necessarily true of all perceptual objects because every one of them is constructed in accordance with the causal category. The necessity of the causal principle is explained by the necessity of the causal category.

Kant never questions the necessity of pure concepts throughout the Transcendental Deduction because it is his explanans. For example, he says, 'I need not insist upon the fact that, for instance, the concept of a cause involves the character of necessity, which no experience can yield' (A112, tr, Kemp Smith). In the *Prolegomena* (§26), he says that appearances constitute only the matter of experience and that its form is provided by the categories and their a priori principles. He also says that they can perform this formal function because they are a priori and necessary. Through this formal function, they provide the basis for objective experience, namely the experience of objects as existing in nature. Hence they are the a priori laws of nature (P §25). In short, the categories are the explanans for the objective experience or knowledge of nature. In summing up his argument for the a priori necessity of the categories, he says, 'I have amply shown that they [the categories] and the principle derived from them are firmly established *a priori* before all experience and have their undoubted objective rightness, though only regard to experience' (P §27). His unwavering conviction in causal necessity may sound highly naïve, given Hume's devastating critique, which is said to have awakened him from a dogmatic slumber. But the eighteenth century physicists never questioned the causal principle. Nor is it questioned by most physicists even today. Although Heisenberg's uncertainty principle is supposed to have injected indeterminacy into quantum mechanics, most particle physicists still assume that its wave functions are deterministic. They believe that quantum indeterminacy obtains only in the localization of wave packets when they collapse in an experimental apparatus. Kant firmly shared his conviction in the necessity of causal laws with all other physicists of his own age. It was beyond their belief that there could be any exceptions to those laws. Hence they firmly embraced determinism together with deism. They could not believe that the operation of physical laws could be altered or suspended even by divine intervention. That is why they could not accept religious miracles. Even Hume categorically denied the existence of those miracles although he was forcefully arguing against the idea of necessary connection. On the efficacy of causal laws, he was as deterministic as Kant and Newton were. If their necessity could never be explained by Hume's empirical theory, Kant thought, their explanans could be found only in the a priori concepts of the understanding.

Kant holds that the concept of causality is necessarily true because it is genetically a priori. This is the same argument he used for the necessity of pure intuitions. In both cases of pure concepts and pure intuitions, he is deriving their epistemic apriority (necessity) from their genetic apriority. This derivation is not a proof, but an assumption, which he never proves. But he has to prove their genetic apriority. He claims to have done it for the pure intuitions in the Metaphysical Expositions and for the pure concepts in the Metaphysical Deduction. He says, 'In the *metaphysical deduction* the a priori origin of the categories has been proved through their complete agreement with the general logical functions of thought; in the *transcendental deduction* we have shown their possibility as a priori modes of knowledge of objects of intuition in general' (B159, tr. Kemp Smith). This sentence refers to two *deductions*: one is supposedly metaphysical and the other one is transcendental. Though the Transcendental Deduction is a familiar title, the Metaphysical Deduction is a totally new one. Kant has never used it as the title of any segment of the *Critique*. Nor does he explain what this new title refers to. He casually claims that the Metaphysical Deduction has proven the a priori origin of the categories by using the logical functions of thought. He is evidently referring to chapter 1 of the Analytic of Concepts, whose official title is 'The Clue to the Discovery of All Pure Concepts of the Understanding'. He now calls it the Metaphysical Deduction. With this new label, it can be paired up with the Transcendental Deduction just as the Metaphysical Exposition is paired up with the Transcendental Exposition in the Transcendental Aesthetic. Just as the Metaphysical Expositions proves the genetic apriority (their a priori origin) of pure intuitions, the Metaphysical Deduction proves the genetic apriority of pure concepts. Since their genetic apriority can secure their epistemic apriority, the categories can function as the explanans in Kant's transcendental arguments.

The logical relation between the Metaphysical Exposition and the Transcendental Exposition parallels the logical relation between the Metaphysical Deduction and the Transcendental Deduction. We have noted that the Metaphysical Exposition is the logical premise for the Transcendental Exposition. Likewise, the Metaphysical Deduction is the logical premise for the Transcendental Deduction. This logical relation is the vital link between the two Deductions, which is usually overlooked by Kant scholars. Because most of them are distrustful of Kant's logical derivation of categories, they usually dismiss it and move on to his transcendental arguments on the assumption that the Metaphysical Deduction has no direct relevance for the Transcendental Deduction. They never suspect that the former is the premise for the latter. I have subjected Kant's categorial derivation to a rigorous scrutiny to show that this vital premise could not be secured by his logical trickery. Hence his transcendental argument cannot even take off the ground.

Let us outline the chain of Kant's transcendental argument. It may be stated in three steps: (1) the objectivity of experience (or the perceptual world), (2) necessity (the epistemic apriority of categories), and (3) the genetic apriority of categories. In the sequence of these three steps, (1) is explained by (2), which takes place in the Transcendental Deduction, and (2) is explained by (3), which takes place in the Metaphysical Deduction. Let us examine the soundness of these three steps. All subjectivists, the Humeans and the Cartesians alike, may reject the first step and claim that there is nothing objective in the perceptual world. We can do nothing about them, but let them wallow in their solipsistic swamps. Technically speaking, there is no way to talk with a solipsist. So we can gladly grant the first step for the Transcendental Deduction. But the move from the first to the second step is questionable. There is no need to explain the objectivity of experience in terms of its necessity. Kant has already established the objectivity of space and time in the Transcendental Aesthetic. Although empirical data are subjective, they can become objective if they can be placed in the objective frame of space and time. Their relation may still remain contingent, but their contingency is not the same as their subjectivity because contingency is perfectly compatible with objectivity. The existence of physical objects may be contingent, but their objectivity can never be affected by their contingency. There is no need to reduce objectivity to necessity. But Kant is compelled to make the reduction because he erroneously believes in the compatibility of objectivity with contingency. The move from the second to the third step is equally questionable because it stands on Kant's assumption that only genetic apriority can secure epistemic necessity. In the Transcendental Aesthetic, we noted, he assumes that the epistemic apriority of space and time is guaranteed by their genetic apriority. He makes the same assumption for the categories. But their genetic apriority has never been proven in the Metaphysical Deduction because it is based on Kant's misconception of the relation between logical and descriptive concepts. Even if we grant their genetic apriority, it cannot guarantee their epistemic apriority as we have noted in the case of pure intuitions. The convertibility of genetic apriority to epistemic apriority is Kant's central dogma, and the Transcendental Deduction is ultimately based on this transcendental dogma.

THE SCHEMATISM

The idea of giving schemata for the categories is not Kant's invention. It is an important legacy from Aristotle. Since his categories are the ultimate generic concepts, they have several species. He calls them the schemata of categories. For example, the primary and the secondary substances are the schemata for the category of substance, and the discrete and the continuous quantities are the schemata for the category of quantity (*Categoriae* 2a11–19; 4b20–1). The Aristotelian schematism provides specific concepts for a generic one. But it is hard to tell whether or not Kant follows this procedure. In the opening of the Schematism, he says that a concept is applied to an object by subsuming the latter under the former and that this operation is possible only when the concept is homogeneous with the object. When they are homogeneous with each other, he says, the concept can be intuited in the object (A137/B176). By 'the homogeneity of a concept with an object', he means the commensurateness of a concept with an object. He goes on to say that the pure concepts are heterogeneous with empirical intuitions. For example, the concept of causality can never be matched with a corresponding impression. Evidently, Kant has in mind Hume's contention that the concept of cause can never be traced back to any impressions. Hence the empirical intuitions cannot be subsumed under the categories. Consequently, the latter cannot be applied to the former. This is Kant's problem of categorical application, for whose solution he offers his theory of transcendental schemata.

Kant's statement on the difficulty of applying the categories to empirical intuitions is a big surprise for his readers, who have gone through the tortuous arguments of the Transcendental Deduction. Those arguments presuppose the application of the categories, without which there is no point in raising the question of their validity. Kant has not even intimated the difficulty of their application in any part of the Transcendental Deduction. Hence some critics have said that the problem of categorical application is nonexistent because objects are not meant to be subsumed under the Kantian categories as they are under the Aristotelian categories. The application of the former lies in their function as the forms of judgement or as the rules of synthesis. This is called the functional view of Kantian categories, which was presented in the Transcendental Deduction. In talking about the problem of subsumption, these critics say, Kant has forgotten the difference of his categories from Aristotle's. Thus, they have detected an obvious fissure between the Transcendental Deduction and the Schematism. Paul Guyer says that the Schematism sounds like the beginning of a new deduction of categories because it shows no trace of the Transcendental Deduction.[5] How to account for this fissure is probably the biggest problem for the Transcendental Analytic.

In the Transcendental Deduction, Kant has claimed that the objects are constructed by the synthetic function of categories. Therefore there can be no problem of their application to objects. The problem of application can arise only for those concepts which are applied to the independently existing objects. This difference can be stated in terms of Kant's distinction between the conformity of concepts to objects and the conformity of objects to concepts. The problem of application can arise in the conformity of concepts to objects, but not in the conformity of objects to concepts. These two types of relation between concepts and objects can produce two models: the construction model for the conformity of objects to concepts and the application model for the conformity of concepts to objects. The central issue for the construction model is the problem of categorial synthesis, which is essential for the construction of objects. I propose the thesis that Kant deploys the construction model first and then the application model and that this transition is marked by the Schematism. The Analytic of Concepts, which includes the Transcendental Deduction, advocates the construction model. The Analytic of Principles, which includes the Schematism of the Pure Concepts and the System of all Principles of Pure Understanding, advocates the application model.

The problem of categorial synthesis is central in the Transcendental Deduction. The problem of categorial application is not even mentioned in the A Deduction, and the word 'apply' or 'application' never appears in it in connection with the categories. But the problem of categorial application is central for the Analytic of Principles. In the B Deduction, to be sure, he talks about the application of categories in §22, §23, and §24, where he stresses that the application of categories is restricted to the objects of senses. But this restriction is not even mentioned in the A Deduction because there is no need for it. In the construction model, the objects are constructed out of empirical intuitions by the synthetic function of categories. This construction process automatically limits the application of categories to the phenomenal world. But there is no such built-in restriction in the application model because it applies the categories to the independently existing objects. When Kant talks about the restriction of categories to the objects of senses, he usually mentions the non-sensible objects or things in themselves (B149, A149/B188). Since the supersensible objects cannot be constructed, we can only try to apply the categories to them. But their legitimate application is impossible because those objects are inaccessible to us.

Kant's talk about the application of categories and its restriction to the phenomenal world in the B Deduction can be taken as the spillover effect of the application model from the Analytic of Principles. The application model in turn was carried over from the *Inaugural Dissertation*, whose central problem was the application of categories to the intelligible world. It predates Kant's Copernican revolution that has produced the construction model. It may also be called the prescription model because its function is supposedly to prescribe a priori laws to nature by the categories. On the other hand, the application model does not prescribe a priori laws. In his *Inaugural Dissertation*, Kant never regarded the application of pure concepts as the prescription of a priori laws to noumena. Likewise in the Analytic of Principles, as we will see later, he does not advocate the prescription of a priori laws to nature. The spirit of his Copernican revolution dictates that the construction model should completely replace the application model. The Transcendental Deduction is sufficient for the Transcendental Analytic; there is no point in reinstating the application model. But old habits die hard. Instead of jettisoning the application model, Kant has tried to retain and assimilate it into the construction model. In some passages, he talks as though the application of categories were inseparably connected with their synthetic function. This is the fusion of his two models that has produced a systematic confusion and complication in the Transcendental Analytic.

In the Schematism, Kant produces the schemata for the categories. A schema for a pure concept is called a transcendental schema, which he calls the third thing. It is said to be homogeneous with both the category and the appearance because it is sensible like empirical intuitions and pure like pure concepts. Therefore it can serve as the mediator between sensibility and the understanding (A138/B177). This is a dubious assertion. He has introduced 'homogeneity' and 'heterogeneity' for describing whether a concept is commensurate or incommensurate with an object. The fact that both pure concepts and pure intuitions are pure concerns only their genetic origin, which has nothing to do with their commensurateness or incommensurateness with each other. If the concept of causality is incommensurate with empirical intuitions, it is even more incommensurate with pure intuition of time or space. It makes no sense to say that one moment of time is the cause of another moment, or that one part of space is the cause of another part. The alleged function of mediation is an impossible one. Moreover, if Kant is to follow his own description of transcendental schemata, he should construct them out of pure intuitions. But he gives only two such schemata, the pure image of space as the schema of quantity and the pure image of time as the schema of the concept of objects, and then constructs all other transcendental schemata out of impure images. Let us now examine all of them.

In naming the schemata of quantity, Kant does not even mention the three categories of quantity: unity, plurality, and totality. He just names space as the pure image of all magnitudes (*quantorum*) and time as the pure image of all objects of senses (A142/B182). The former is the transcendental schema for the

Aristotelian category of quantity, and the latter is the transcendental schema for the concept of object. As we noted earlier, these two categories are not on Kant's table of categories. Then Kant gives number as the pure schema of magnitude (*quantitatis*). Number is a concept, whereas space and time are pure intuitions. Kant is using these two media to produce two kinds of schema: the concept-schema and the image-schema. The first schema of quantity is an image-schema, and the second schema of quantity is a concept-schema. These two schemata correspond to Aristotle's two schemata of quantity, the continuous and the discrete quantity. In the name of schematism, Kant is replacing his three categories of quantity with the Aristotelian categories of quantity. We have already noted that Kant's three categories of quantity cannot be derived from the logical quantifiers. But that is not his only problem with the categories of unity, plurality, and totality. They are insufficient to discharge the function of quantitative categories, especially the concept of continuous quantity. Kant can amend their insufficiency only by replacing his categories with Aristotle's. This is his shameless play of substitution.

Kant does not give schemata for all three categories of quality, either, but only for the category of reality. He defines it as the quantity of something insofar as it fills time, namely, sensation and the object of sensation, which is called the transcendental matter (A143/B182). He is defining the schema of a pure concept by the empirical content of time rather than by the pure intuition of time. This goes against his initial contention that the pure concepts cannot be applied directly to empirical intuitions. What is even more surprising is that the schema of reality turns out to be the quality of sensation or its substratum. Thus he has introduced the Aristotelian category of quality to replace his three pure concepts of quality. This is the same trick of categorial substitution that he used for the quantitative categories. He then says that the quality of sensation or its substratum can be quantitatively measured. This is his conversion of the category of quality into another category of quantity, which will later be called intensive magnitude in the Anticipations of Perception. This conversion eliminates all qualitative categories from his table of categories.

Kant defines the schema of substance as permanence of the real in time, which is represented as the substrate of empirical intuitions. This definition fuses the schema of substance with the schema of reality because 'the real in time' is the schema of reality. The schema of substance involves the empirical content of time as much as the schema of reality. The substrate of empirical intuitions appears to be the same as the transcendental matter that corresponds to sensations. What is new with the schema of substance is the concept of permanence. Where does this concept come from? Is it a priori or empirical? It cannot be empirical because Kant holds that nothing with empirical intuitions is permanent. Nor can it be a pure concept of the understanding because it cannot be found in his table of categories. The same questions arise for the concept of substrate. This concept cannot be empirically derived, either, because the substrate cannot be perceived. Nor can it be a pure concept because it cannot be found in Kant's table of categories. These questions are concerned with the question of what epistemic resources Kant is using for the production of his transcendental schemata. If these two concepts of permanence and substrate are neither a priori nor empirical, then they must have been created by Kant or someone else. The formation of new concepts is one of the important operations that take place in the name of transcendental schematism. But it is seldom noticed because it is never named. The concept-formation performs a similar service as the concept-substitution. Both of them provide the basic ontological concepts that are not available on Kant's table of categories. He also uses 'the real' in defining the schema of causality, 'the real upon which, whenever posited, something always follows' (A144/B183). He is now using two empirical concepts, 'reality' and 'succession', in defining a transcendental schema. The schema of community is the combination of the schema of substance with the schema of causality because it is the concept of mutual interaction of substances.

The schema of possibility is the agreement of the synthesis of different representations with the conditions of time in general. This is Kant's transformation of the Leibnizian category of possibility. Whereas the Leibnizian possibility requires only logical consistency on the conceptual level, the Kantian possibility expands this requirement to include agreement with the conditions of sensibility. Kant defines the schema of actuality as existence at a determinate time, and the schema of necessity as the existence of an object at all times. These two schemata deviate from his earlier assertion that his modal categories do not concern the content of judgement because they are not ontic but epistemic (A74/B100). The ontic modality concerns the nature of an object or rather its ontological status. The traditional modal concepts have been ontic. But Kant wants to restrict his modal concepts to the epistemic function. He insists that they are concerned only with our epistemic relation to a judgement, not with its content. But his modal schemata of actuality and necessity are ontic, although the schema of possibility is not. It concerns the nature of an object whether it exists at some definite time or at all times. Kant is confused between the two types of modality, and his confusion will show up again later in his exposition of modal principles.

The transcendental schemata are sometimes called the schematized categories, while the original categories are called the unschematized categories. These two sets cannot be paired up in a one-to-one relation. There are twelve original categories, which are grouped into four triplets. But Kant has given two schemata (the continuous and the discrete quantity) for the three unschematized categories of quantity. He calls only one of them a schema and the other a pure image. In the Axioms of Intuition, he will use the concept of extensive magnitude as the only schematized category of quantity. Thus he winds up with one schematized category for the three unschematized categories of quantity. Again, he gives only one schematized category of intensive magnitude for the three unschematized categories of quality. He has reduced the number of categories in the first two triplets from six to two. This reduction is dictated by his substitution of the Aristotelian categories of quantity and quality for his own unschematized categories. He has given six schematized categories for the remaining six unschematized categories of relation and modality. Thus he has given only eight schematized categories altogether. In his summation, he divides them into four groups: the time-series, the time-content, the time-order, and the scope of time. Only the schemata of time-series are made of pure intuitions. All other schemata are made of the empirical content of time. The time-content is empirical, and so is the time-order because the temporal order of events is empirical. So is the scope of time. In the three quarters of transcendental schemata, Kant has directly applied the pure concepts to empirical intuitions. That goes against his initial claim that they cannot be directly applied to empirical intuitions.

After the summation, Kant says that the categories have no

meaning at all until they are given reference to objects by their schematization (A146/B186). Evidently, he is now thinking of the unschematized categories as their logical functions of judgement. Prior to their schematization, he says, the categories have only logical functions (A147/B186). So he says that the schematism of sensibility realizes the categories, that is, they become generic or material concepts with meaning. This is the opposite of what he said at the beginning of Schematism. He began with the problem of subsumption that arose for the categories as generic concepts. But he now talks as though he had completely forgotten the problem of categorial subsumption. He ends the Schematism by describing it as the conversion of logical concepts into generic ones. He is now recovering his double function theory of categories. He has said that the categories are originally the logical concepts embedded in the forms of judgement and then become the rules of synthesis. But he has never explained how the categories are transformed from logical concepts to the rules of synthesis. This transformation was presupposed for the A Deduction, but Kant skipped over it. The B Deduction was more faithful to Kant's double function theory of the categories than the A Deduction. The two stages of the B Deduction traced the two stages of the categorial function, first the logical function and then the synthetic function. Even there Kant did not explain the conversion of logical concepts into the rules of synthesis. This is the vital link missing from both the A and the B Deduction. He is now trying to provide that link by saying that the schematism is the mechanism for converting logical concepts to generic concepts. But such a conversion is a logically impossible operation because those two types of concepts have nothing in common. These confusions arise from his double function theory of the categories or his identity theory of logical and descriptive concepts.

A PRIORI PRINCIPLES

Kant generates eight a priori principles from the eight schematized categories. These principles are supposed to establish the objective perceptual world for the transcendental apperception. The first one is The Axioms of Intuition: 'All appearances are, in their intuition, extensive magnitudes' in the A edition, and 'All intuitions are extensive magnitudes' in the B edition. Kant begins the proof of this principle by stating that all appearances are given through the pure intuitions of space and time and that the consciousness of the synthetic unity of space and time becomes possible through the category of magnitude. Then he defines extensive magnitude as the representation of a whole produced by the extensive synthesis of its parts, that is, by the successive addition of homogeneous parts (A162/B203). This definition is ambiguous about the origin of extensive magnitudes. It may mean that the extensive magnitude of a whole is produced by the successive addition of its parts or that the former is measured by the latter. Depending on these two meanings, the extensive synthesis should be understood as the device (1) for producing extensive magnitudes or (2) for measuring them. (1) appears to be supported by Kant's claim that a line cannot be represented without drawing it in thought by successively adding all its parts (A162/B203). If a line is produced by an extensive synthesis, so is its extensive magnitude. But do the parts have any extensive magnitudes in their own right? If they do not, their successive addition cannot produce the extensive magnitude of the whole. So we had better assume that the parts have their own extensive magnitudes. In that case, their extensive magnitudes cannot be products of extensive synthesis because the former are presupposed for the latter.

Kant may say that the extensive magnitude of each part is also produced by an extensive synthesis. That will turn the extensive synthesis into an infinite regress, which cannot be executed by the human understanding. So we have to favour (2) over (1) in our interpretation of the extensive synthesis. We have to distinguish between extension as a primitive property and its magnitude. The former can exist apart from measurement, but the latter is produced by measurement, which depends on the extensive synthesis. This may be the best way to interpret Kant's theory of extensive synthesis. He holds that pure intuitions have extensive magnitudes because they are apprehended by extensive synthesis. He further holds that all empirical intuitions gain extensive magnitudes because they are placed in space and time.

The Axioms of Intuition is supposed to explain how mathematical axioms are generated by extensive synthesis. But this account contradicts the one given in the Transcendental Aesthetic, where Kant appealed to our spatial intuition for the recognition of the truth that the straight line is the shortest distance between two points. He now attributes the truth of the same axiom to extensive synthesis. Evidently, he assumes that the extensive magnitude of every line is generated by extensive synthesis. Therefore, the truth of the axiom that a straight line is shorter than a crooked line between two points is based on the extensive synthesis. This is a quantitative account of the axiom because extensive synthesis is the operation for measuring the extensive quantity of two lines. On the other hand, his earlier account of the same axiom was a qualitative one because it was based on the intuitive inspection of the quality of two lines. But we have just noted that the extensive magnitude cannot be generated by the extensive synthesis. We can directly appeal to our spatial intuition to know that a straight line is shorter than a crooked one. We can compare their lengths in our intuition, without drawing them by extensive synthesis as Kant claims. Hence extensive synthesis appears to be gratuitous and circuitous for recognizing the truth of the axiom. The theory of extensive synthesis also contradicts his theory of pure intuitions given in the Transcendental Aesthetic, where he said that the whole space and time precede their parts. But the theory of extensive synthesis says that the whole is produced by the successive addition of parts. Neither of these two views is faithful to his view of space and time as *quanta continua* (A169/B211). Both the successive addition and division can be performed equally well on the manifold of space and time. Neither of them can have priority over the other.

The Anticipations of Perception is the rule of synthesis for intensive magnitude, which parallels the rule of extensive synthesis. Although a sensation is not subject to the successive synthesis from parts to the whole, Kant holds, it is capable of gradually diminishing to nothing. The quality of sensation is a continuous quantity just like space and time, but it is not extended. Therefore its quantity is called intensive magnitude. Kant attributes intensive magnitude not only to sensations, but also to their substrates, which he calls the real. It is clearly a matter of empirical discovery whether the intensity of a sensation and the quality of its substratum is continuously variable. But Kant pronounces it as an a priori principle, that is, we can a priori anticipate that sensations and their substrata must have intensive magnitudes. Nor is there any a priori way of knowing that 'the real' is the substrate of sensation and that it has an intensive magnitude. Kant's proof of the

Anticipations of Perceptions is a string of empirical assertions. In the concluding paragraph, he admits that the alleged a priori anticipation is indeed strange (A175/B217). He is chiefly concerned with the objective determination of empirical intuitions. The common function of all his a priori principles is to establish the objectivity of appearances for the transcendental apperception. In the Anticipations of Perception, he is assuming that the quality of empirical intuitions can be made objective by their quantitative determination. For example, the hotness of water is a subjective feeling, but its temperature is an objective measurement. This may be the way to convert empirical intuitions from subjective feelings into objective facts. Kant evidently thinks that this conversion can be accomplished by the synthesis of intensive magnitude. But it is impossible to know a priori that the quality of subjective sensations and their substrates can be quantitatively determined. Hence the Anticipations of Perception is only an a priori conjecture.

Kant's formulation of the First Analogy is quite different in the two editions of the *Critique*. In the first edition, it asserts the permanent substratum for the changing appearances. In the second edition, it asserts the permanence of the substance in its quantum, the conservation of matter. The First Analogy is the extension of the Anticipations of Perception. The latter asserts the existence of the real as the substrate of sensation; the former asserts its permanence. But the concepts of the real and the permanent substrate are not empirical in the Humean sense, that is, they cannot be derived from impressions. How then has Kant obtained these concepts? This is the first question for the First Analogy. He may say that the concept of a permanent substance has been obtained by transcendental schematization, that is, by adding the concept of permanence to the logical concept of subject. Then he has to explain how he has gained the concept of permanence. This concept cannot be contained in the concept of substance. If it were so contained, 'The substance is permanent' would be an analytic proposition. The concept of permanence cannot be derived empirically because there is nothing permanent in the world of impressions. Then its origin must be a priori. But it cannot be found in Kant's table of categories. So there is no way of telling whether or not Kant would regard the concept of permanence as a priori. Nor can he say that the concept of permanence is his own invention because it goes back to ancient Greece.

This is another case of showing that his table of categories as a system of pure concepts is neither systematic nor complete. There is one more serious problem with Kant's conception of substance. Its permanence can be taken to be absolute or relative. The Aristotelian substance is not absolutely permanent; it can come into existence and go out of it. But Kant sometimes gives absolute permanence to his substance by denying its coming into being and its ceasing to be (A188/B231). It is also hard to determine whether he admits only one or many substances. Sometimes he uses 'substance' as a mass noun which indicates no number; sometimes he uses it as a count noun in its plural form ('substances'). These ambiguities make it hard to follow his arguments for the First Analogy. His argument begins with the premise that time does not change. That is an axiomatic truth. Changes take place in time. His next premise is that time cannot be perceived. This appears to go against his original argument that time is an object of a priori intuition, as we noted earlier. He then argues that there must be the permanent substratum of appearances because the temporal relation of succession and coexistence (or simultaneity) can be perceived only in the permanent substance (A182/B225). He also claims that even the temporal property of duration can be perceived only in the permanent substance because all appearances are ephemeral (A183/B226). This is his proof for the existence of substance. He finally concludes that the unity of time is secured by the unity of the permanent substance. If there is more than one substance, he claims, there must be more than one system of time (A186/B229). At this point, he surely accepts only one permanent substance for the whole world, and he refines his conception of substance as permanent matter, which can never be diminished or destroyed. He concludes his theory of substance by saying that all changes are only alterations of one permanent substance (A187–9/B230–2).

Kant's one substance appears to be virtually identical with Spinoza's substance minus the attribute of thought. But I cannot make any sense of his argument that the permanent substance is required to make the passage of time perceivable. Even if time is not perceivable as he says, the permanent substance cannot be any more perceivable than time itself. The substratum of appearances is inaccessible to any intuition, pure or empirical. How can the unperceivable substance make the unperceivable time perceivable?

Kant never recognizes this problem. Instead, he baldly claims that the permanent substance is required for all types of temporal relations – duration, succession, and simultaneity. Let us consider the duration of a sound. I can perceive it in time, but I cannot associate it with any permanent unperceivable substance. If the permanence of substance is understood as the conservation of matter, I cannot see how it affects my perception of the duration of a sound. On Kant's theory, time is the form of appearances, that is, their temporal relations are perceived in time. Now he says that those relations can be perceived only in the substance. This contradicts his theory of pure intuitions in the Transcendental Aesthetic, where he argued for the original unity of space and time. He now says that the emergence of a substance and its disappearance will remove the condition for the empirical unity of time (A188–9/B231–2). If the unity of space and time is dependent on the unity of substance, then space and time should be the properties of substance. This is the view of Spinoza and Leibniz, which Kant rejected in the Transcendental Aesthetic. It appears that he has completely forgotten what he had said in the Transcendental Aesthetic. This is one of the reasons for the patchwork theory, that is, he organized the *Critique* by putting together various portions written over so many years that he could not secure their continuity and coherence.

The Second Analogy is Kant's causal principle. The First Analogy leads us to expect him to use the concept of substance in his discussion of the temporal succession of cause and effect because he has said that the permanent substance is the matrix for all temporal relations and that all changes are only alterations of the permanent substance. But this expectation is defeated in the first edition. Only in the second edition does Kant mention the First Analogy as a preliminary for his proof of the Second Analogy (B232–4). But this preliminary is only perfunctory. His theory of substance is never used in his proof of the Second Analogy. He tries to build the proof on the distinction between the subjective succession of appearances and their objective succession. The former is the connection that takes place in the subject; the latter is the connection that takes place in the object. He explains this point by the perception of a house and a boat. When I see a house, I can first see its front and then its back, or reverse the sequence of these two perceptions. This is the subjective succession, which does not take place in the house itself. On the other hand, when I see a boat floating down a river, I can first see it upstream and then see it downstream. The sequence of these two perceptions is not only in the subject, but also in the object. There are two kinds of sequence: reversible and irreversible. Kant holds that the objective sequence is irreversible because it is in the object whereas the subjective sequence is reversible because it is in the subject. Then he makes the problematic move of claiming that the irreversible sequence is the determination of the causal principle. Therefore the causal principle is necessary for knowing the objective sequence. This is supposed to prove its necessity for the possibility of experience, which is defined as the knowledge of objective phenomena. This is the gist of Kant's proof.

Kant's distinction between reversible and irreversible perceptions is the first premise for his proof. But it has been questioned. Suppose that you first see the front of a house and then its back, and then come back to the front. Your perception of the house will go through the front-to-back sequence and the back-to-front sequence. But the second sequence cannot be the reversal of the first sequence because your second perception of the front is a different perception from the first one. All perceptions are irreversible by their nature. Is there then no difference between perceiving a house and a boat? Some commentators have tried to state their difference as the perception of an enduring object (a stationary house) and that of an ongoing event (a floating boat). This is not quite right, either. The perception of a boat also involves an enduring object (a boat) as much as the perception of a house does. There is no point in restricting the concept of an event to the motion of a boat, either. The stationary house is as much an event as the floating boat. Suppose that the house has been standing on its site for ten minutes. That is an event of ten-minute duration. The house has been acted on by all the forces of the universe just as the floating boat has been. All objects of perception are events, which take place in the space–time continuum. All perceptions are also events. Therefore, neither the events nor their perceptions are reversible. There is no reversible sequence of events, and that eliminates the first premise for Kant's proof.

For the sake of argument, let us grant the distinction between the reversible and the irreversible succession. Can it be used to prove the causal principle? Kant says that the causal principle is necessary for determining an irreversible succession. If he is right, we cannot determine the objective sequence of two events until we discover their causal connection. That is completely counter-intuitive. We usually recognize the irreversible sequence of events without knowing their causal connection. I can see a bird flying into my yard and then another bird flying away. I can recognize the sequence of these two events without knowing their causal connection. Kant's claim that the causal principle is necessary for the recognition of objective sequences is to place the cart before the horse. The normal causal investigation begins with the temporal determination of two succeeding events and then proceeds to the discovery of their causal connection. In some cases, the investigation shows that there is no causal connection between those events. In that case, we have to say that the sequence of those two events is subjective. If Kant is right, we cannot say that one event has objectively succeeded another until we determine their causal connection. But we cannot begin the study of their causal connection before determining their objective sequence. This vicious circle is the result of placing the cart of causal determination before the horse of time-determination. It can be broken only by recognizing that the determination of an objective succession does not depend on the causal principle. Thus Kant's proof falls apart even if we grant the questionable distinction between the reversible and the irreversible successions. There can be no a priori proof of the causal principle. Nor can it be derived from impressions as Hume has shown. Hence we have to take it only as a hypothesis that belongs to theory-formation. But Kant never considers the need for the formation of concepts or theories. Instead he just assumes that all our epistemic apparatus must come either from a priori or from a posteriori sources. Therefore he tries to squeeze all his concepts and principles into one of these two permanent compartments. This is one of the fatal defects in his architectonic manoeuvres.

Kant states the Third Analogy differently in the two editions. In the A edition, it asserts the mutual interaction of all substances. Unlike the First Analogy, the Third Analogy clearly admits the plurality of substances. But it is surely beyond a priori knowledge whether there exists only one or more than one substance. It is even more so that their coexistence entails their interaction. Probably for this reason, Kant has rephrased the Third Analogy for the B edition, which says that the coexistence of substances can be perceived only by their mutual causation. In his proof, Kant says that things are coexistent when their perceptions are reciprocal. For example, I can first see the moon and then the earth and then reverse this procedure. The reciprocal perceptions are what he called the reversible perceptions and branded as subjective in the Second Analogy. But he now says that they can be objective, too, and that the objective reciprocal perception means the coexistence of substances. Then he gives the transcendental argument that the principle of mutual causation is indispensable for recognizing the objectivity of reciprocal perceptions. This argument runs in parallel to his proof for the causal law: the recognition of two coexisting objects requires the law of reciprocal causation just as the recognition of objective sequence requires the causal law (A212/B259). Kant's argument for the Third Analogy is as faulty as his argument for the Second Analogy. Moreover, he does not even mention the permanent substance for the proof of the Third Analogy any more than for that of the Second Analogy, totally ignoring his earlier contention that the permanent substance was the common basic framework for all temporal relations. If there is only one substance as he said in the First Analogy, it cannot coexist with any other. If there are many substances, they must coexist at all times because they are permanent. Hence there is no need for the proof of their coexistence. Even if they coexist eternally, their coexistence cannot be perceived because they are unperceivable. Thus, all three Analogies of Experience turn out to be Kant's a priori speculations about the unperceivable objects.

Kant makes a general observation on the three Analogies just before giving his proofs. He assigns the constitutive function to the Axioms of Intuitions and the Anticiptions of Perception. They are the rules of synthesis for the constitution of objects. But the three Analogies are not constitutive of objects (A179–80/B222). Hence they are called the regulative principles. Kant says that they apply only to the relations of existence, that is, they apply only to the relations of existing objects. He says that their existence cannot be constructed. The constitutive principles are for constructing perceptual objects; the regulative principles are for determining the relation of existing objects. The latter principles are used to discriminate the objective relation of representations from their subjective relation. This is surely a different function from the function of constructing objects. I have earlier proposed the distinction between Kant's construction model and his application model. The constitutive principles belong to the construction model; they are constitutive of objects. The regulative principles belong to the application model; they are applied to existing objects. I can now more clearly delineate the operation of these two models in the *Critique* than in my initial sketch.

In the Transcendental Deduction, Kant's deployment of the construction model is largely limited to the three categories of Relation. They are the rules of synthesis that perform the constitutive function. They can perform this function because they are relational concepts that can combine the manifold of intuitions. But the categories of Quantity and Quality cannot function as the rules of synthesis because they are monadic concepts. For example, the pure concept of reality or negation cannot be a rule of synthesis. The same is true of the concept of unity, plurality, or totality. They can be used jointly in the synthesis of intuitions, but none of them can singly operate as a rule of synthesis. In the Analytic of Principles, Kant converts these monadic concepts to two relational concepts of extensive and intensive magnitude ('extensive' and 'intensive' are relational adjectives), and produces the Axioms of Intuition and the Anticipations of Perception, which can perform the function of construction by their extensive and intensive syntheses.

The categories of Relation also go through their functional transformation in the Analytic of Principles. Whereas Kant assigned to the categories the function of prescribing a priori laws to nature, he does not assign this awesome function to the three Analogies. But he may appear to make the same argument in the Analogies of Experience that he made in the Transcendental Deduction. He argues for the necessity of a priori principles for the possibility of experience in the Analogies of Experience, as he argued for the necessity of categories for the possibility of experience in the Transcendental Deduction. But the possibility of experience is achieved in different ways in the two cases. As we noted earlier, 'experience' means the knowledge of objective objects and their relations. In the Transcendental Deduction, the categories make experience possible by constructing objective objects from subjective impressions. But the three Analogies make experience possible by discriminating the objective connection of appearances from their subjective connection. Their objective connection is not constructed, but only identified by the application of a priori principles to the independently existing objects such as a stationary house or a floating boat. In the construction model, these objects cannot even exist until they are constructed by the synthetic act of the transcendental subject. And their construction prescribes a priori laws to nature. But Kant does not even mention this prescriptive function in the Analogies of Experience. Only in the Postulates of Empirical Thought, he casually says, 'The understanding gives a priori the rule to experience as such only according to the subjective and formal conditions of both sensibility and apperception, the conditions which alone make experience possible' (A230/B283, tr. Pluhar). He is talking about a single rule that cannot be identified with the a priori laws of nature because it is the rule that brings together all appearances into one experience. Thus the three Analogies belong to the application model, whereas the Axioms of Intuition and the Anticipations of Perception belong to the construction model. The modal categories and principles belong to neither because their function is not ontic but only epistemic. They concern not the objects of experience, but only our modes of knowledge.

The Postulates of Empirical Thought are Kant's modal principles. He gives no proofs for them because they are only definitions. They do not concern the content of our knowledge, but only its epistemic modality. The First Postulate defines the possible as that which agrees with the formal conditions of experience, that is, the formal conditions of sensibility and the understanding. This is stronger than the Leibnizian concept of possibility, which is logical, that is, whatever is free of logical contradiction is regarded as possible. The Kantian possibility is the real or empirical possibility; it is whatever is really possible in the empirical world. Kant explains their difference by the example of a figure bound by two straight lines. This figure is logically possible because it can be conceived without contradiction. But it is not possible in the empirical world because it is incompatible with the formal condition of sensibility, namely, space. We can think of an object that is impossible because it is incompatible with the formal conditions of the understanding; for example, a random event that is not subject to the causal principle. It is a logical possibility, but not a real one because it violates the formal conditions of the understanding.

The Second Postulate defines the actual as that which is bound up with the material conditions of experience. Those material conditions are the conditions of perception. Whatever is perceivable is actual. The Second Postulate differs from the schema of actuality given in the Schematism, where Kant defined it as existence at some definite time. I pointed out that this definition was ontic rather than epistemic. The new definition of actuality makes it clearly epistemic by linking it to the material conditions of experience. The first two Postulates stand in the relation of form and content (or matter). They are complements to each other. The Third Postulate is again different from the schema of necessity given in the Schematism, where necessity was defined as existence of an object at all times. That was ontic rather than epistemic. Kant formulates the Third Postulate by the combination of the first two Postulates. This can make the Third Postulate fully epistemic because the first two Postulates have been defined in epistemic terms. In his exposition, however, Kant does not explain how necessity can be generated by the combination of possibility and actuality. Instead, he converts the modal necessity to the causal necessity. He calls it the material necessity in existence (A227/ B279). But this is an ontic necessity. He is back in the confusion between epistemic and ontic modalities. He has repeatedly insisted that his modal principles are epistemic, that is, they are concerned with the modes of knowledge and not with its content. But the material necessity belongs to the content of judgement. Kant is now transferring the causal necessity from the Analogies of Experience to the Postulates of Empirical Thought and renaming it as an epistemic necessity. Thus he can never get over his confusion between epistemic and ontic modalities.

By restricting modalities to their epistemic function, Kant is rejecting their ontic function, which has been exploited in the metaphysics of Descartes and Leibniz. Beyond and above the actual entities, these philosophers have counted the possible and the necessary entities as the proper objects of knowledge. Hence they believe that the domain of philosophy is wider than that of natural science, which is restricted to the actual world. They have investigated the nature of God as the necessary being and advocated the independent existence of mind on the ground that the separation of mind and body is possible. These metaphysical claims are based on the modal concepts of necessity and possibility. This type of modal argument has been revived in contemporary philosophy. Some philosophers say that the mental and the physical are two independent properties because they can be separated in some possible worlds. For Kant, these possible worlds are only fictions; the actual world is the only really possible one. This is his restriction of knowledge to the actual world, which goes together with his restriction of the categories to the world of experience. There is no other domain of objects for human knowledge than the world of experience. The modal categories cannot lead to the modal ontology of possible and necessary entities because they can be used only for describing the epistemic status of our knowledge of the actual world. This is Kant's rejection of modal metaphysics.

In his exposition of the Second Postulate, Kant presents his argument against subjective idealism. This is his famous Refutation of Idealism. This was originally included in the Fourth Paralogism of the A edition, but he has revised and relocated it in the B edition. But he does not give his reasons for its relocation. In all probability, as we will see, he is unsure of its proper location. He divides idealism into two types: the problematic idealism of Descartes and the dogmatic idealism of Berkeley. He reminds us that the ground of the latter has been undermined by his Transcendental Aesthetic. We have already noted why Kant's transcendental idealism is an effective counter to Berkeley's empirical idealism or phenomenalism. After this quick disposal of Berkeley, Kant focuses his attention on Cartesian idealism, according to which one can be certain only of one's own thought and existence, but never of the existence of external objects. Kant assumes that these external objects are the objects located in space and then tries to dissolve Cartesian doubt by invoking his First Analogy. His refutation begins with the sentence, 'I am conscious of my existence as determined in time' (B275). Then he argues that all determination of time requires the permanent, as he argued in the First Analogy. Since the consciousness of one's existence depends on the existence of the permanent, he claims, the former proves the latter. The existence of the permanent is none other than the existence of an external object. Therefore, the existence of an external object is as certain as the existence of one's own self.

If Kant's refutation is sound, it can forever silence Cartesian doubt. But his refutation is as flimsy as his argument for the First Analogy. He identifies the permanent substance with the Cartesian external object because he takes the latter as the substrate of sensations. But we have seen that his proof for the substrate is shoddy and flimsy. The external objects, whose existence is doubted by Descartes, belong to what he calls formal reality, which lies beyond our sensibility. Hence the Cartesian external objects are equivalent to Kant's things in themselves. Kant cannot be certain about the Cartesian external objects any more than he can be about his noumena. Instead of taking Cartesian idealism as an opponent of his transcendental idealism, Kant should have recognized their affinity. After all, his transcendental idealism is his restatement of Cartesian representationalism.

THE TRANSCENDENTAL DIALECTIC

In the Transcendental Analytic, Kant has repeatedly warned that his a priori concepts and principles must be limited to the world of phenomena. Once their use is extended beyond this limit, he will now show, human reason becomes dialectical and spins out dubious arguments. This is the art of transcendental dialectic that has produced three a priori sciences: rational psychology, rational cosmology, and rational theology. Kant assigns these dialectical sciences to reason and natural sciences to the understanding. The three rational sciences are built on the concepts of the self, the world, and God. They are the pure concepts of reason, which Kant calls the transcendental ideas of pure reason to stress their difference from the categories of the understanding. His derivation of transcendental ideas is as tricky and as devious as his derivation of the categories. He says that their origin lies in the forms of syllogism (A321/B378). He takes syllogism as the logical device for articulating the relation between the condition (the premise) and the conditioned (the conclusion). Whereas syllogism descends from the condition to the conditioned, prosyllogism ascends from the conditioned to the condition and tries to reach ever higher and higher premises. This logical ascent cannot stop until it reaches the ultimate condition or the unconditioned condition. Kant recognizes three forms of syllogism and prosyllogism: categorical, hypothetical, and disjunctive. The three forms of prosyllogism are the logical extensions of the three Analogies of Experience in search of the unconditioned condition. Kant says that those extensions lead to the three transcendental ideas of the self, the world, and God, when they are used in search of the unconditioned condition. He assigns the concept of the self to the categorical synthesis (or syllogism), the concept of the world to the hypothetical synthesis, and the concept of God to the disjunctive synthesis (A323/B379). This is an arbitrary assignment. If these three syntheses are extensions of the three Analogies of Experience, all of them are concerned with the world of experience. Therefore, their extended use should jointly produce the transcendental idea of the world. On the other hand, the self is the transcendental subject. It is the subject of experience, not its object. Therefore, the extended use of the three syntheses can have nothing to do with the transcendental idea of the self. The disjunctive synthesis is the principle of community for the interacting substances. It is simply inexplicable how this can lead to the transcendental idea of God. Kant's derivation of transcendental ideas is as arbitrary as his derivation of the categories. Fortunately, this has nothing to do with his critique of the three rational sciences built on those transcendental ideas. So we will proceed to examine his critique.

Transcendental Psychology

Kant summarizes rational psychology in four Paralogisms. When a syllogism produces an erroneous inference by equivocation, it is called a paralogism. The central contention of the four Paralogisms is the Cartesian–Leibnizian view that the soul is immortal and imperishable because it is a simple substance. The common base for all four Paralogisms is 'I think' (A341/B399). It is a pure thought that contains nothing empirical. Hence, Kant says, rational psychology differs from empirical psychology. The First Paralogism claims that the soul is a substance because it is the subject of thought and cannot be a predicate. But the concept of substance can be applied only to the object of experience and not to the thinking subject because the latter is not an object of experience. It is only a logical subject (A350). The First Paralogism stands on the equivocation of the term 'substance'. The Second Paralogism claims that the soul is simple because it is a simple substance. This is a further elaboration of the First Paralogism. Kant says that the Second Paralogism mistakes the unity of a thinking being for its simplicity. If to be simple means to contain no parts, the self cannot be simple because it contains many representations. But their unity should not be mistaken for simplicity. The Third Paralogism claims that the self is a person because it is conscious of its numerical identity. Kant says that the identity of consciousness is mistaken for the identity of a thinking subject. The former is only a formal condition of all thoughts and has nothing to do with the latter (A363).

The Fourth Paralogism does not really concern the nature of the self. It is addressed to the Cartesian doubt about the existence of external objects. Therefore it does not really belong to rational psychology. So Kant rewrote it as the Refutation of Idealism and relocated it in the B edition. He also rewrote the other three Paralogisms for the B edition, highlighting his central argument against them all, namely, the category of substance cannot be applied to the thinking subject for two reasons. First, the thinking subject is the subject of thought and not its object. Second, it is not a real but a logical or ideal entity. Throughout his criticism of rational psychology, he takes the thinking subject as the transcendental subject, which provides the transcendental unity of apperception. This is his transcendental psychology that replaces rational psychology. But it should not be mistaken for Kant's whole theory of the self or the subject. In fact, many scholars have expressed their dissatisfaction with it by taking it as his whole theory. But it is only one dimension of the self, namely, the self as a thinking subject. It is limited to the domain of theoretical reason.[6] Kant's theory of practical reason will show the self as the subject of action. His theory of aesthetic experience will show still another dimension of the self.

Transcendental Cosmology

Rational cosmology is literally dialectal. Every one of its assertions is matched by a counter-assertion. Kant summarizes its dialectical conflict in four pairs of antinomies. The First Antinomy is the dispute on whether the world is finite or infinite in space and time. The thesis argues for its finitude, and the antithesis for its infinitude. Kant gives the proof for both the thesis and the antithesis. For the proof of the thesis, let us suppose that the world had no beginning. Then an eternity must have elapsed. But that requires an infinite number of syntheses, which can never be completed. Hence the world must have had a beginning. Kant's argument for the thesis is based on the alleged absurdity of assuming the eternity of the world. But it is highly dubious. There is no reason to assume that the elapse of time depends on the synthesis of successive series. The synthesis is the mechanism for experiencing time, which cannot be equated with the flow of time. It is anachronistic for Kant to use his notion of synthesis in proving a thesis in rational cosmology because this notion was not available for the rational cosmologists. Even on his theory, space and time are pure intuitions that exist prior to the act of synthesis. If the existence of time does not depend on the synthesis of its manifold, its flow cannot depend on it, either. If the world had no beginning, to be sure, an eternity must have elapsed. That may sound absurd only if the finitude of time is presupposed. But Kant has argued for infinite time in the Transcendental Aesthetic.

Even if the passage of time does depend on the act of synthesis, it cannot be an individual act. If the passage of time depends on the individual synthesis, it will be privatized for each individual. Therefore, the passage of time must depend on the synthesis of the transcendental subject. Since it is a logical subject, its synthesis may not even take time because it is a logical operation. The synthesis of infinite series should be like the logical operation of generating a transfinite number. Hence the infinite synthetic operation should be possible for the transcendental subject. Even if its synthesis takes time (I wonder how much time it takes for each act of synthesis), Kant has already given the transcendental subject an infinite amount of time in the Transcendental Aesthetic. For these reasons, Kant has given only a pseudo-proof for the finitude of time. His proof for the infinitude of space is not any better because it is again based on his notion of extensive synthesis: Infinite space is impossible because it requires an infinite series of syntheses. His proof for the finitude of space is as faulty as his argument for the finitude of time. For the proof of the antithesis, Kant supposes that the world is finite. If it is, it must be bounded by empty space and empty time. This is the absurd consequence of the supposition, he says. The beginning of the world cannot be preceded by an empty time because nothing can come into being in an empty time. Neither can the world be limited by an empty space because the world cannot be related to such a non-entity. Kant can say that a finite universe must be surrounded by empty time and space, because he presupposes that space and time are infinite. But he does not prove the latter point. On the contrary, he uses the impossibility of infinite space and time for his proof of the thesis. Hence his arguments are inconsistent and devious. Thus, his proofs for both the thesis and the antithesis are illegitimate.

The Second Antinomy is the dispute on the ultimate nature of physical matter. Both the thesis and the antithesis stand on the premise that material substances are composite entities. The point of their dispute is whether they are infinitely divisible. The thesis holds that they must be composed of simples, which cannot be divided further. The antithesis holds that there are no simples. The proof of the thesis holds that a composite must be made of simples because it is an aggregation of simples by definition. So this is an argument by definition that evades the question. The composite should be defined not as an aggregation of simples, but as that of parts. This definition cannot settle the question of whether those parts are further divisible. Kant gives two arguments for the proof of the antithesis. First, since space is infinitely divisible, matter that occupies it is also infinitely divisible. This is a poor argument. There is no way to infer the nature of matter from the nature of space. The second argument for the antithesis is not any better: There are no simples because they cannot be encountered in possible experience. But there is no a priori way of settling whether or not simples can be encountered in possible experience, because this is an empirical question. Hence Kant's alleged proofs for both the thesis and the antithesis are again illegitimate.

The Third Antinomy concerns the conflict between freedom and necessity. The thesis argues for the existence of freedom alongside the causal necessity. The antithesis argues for universal determinism and denies the existence of freedom. Kant tries to prove the thesis by saying that the causal principle in its unlimited application falls into self-contradiction. If the causal principle has absolute universality, it would be impossible to give a complete causal account of any event because such an account would require an infinite series of syntheses. This is the same argument

for the impossibility of completing an infinite number of syntheses, which we have already branded as dubious in the First
Antinomy. Granted that every causal account is incomplete, its
incompleteness cannot be the same as its self-contradiction. The
proof of the antithesis is based on the Second Analogy. There can
be no freedom because its existence would nullify the causal principle and disrupt the possibility of experience. Determinism rules
everywhere if the causal principle holds everywhere. But we have
already noted that Kant has failed to give an a priori proof of the
causal principle. To that extent, Kant's proofs for both the thesis
and the antithesis are defective. The Third Antinomy reappears in
the Fourth Antinomy, which is the dispute over necessary vs. contingent being. Kant's distinction of these two entities is not traditional. He defines them in terms of causal necessity. The existence
of a contingent being is causally conditioned; the existence of a
necessary being is causally unconditioned. A necessary being is
causally independent; a contingent being is causally dependent.
Because the dispute over these two entities is the same as the
dispute over freedom vs. necessity, the Fourth Antinomy turns
out to be a repetition of the Third Antinomy. Kant's proofs for
the former are not any better than his proofs for the latter.

Kant says that the antinomies are not 'a mere mock fight'
(A464/B492). But his proofs of their theses and antitheses are so
flimsy that they do look like a mock fight. He still says that these
antinomies are not merely sophistical arguments, but the inevitable conflicts of pure reason. After the presentation of the antinomies and their proofs, however, he gives a different account of
their origin (A462–76/B490–504). He now attributes the theses to
the rationalists and the antitheses to the empiricists. In that case,
the antinomies do not reflect the inner conflict of pure reason, but
are the metaphysical disputes between two parties, whose interests
go well beyond the theoretical interest of pure reason. Kant says
that the theses are favoured by those who care about religion and
morality. The interests of religion and morality surely lie outside
the province of theoretical reason. Whereas the theses are friendly
for morality and religion, Kant says, the antitheses are hostile to
them. He assumes that morality requires freedom that is affirmed
by the thesis of the Third Antinomy and denied by its antithesis.
In talking about religion, he chiefly has in mind Christianity,
which advocates the finite world and its creation by God. In that

case, the parties to the cosmological disputes cannot be neatly divided into the two camps of rationalists and empiricists. There is no reason to assume that morality is warmly supported only by the rationalists and coldly rejected by the empiricists. Neither is it any easier to align the allegiance of rationalists and empiricists for or against religion. But the important point is Kant's recognition that there are many extra-theoretical interests that have motivated the transcendental dialectic. When these interests are taken into account, the antinomies are the disputes involving various parties and their interests. When they are not, the same antinomies can be seen as the inner conflict of theoretical reason. So there are two ways of understanding the cosmological antinomies.

Kant says that the solution of antinomies can never be found in experience because they transcend the domain of experience (A484/B512). The world, which is the object of dispute in the antinomies, can be defined as the totality of all phenomena. But those phenomena are the products of our synthesis. Therefore the world stands not as a complete object, but only for the transcendental idea that is being realized in the endless syntheses of experience (A479/B507). This is the heart of Kant's transcendental cosmology. He attributes the cosmological antinomies to the transcendental illusion that the world is an independent object. If the world were such an object, he says, it would be either finite or infinite. Therefore, it would be impossible to prove both the theses and the antitheses because both of them cannot be true. So he takes the cosmological antinomies as the confirmation of his transcendental idealism (A506/B534). This contention stands on the supposition that he has proven both the thesis and the antithesis of each antinomy. But he has failed to do it. Therefore he cannot use the antinomies to support his transcendental idealism. There is no way to prove both the thesis and the antithesis of an antinomy because they are contradictory of each other. On the dialectical level, at most, each of them can be entertained as a plausible hypothesis although they are in conflict with each other. Kant has tried to convert their plausibility into a logical proof. That is an impossible task. A dialectical question cannot be settled not because both its thesis and antithesis can be proven, but because neither of them can be proven by pure reason alone.

Kant proposes to resolve the antinomies by replacing rational cosmology by his transcendental cosmology. He says that all four antinomies stand on the general premise that the entire series of conditions is given if the conditioned is given (A497/B525). But this is an illusion. The series of conditions is not given; it has to be achieved by regressive synthesis, which can go on endlessly. This is Kant's general premise for the solution of cosmological antinomies. On this premise, he holds that the world is neither finite nor infinite. It is neither limited nor limitless in space; it has neither a beginning nor no beginning. This is Kant's solution for the First Antinomy: Both the thesis and the antithesis are false. But this resolution is faulty because it is based on his dubious notion of regressive synthesis, as we noted earlier. His own theory of space and time dictates that the world is infinite in space and time. Of course, that does not settle the extent of the empirical world. Kant indeed talks about 'the empirical regress' (A518/B546). But the outcome of empirical syntheses can be settled only by empirical investigations. Hence it is an empirical question whether the empirical world is finite or infinite. There can be no a priori solution for this question. Kant offers a similar solution for the Second Antinomy. The division of matter is also a process of regressive synthesis that can go on indefinitely. Therefore, Kant holds, both the thesis and the antithesis are false. But the continuous division of matter is a series of regressive empirical syntheses, and its outcome is an empirical issue. There can be no a priori resolution of this question, either.

For the resolution of the Third Antinomy, Kant says that both its thesis and antithesis can be true. This resembles Leibniz's reconciliation of freedom and necessity. Leibniz holds that there are two domains of discourse, the realm of matter (or nature) and the realm of spirit (or grace). The former is governed by necessity, and the latter by freedom. Because these two realms are in pre-established harmony, Leibniz says, human behaviour can be viewed as a free action in the realm of spirit and as a causally determined motion in the realm of matter. Kant has his own two worlds: Human beings are causally determined as natural entities in the phenomenal world, but they are free as rational beings in the noumenal world. He recognizes two characters of human beings. As phenomenal entities, they have an empirical character; as noumenal entities, they have an intelligible character (A539/B567). Reason belongs to the intelligible character; it is not an appearance (A553/B581). Therefore, reason is not subject to time

(A551/B579). This is a baffling statement. If reason is a noumenal entity, how can it operate in the phenomenal world? All noumena are said to be inaccessible to both human sensibility and intellect, because they are situated beyond space and time. But reason belongs to our intellect and we can witness its operation. The appearance of reason in our experience is a huge unexplained mystery in Kant's transcendental idealism.

He holds that reason is the agent of free action because it is located in the world of noumena that stands above causal necessity. It is the cause of its own action, and this is the causality of reason and its freedom. This is his theory of transcendental freedom. But this should be called transcendent freedom. At this point, Kant's transcendental cosmology becomes transcendent. This is an illegitimate move that goes against his own restrictions on transcendental philosophy. If noumena are unknowable as Kant says, there is no way to know whether reason is free or unfree as a noumenal entity. He may say that reason is not subject to causal determination because the causal principle is restricted to the phenomenal world. But the noumenal world may have its own causal principle. In defence of Kant, it is often said that he is asserting only the possibility of freedom rather than its reality in the noumenal world. But he has no right to talk about its possibility, either. In the Postulates of Empirical Thought, he restricted his own conception of possibility in distinction from the Leibnizian logical possibility. The Kantian possibility must fulfil the formal conditions of experience. Because noumena cannot fulfil these conditions, he has no right to talk about the possibility of freedom in the noumenal world.

How can reason act in the world of noumena? It appears impossible to talk about any action, free or unfree, in the noumenal world because it is beyond time and space, the basic conditions for human action. Since reason is supposed to act beyond time and space, Allen Wood calls it a timeless agency, a contradiction in terms.[7] Its choices and actions are supposedly non-temporal. Kant admits the impossibility of action in the noumenal world because nothing happens there, but says that reason can have its effect in the phenomenal world (A541/B569). This is the effect of reason without its action. It is the mystery of Kant's transcendental freedom, which is further compounded by his theory of double causation. All human actions can be explained fully in terms of the empirical characters of agents that have been formed by causal necessity. They can also be explained fully in terms of their intelligible characters that are beyond causal necessity. This should not be mistaken to mean that all human actions can be explained partly by the intelligible characters of agents and partly by their empirical characters. Let us suppose that John has done a marvellous deed. His empirical character that had been formed as a natural being was the necessary and sufficient condition for his deed. It would have taken place whether his reason intervened or not. When his reason intervened as a noumenal agent, however, it dictated exactly the same act as its necessary and sufficient cause. What a remarkable coincidence and redundancy! On this point, Kant accepts Leibniz's theory of pre-established harmony. Hence his transcendental resolution of the Third Antinomy is his restatement of Leibniz's theory. But Kant's theory has one fatal defect that is not in Leibniz's theory. The latter recognizes two domains of discourse, but Kant recognizes only one by placing the noumenal world beyond the reach of human sensibility and language (the categories). Hence his discussion of noumenal action and freedom is semantically impermissible.

Some commentators have called Kant's theory of freedom compatibilism because the noumenal freedom is compatible with the determinism of phenomena. But his theory does not belong to compatibilism in its normal sense, which presupposes neither the demarcation between phenomena and noumena, nor the theory of double causation. In the normal sense of compatibilism, the will is regarded as free even though it is determined by causal chains of the phenomenal world. In order to bring Kant's theory of freedom close to this normal sense of compatibilism, Hud Hudson adopts the two-aspect interpretation of phenomena and noumena: The rational self and the empirical self do not belong to two separate worlds because they are two aspects of one and the same self.[8] But the two-aspect theory makes Kant's position not more sensible but, rather, more absurd because it makes the human agency free in the noumenal aspect and unfree in the phenomenal aspect. These two aspects cannot belong to the same human being because they are contradictory of each other. Kant has tried to avoid this outright contradiction by assigning freedom and determinism to two different worlds.

There is an even more troublesome problem for the two-aspect account of Kantian compatibilism. The phenomenal aspect is defined by the human epistemic condition; the noumenal aspect is free of this restriction. We can say that we are determined in our phenomenal aspect because it depends on our epistemic condition. We can know whatever depends on our epistemic condition. But we cannot say anything about our noumenal aspect because it has no link to our epistemic condition. We can never know anything that is not linked to our epistemic condition. Therefore, we cannot even say that we have the noumenal aspect. Even if we have it, we cannot say that our noumenal aspect is free or rational. Thus one of the two aspects turns out to be a total blank. This is the inevitable consequence of the two-aspect theory on Kantian compatibilism. Although Henry Allison is a champion of the two-aspect interpretation, he does not endorse Kantian compatibilism and advocates an incompatibilist reading of Kant's theory.[9] Kant indeed gives the impression that his theory of freedom is a version of incompatibilism, when he ridicules freedom in a deterministic world as the freedom of a turnspit and stresses the power of free will for initiating a new series of events $(C_2$ 96–7). But it makes little sense to place the label of incompatibilism on his theory. Incompatibilism is defined as the theory of freedom incompatible with determinism. But Kant's theory is compatible with determinism. It is simply misleading to attach the label of either compatibilism or incompatibilism to his theory because their standard meanings have been formulated in the context of the phenomenal world, whereas Kant's theory of freedom was formulated in the context of two worlds.

We have already noted that the Fourth Antinomy is a repetition of the Third Antinomy. Kant's resolution of the former follows his resolution of the latter: both the thesis and the antithesis can be true. But the scope of the Fourth Antinomy is broader than that of the Third Antinomy. The latter was in search of the ultimate condition for every phenomenal object; the former is in search of the ultimate condition for the entire phenomenal world. Because the phenomenal world is only a representation, Kant says, it cannot be the ultimate condition for its own existence. He identifies this ultimate condition as the noumenal world. This argument has nothing to do with the problem of regressive synthesis, because it is a restatement of his argument for the things in themselves in the Transcendental Aesthetic. At this point, Kant's transcendental cosmology again becomes transcendent. His transcendental cosmology says that the empirical world is only a representation. This questionable view is based on his questionable theory of space and time, as we noted earlier in the Transcendental Aesthetic. His transcendent cosmology has one strange consequence. Every entity of the noumenal world is free because it stands above the causal chain that governs the phenomenal world. It is also a necessary being because Kant defines a necessary being as an entity whose existence is not causally determined. By this definition, all human beings are necessary beings in the world of noumena. They could not have been created by God because their creation would have made them contingent beings. It is probable that there is no distinction between God and his creatures in the noumenal world because it is situated beyond space and time. Leibniz has a principle of individuation for all possible worlds, but Kant does not. He can meaningfully talk about individuation only in the phenomenal world, but not in the noumenal world. Nor can he tell whether the noumenal beings are necessary or contingent because it is impossible to know whether or not they are subject to the causal principle. Therefore, Kant's resolution of the Fourth Antinomy is not any more sensible than his resolution of the Third Antinomy. The Fourth Antinomy is sometimes misunderstood for a dispute on the existence of God. But God is not even mentioned in the cosmological discussion. The problem of God will be taken up in transcendental theology.

Transcendental Theology

Kant calls the concept of God the ideal of reason and gives it many definitions (A572–8/B600–6). In the context of the possible, he defines God as the sum of all possibilities and as the source of all possibilities. In the context of the actual, he defines God as the substratum of all realities, as the ground and cause of all realities, and as the sum of all realities. These three definitions are extensions of the three Analogies (A576/B604), and they deliver three different conceptions of God. But he says that the concept of God as the substrate of all realities is the most important one. He calls such a God 'the All' and identifies it with the thing in itself. He also calls it *ens realissimum*. His conception of God is not always theistic. Some of his concepts are pantheistic; for example, God as the sum of all realities or as 'the All', which later became Goethe's favourite expression for his pantheistic God (*Faust* 6256). In spite of this broad range in his conception of God, he discusses only three proofs for divine existence in his criticism of rational theology: the ontological proof, the cosmological proof, and the teleological proof. He will explain why none of them is valid.

The ontological proof that Kant scrutinizes is quite different from Anselm's original version, which takes as its premise the concept of a being greater than any other being. If it does not exist, it cannot be as great as the one that exists. Then it cannot be the greatest being, which contradicts the original premise. We must accept the existence of God to avoid this contradiction, so Anselm argues. Kant's version of the ontological proof is based on the premise that God is an absolutely necessary being, an entity that exists necessarily. If it does not exist, it contradicts the premise. Therefore God must exist. The concept of a necessary being can be used to prove its existence, just like the concept of the greatest being. The two versions of the ontological proofs follow the same line of argument. Kant's famous critique of this argument is that existence is not a real predicate. But his opponents have rejected this contention. Consider Descartes' statement, 'I think, therefore I exist'. In the sentence, 'I exist', the word 'exist' is clearly a predicate of the subject 'I'. This grammatical fact cannot be denied by anybody, including Kant. But we have to distinguish the use of 'exist' as a predicate assigned to an object from the one assigned to a concept. When we say 'I exist', 'You exist', or 'London exists', we are assigning the predicate 'exist' to an object called I, you, or London. But Kant is talking about assigning existence as a predicate in a concept.

A concept can contain many predicates. Take the concept of a horse. It contains many attributes, each of which can be described by a predicate. But existence is not one of them. This is Kant's point when he says that existence is not a predicate. He should have said that existence is not a predicate contained in a concept. If we assign existence as a predicate to the concept of a horse, we will have the concept of existent horse. Is that different from the concept of non-existent horse? Are these two in turn different from the concept of horse? Kant would say that the concept of existent horse and the concept of non-existent horse are equally bogus, because the concept of horse can contain neither existence nor non-existence as its predicate. Instead of assigning existence as a predicate to a concept, we assert the existence of objects that fall under the concept. This is the relation of a concept to an object, which Kant calls synthetic, because the existence of objects lies outside the concept. This point is indicated by the existential quantifier in predicate logic, which is different from predicate symbols. If existence were a predicate, it would be designated by a predicate symbol.

When Anselm says that an existent God is greater than a non-existent God, he is not comparing two Gods, one existent and one non-existent, but two concepts or definitions of God. Hence his statement should be taken to mean that the concept of an existent God is greater than the concept of a non-existent God. Thus the predicates of existence and non-existence are included in these two concepts of God, but their inclusion is not logically permissible because they cannot be predicates in a concept. By their inclusion, the existence of God can be easily proven from the definition or concept of God. But the proof is circular and analytic because the existence of God is already contained in the concept of God. This is the logical essence of the ontological proof, according to Kant. The same analytic and circular reasoning governs the ontological proof that is based on the concept of God as the necessary being because this concept contains the predicate of necessary existence. The existence of God can be proven even from the definition of God as a contingent being. If God is defined as a contingent being, it must exist contingently. You can include all kinds of existence not only in the concept of God, but also in the concept of a horse. The concept of a horse as a necessary being entails the proposition that a horse necessarily exists just as the concept of a horse as a contingent being entails that a horse contingently exists. But we can never settle the question of existence by building it into our concepts because our conceptual power has no control over the existence of objects. It is only a verbal trick to solve the question of existence by building it into our concepts. This is the central point in Kant's rejection of the ontological proof.

Unlike the ontological proof, the cosmological proof is more than a verbal trick. Its premise is not the concept of God, but the contingent existence of the world. The search for its ultimate cause was already introduced in the Fourth Antinomy. Its argument is not analytic but synthetic. But no synthetic proposition can be validated without empirical intuitions. Hence there is no way to validate the cosmological proof. It can be accepted only as a plausible view of God's existence in the noumenal world, which transcends human experience. Even then it can give no indication of what kind of being God is. All it can say is that God is the ultimate cause of the world, which may be conscious or unconscious, a person or a thing. It cannot deliver the traditional concept of God as the most perfect being. On this regard, the teleological proof can fare better because it conceives God as the author of the order and beauty of the world. For that reason, Kant says, the teleological proof deserves to be mentioned with respect. But he points out that the existence of a divine designer for the natural order cannot be proven without accepting the cosmological proof. Since the latter is impossible, the former is equally impossible. Thus all three proofs fail. But Kant says that their failure does not prove the non-existence of God, either. The impossibility of rational theology only shows that the proof of God is beyond the scope of rational discourse. Hence rational theology is a pseudo-science. Kant believes that true theology belongs to the domain of rational faith, which should be kept apart from rational knowledge. Whereas rational knowledge belongs to the domain of proof, rational faith belongs to the domain of plausibility. This is Kant's transcendental theology.

After concluding the transcendental theology, Kant attaches a long appendix on the regulative use of transcendental Ideas. Although they cannot perform a constitutive function, he says, they can perform a regulative function for our knowledge. Though the transcendental Ideas of the soul, the world, and God cannot produce knowledge because they cannot be backed up by intuitions, they can still aid our attempt to systematize empirical knowledge. This is their regulative function. Guided by the transcendental concept of self, we can seek the systematic unity of all appearances concerning the empirical self. The same regulative function is performed by the transcendental concept of the world. Although the concept of the world is only an Idea to be realized by the endless series of syntheses, its empirical investigation and systematization should be conducted as though the world were a completed system. The transcendental concept of God drives us even further than the systematic unity of physical science on the mechanical level and prompts us to think of the world as the design of God. Kant calls it the purposive unity of nature (A686/714). The concept of natural purpose is the concept of natural teleology, which transcends mechanical causation. This concept can be linked to the concept of God as the cosmic author of design. But the concept of intelligent design by God is only an Idea, which cannot be substituted for the empirical inquiry of organic functions. The substitution makes the concept constitutive rather than regulative; it is the substitution of a hollow concept for scientific research. It leads to the illusion that scientific knowledge can be gained without scientific labour. This scientific illusion is even worse than the transcendental illusion of rational cosmology. This is Kant's admonition against mistaking the regulative function of transcendental Ideas for their constitutive function.

CHAPTER 2

PRACTICAL REASON

(ETHICS, POLITICS, AND RELIGION)

Kant distinguishes practical philosophy from theoretical philosophy. The latter is concerned with what is; the former is concerned with what ought to be done. Theoretical philosophy is descriptive; it describes what is. Practical philosophy is normative; it sets the normative standards for what ought to be done. Practical philosophy belongs to practical reason, and theoretical philosophy to theoretical reason. These two are not two types of reason, but its two functions. Kant examined the theoretical function of pure reason in the *Critique of Pure Reason* and then presented his practical philosophy in three separate works, the *Groundwork for the Metaphysics of Morals* (1785), the *Critique of Practical Reason* (1788), and the *Metaphysics of Morals* (1797). The central question in these works is the nature of normative standards. This was already an important topic in the first *Critique*. When he introduced the pure concepts of reason in the Transcendental Dialectic, they included Platonic Ideas (A313–20/B370–7). He described them as the archetypes that transcend the world of senses. They are the ideals of perfection that can never be fully realized in the world of phenomena. They fulfil a much higher need than the categories. The latter is for knowing the world of appearances; the former is for the practical task of governing our life. Kant names two Platonic Ideas: the Idea of Virtue and the Idea of Republic. The former is the ideal of a perfect individual; the latter is the ideal of a perfect community. He stresses that these ideals of pure reason can never be derived from experience, for example, the Idea of Virtue by empirically examining virtuous persons, because there is no way to recognize such persons without appealing to the Idea. But he does not recognize the need of eternal archetypes for understanding the phenomenal world and regards Plato's postulation of the Ideas even for plants and animals as no more than his rhetorical flourish. He believes that Plato is chiefly concerned with the role of Ideas as the transcendent normative standards in the world of practice (A314/B371). In his *Inaugural Dissertation*, he had already adopted Platonic Ideas. One year before the *Dissertation*, he had recorded in *Reflexion* 5037 that a great light had dawned on him (KGS 18:69). Some scholars believe that the 'great light' was his discovery of Platonism because the *Dissertation* abounds with allusions to Plato, which were absent from his earlier writings. Kant extensively used Platonic Ideas in the *Dissertation*. To be sure, he frees his theoretical philosophy from those Ideas in the first *Critique*, but he still retains them for his practical philosophy.

Although Kant calls Platonic Ideas the transcendental concepts, they are not transcendental but transcendent. Hence they are fundamentally different from those transcendental ideas that produce dialectical illusions, namely, the concepts of the soul and the world. These two concepts are neither transcendent nor normative. They are formed by extending the categories and their rules of synthesis beyond the phenomenal world. Their ultimate origin is the understanding. Hence theoretical reason is really an extension of the understanding. But normative Ideas can never be formed by such an extension because they are eternal archetypes. They belong not to the understanding, but to reason proper. This is Kant's division of labour between theoretical and practical reason. Although he presents it as a division within pure reason, it is ultimately reducible to the demarcation between the understanding and reason. This demarcation is uniquely Kantian. Nobody has ever divided human intellect in this manner before or after him. Hence many have questioned its legitimacy and regarded it as another kink in his architectonic. But Kant's demarcation between the two levels of intellect is determined by the two sets of its primary interests. One set is normative and prescriptive; the other set is descriptive and cognitive. Because human reason can never be content with the satisfaction of the latter alone, Kant holds, it is destined to strive for the realization of the former, the transcendent normative ideals.

Normative standards, however, are not transcendent in every case. There are positive norms as well, which are instituted by political or religious authorities as positive laws and religious rules. Even a code of conventional morality is a positive norm. Some philosophers claim that there are no transcendent norms but only positive ones. Their position may be called normative positivism. Kant brands it as extremely reprehensible because it derives *what ought to be* from *what is* (A319/B375). On the other hand, to accept transcendent norms is normative Platonism, which may also be called normative transcendentism. Normative Platonism should be distinguished from other types of Platonism such as mathematical Platonism and cosmological Platonism because one can endorse the former without the latter. By accepting transcendent norms, however, the Platonists do not reject positive norms. On the contrary, they hold that transcendent norms can be realized by their translation into positive norms because the former are too general to serve as practical guides. But they insist that transcendent norms are the ultimate grounds for instituting, criticizing, and justifying all positive norms. On the other hand, the normative positivists hold that the ultimate ground for positive norms is not transcendent but empirical. But Kant believes that the empirical derivation and justification of positive nouns is reprehensible because it grounds what ought to be on what is. He regards Plato as the father of normative transcendentism and Epicurus as the father of normative positivism (A471/B499).

While the rationalists illegitimately extend their speculation beyond the domain of sensibility, Kant says, the empiricists are guilty of dogmatically denying supersensible normative Ideas. But those Ideas provide the ultimate principles of morality, legislation, and religion (A318/B375). Hence the transcendent Ideas are the necessary conditions for the possibility of practical life, just as the categories of the understanding are the necessary conditions for the possibility of experience in the phenomenal world. Thus Kant has given two transcendental arguments: one for the categories and the other for the transcendent norms. In comparison with the transcendental deduction of the categories, the latter is so short and brief that even its existence is seldom recognized in Kant scholarship. But there is a neat parallel between these two transcendental arguments. Both of them follow the same line of argument as that of Plato's for the existence of transcendent Ideas as the explanans of phenomena. Kant has appropriated Plato's transcendent account as his transcendental account, but has divided it into two types: one for the understanding and the other for practical reason. The former is his account for the possibility of objective experience in the domain of subjective impressions; the latter is his account for the possibility of objective normative standards in the domain of practical reason. Without transcendent norms, he believes, our practical world would fall into the chaos of subjective inclinations just as our perceptual world would be mired in subjective sensations without the categories.

KANT'S ETHICAL PLATONISM

In the Canon of Pure Reason (A797–819/B825–47), Kant discusses how the transcendent Ideas can be used in practical life. Throughout the *Critique*, he uses the word 'canon' in contrast to 'organon'. The latter means the instrument for producing knowledge; the former means the rule for using cognitive powers. He says that the transcendental analytic has given the canon for the pure understanding, that is, why the categories can be legitimately applied only to appearances (A796/B824). But there is no canon for pure reason in its speculative function because it can produce no synthetic a priori truths as the understanding does. Although his critique of pure reason in its theoretical function is negative, he recognizes its positive function in the practical domain. Therefore practical reason can have its own canon. This is the important difference between practical and theoretical reason. Kant explains this point by using the concept of freedom (A798/B826). It cannot be used for the theoretical understanding of human actions because the phenomenal world allows no room for free will. But practical life is inconceivable without freedom. Freedom in practical life is practical freedom; it is the power of choosing freely without being constrained by natural impulses. The existence of this power can be proven through experience (A802/B830). He says, 'We thus cognize practical freedom through experience, as one of the natural causes, namely a causality of reason in determination of the will' (A803/B831, tr. Guyer and Wood). In that regard, he notes, practical freedom is altogether different from the transcendental freedom that totally transcends the natural world. This is a big surprise. In the Third Antinomy, he had stressed their inseparable connection: 'The denial of transcendental freedom must, therefore, involve the elimination of all practical freedom' (A534/B502). As we noted in the last chapter, the concept of transcendental freedom makes no sense because it entails the concept of a timeless agent choosing and acting beyond time. Kant is getting out of this rigmarole by separating practical freedom from transcendental freedom and by placing the former in the phenomenal world.

Kant's description of practical freedom as the power of choosing without being coerced by natural impulses is a Platonic legacy along with Platonic Ideas as the transcendent normative standards. Practical freedom makes practical laws, which are distinguished from the theoretical laws that govern nature. Kant divides practical laws into pragmatic laws and moral laws (A806/B834). Pragmatic laws are the laws of prudence; they are concerned with happiness. They are the technical rules that make use of empirical laws governing our desires and passions and the natural and cultural means for the satisfaction of those desires and passions. But there is no empirical basis for moral laws because they take no account of desires. They are a priori laws based on the Ideas of pure reason (A806/B834). Kant conceives of moral law in a political framework. The function of moral law is to harmonize the freedom of each individual with the freedom of others. This idea is derived from the Idea of a republican constitution, which allows '*the greatest possible human freedom* in accordance with laws by which *the freedom of each is made to be consistent with that of all others*' (A316/B373, tr. Kemp Smith). These laws are initially proposed as maxims, the subjective rules of behaviour. When these subjective rules are in accord with the Ideas of pure reason, they can be accepted as the objective laws of a community. Thus, Kant's conception of morality covers both the life of individuals and that of their community. It is as comprehensive as Plato's conception of justice in the *Republic*.

Kant introduces the concept of the highest good as his ultimate normative Idea. It has two parts: happiness and morality as the worthiness for happiness. The moral good is not sufficient for human beings because they need happiness. But happiness alone cannot be the highest good for rational beings. They should be morally good to deserve happiness. Their happiness should be commensurate with their morality. This rational ideal of concord between morality and happiness is contained in the concept of the highest good. Kant says that it can be realized in a perfect community of rational beings, where they are the authors of their own morals and happiness (A809/B837). In such an ideal community, he says, 'all the actions of rational beings take place just as if they had proceeded from a supreme will that comprehends in itself, or under itself, all private wills' (A810/B838, tr. Kemp Smith). But such an ideal community is only an Idea, which can never be realized in this world because it can offer no guarantee for the proportionate apportionment of happiness with morality. It can be realized only in the supersensible world, which is governed by the morally perfect ruler (A812/B840). Kant calls it a *corpus mysticum* (mystical body) of rational beings (A808/B836). So he postulates the supersensible world as a moral kingdom. This is his moral theology, with which he replaces his transcendental theology. The latter was negative; it was a critical rejection of rational theology. But his moral theology is positive; it affirms the existence of God for moral reasons. The highest good is demanded by pure reason. If it cannot be realized, Kant holds, pure reason is demanding what is impossible. This is the absurdity of practical reason, and it can be averted only by his moral theology. For Kant, practical reason has its own logic just as theoretical reason has its own.

THE CATEGORICAL IMPERATIVE

Kant's moral theory is best known for the categorical imperative, which was presented in the *Groundwork for the Metaphysics of Morals*. This work came as a big surprise for his readers four years after the *Critique of Pure Reason*. Toward the end of this book, he said,

> Now the philosophy of pure reason is either **propaedeutic** (preparation), which investigates the faculty of reason in respect of all pure *a priori* cognition, and is called **critique**, or, second, the system of pure reason (science), the whole (true as well as apparent) philosophical cognition from pure reason in systematic interconnection, and is called **metaphysics**. (A841/B869, tr. Guyer and Wood)

After this remark, Kant names two branches of metaphysics: metaphysics of nature and metaphysics of morals. The *Critique* was only a preparation for writing these two metaphysical treatises. Even in the Introduction to the *Critique*, he called this work the *propaedeutic* to the system of pure reason (A11/B25). When he was writing the *Critique*, he never intended to write two more *Critiques* because the first *Critique* was designed as a critical examination of the entire human reason, theoretical and practical. In that work, he has clearly defined the division of labour between the understanding and reason. The power of theoretical reason is limited to the understanding, which cannot transcend the domain of sensibility. Nor does the understanding have the power to derive normative standards from the empirical world. That power belongs to pure reason, whose proper function lies not in the theoretical domain, but in the practical domain. When pure reason gets involved in the cosmological antinomies and other metaphysical speculations, it is forgetting its proper function in the practical domain.

Most students of Kant are so impressed with his negative criticism of pure reason in the Transcendental Dialectic that they may not even notice that he also stresses its positive function. This is mostly due to Kant's own faulty procedure of exposition. He gives only a few paragraphs to the normative function of transcendent Ideas in the Transcendental Dialectic (A313–18/B370–5) and then tucks the practical function of pure reason in the Canon of Pure Reason in the Transcendental Doctrine of Method. Most of his readers never even get to this part of the *Critique* because they run out of patience well before reaching it. Since Kant's *Critique of Pure Reason* had been presented as a propaedeutic for his metaphysical treatises on nature and morals, his readers waited for the publication of these two volumes. Instead of these two awaited volumes, however, he published the *Groundwork for the Metaphysics of Morals* (1785) and the *Metaphysical Foundations of Natural Science* (1786). In these two works, he claims to lay the foundations for the metaphysics of morals and the metaphysics of nature. But that is a big surprise. Those foundations had supposedly been laid out in the *Critique*, his labourious propaedeutic. For normative philosophy, he had presented transcendent normative Ideas as the foundation of all morals in the *Critique*. But that foundation is not even mentioned in the *Groundwork for the Metaphysics of Morals*. He had evidently abandoned the old foundation and prepared a new one. His readers and critics were so surprised that they demanded an explanation. So he had to write the *Critique of Practical Reason* (1788). Thus the second *Critique* was born against Kant's original intention of writing only one *Critique of Pure Reason*.

What new foundation does Kant lay out for his normative theory in the *Groundwork*? He calls it the autonomy of rational will: pure reason prescribes moral laws without relying on any authority other than its own. He has inherited Rousseau's concept of political autonomy: one is free as long as one obeys the laws of one's own making. Kant is now turning this political concept into the concept of moral autonomy: practical reason is free and autonomous as long as it obeys the moral laws of its own making. How to make moral laws is not a new problem for Kant. In his ethical Platonism, he had maintained that practical reason prescribes moral laws in accordance with normative Ideas. But Platonic legislation would fail to meet his new standard of rational autonomy. He recognizes two types of heteronomy: empirical and rational (GMM 442). Pure reason loses its autonomy when it derives moral principles from empirical sources, for example, the principle of happiness or moral sense. The same thing happens to pure reason, he holds, even when it obtains moral principles from rational sources, for example, the rational concept of perfection or perfection in accordance with the will of God. The rational concept of perfection is the concept of virtue in accordance with Platonic Ideas. If the rational concept of perfection is a concept of pure reason as he taught in the first *Critique*, it cannot be a heteronomy of pure reason to rely on this concept in its moral legislation. But Kant never considers this point. Instead, he looks upon it as an authority as alien to pure reason as the authority of God. He now proclaims that the autonomy of pure reason means to make moral laws only under the Idea of Freedom (GMM 448). Therefore the Idea of Freedom and moral legislation are interchangeable (GMM 450). This radical concept of rational autonomy is the new foundation for his moral theory and generates the difficult problem of how to derive all moral laws solely from the concept of freedom.

Kant's new concept of freedom is different from the Platonic concept of practical freedom, which he had dissociated from transcendental freedom. Kant identifies the new concept with transcendental freedom (GMM 452). That brings back the mystery or nonsense of a noumenal agent exercising its transcendental freedom in the timeless world. Probably to avoid this embarrassment, Lewis White Beck proposes, Kant drastically changes his way of talking about the relation between phenomena and noumena in the *Groundwork*.[1] Instead of assigning them to two separate worlds, he regards them as two aspects of one thing. The intelligible (noumenal) and the empirical (phenomenal) characters are two aspects of one person, because a rational human being belongs to both the intelligible and the empirical worlds (GMM 451–3). He says that they represent two standpoints (GMM 458). These remarks have been the main inspiration for the one-world interpretation of phenomena and noumena, which we considered in the last chapter. But this new way of describing only aggravates the relation between phenomena and noumena as we noted in the last chapter, as long as noumena are ensconced beyond space and time. If the noumenal aspect of human beings is unknowable, there is no reason to say that it is free. Kant's only reason for saying so is that human beings act under the idea of freedom, that is, they act with the awareness of their freedom. But this awareness can be as naïve as the awareness of direct realism. Even cats and dogs may feel it. The very idea of causal determination is an outcome of deep reflection, which is never available to naïve consciousness.

Kant further articulates his theory of rational autonomy by his demarcation between inclination and reason. Inclination includes desires and passions, all those elements in the empirical dimension of human beings. Their satisfaction is called happiness, the ultimate principle of inclination. Pure reason loses its autonomy whenever it is dictated by inclination. The distinction between the autonomy of rational will and its heteronomy can further be illustrated by the distinction between the categorical and the hypothetical imperatives. The categorical imperatives are unconditional; the hypothetical imperatives are conditional. The conditions for hypothetical imperatives are set by inclination, namely, by its principle of happiness. For example, 'If you want to stay healthy, you ought to exercise regularly' is a hypothetical imperative. The condition of this imperative is the desire to stay healthy, which belongs to inclination. On the other hand, the moral imperative, 'You ought to tell the truth', is categorical because it is free of all conditions. The hypothetical imperatives are consequential; they are obeyed for their consequences. But the categorical imperatives are obeyed not for their consequences, but for their own sake.

The hypothetical imperative belongs to rational heteronomy because its original source is inclination. The categorical imperative belongs to rational autonomy because pure reason is its only authority. The categorical imperative defines moral duty and its absolute value, and the morally good will is to do the duty dictated by the categorical imperative. The distinction of these two imperatives looks similar to the distinction that Kant made between pragmatic law and moral law in the Canon of Pure Reason. Pragmatic laws are based on desires and feelings because they are the rules of prudence for securing happiness. Hence they are binding only conditionally like the hypothetical imperative. On the other hand, moral laws are binding unconditionally like the categorical imperative because they take no account of desires and feelings (A806/B834). But Kant never associated these two types of law with the autonomy and the heteronomy of rational will. He gave the impression that pure reason could exercise its practical freedom in managing both moral and pragmatic laws as long as it could control desires and passions. Practical freedom means practical autonomy. But it cannot meet the radically new requirement of rational autonomy.

Kant's new standard of rational autonomy is so radical that it has been called his second Copernican revolution. His first Copernican revolution was executed in the first *Critique*, where he shifted the centre of human cognition from the object to the subject. In the second Copernican revolution, he shifts the centre of moral authority from the object of the will to the will itself. When the will is determined by its object, it becomes heteronomous. But it is autonomous when it determines its object. Kant's ethical Platonism followed the pre-Copernican tradition of seeking the conformity of moral laws to objects, namely, Platonic Ideas. In his new Copernican model of ethics, practical reason prescribes moral laws on its own authority just as the understanding prescribes a priori laws to nature. In the last chapter, we called it the construction model in distinction from the application model. Kant's ethical Platonism followed the application model; practical reason applied Platonic Ideas to practical life. Just as a priori laws of nature are dictated by the forms of understanding, so the moral laws will be dictated by the form of practical reason, the principle of logical consistency. Only this formal principle can satisfy the requirement for his radical concept of rational autonomy. There are two types of rational principle: substantive and formal. Platonic Ideas are substantive rational principles. Freed from those Ideas, practical reason becomes its own formal rational principle, that is, the pure form of autonomy without substantive content. Therefore practical reason can take two forms: formal rationality and substantive rationality. This distinction is analogous to the one between the formal (logical) and the substantive (material) function of the categories. In his new theory of rational autonomy, Kant is announcing formal rationality as his new foundation for moral theory. This may be called Kant's ethical formalism in distinction from his ethical Platonism.

How can a purely formal reason make practical laws without substantive standards? This is Kant's new intractable problem of moral legislation. He tries to resolve it in his extended discussion of the categorical imperative in the *Groundwork*. The categorical imperative does not directly give moral laws or commands. It dictates the procedure for adopting maxims for moral laws. The maxims are the subjective rules of behaviour. To the confusion of his readers, Kant gives three or four different formulations of the categorical imperative. Kant scholars are not even sure exactly how many formulations can be found in the *Groundwork*. But each of them is a different way of determining whether or not any given maxim can be adopted as a moral rule. Hence each of them explains the function of the categorical imperative as the generative principle of moral laws. Thus the categorical imperative is the procedural device for the construction of moral laws. Kant illustrates how the procedure works, by using four concrete cases: (1) committing suicide, (2) making false promises, (3) developing natural talents, and (4) helping others in need.

The first formulation of the categorical imperative is: *Act only in accordance with that maxim through which you can at the same time will that it become a universal law* (GMM 421, tr. Gregor). This is known as the formula of universal law, which Kant regards as interchangeable with the formula of universal law of nature. The latter can be stated by changing 'universal law' at the end of the first formula to 'universal law of nature'. Kant applies it to the four sample cases. He says that the maxim for the first case is: shorten your life when its continuance threatens more evil than it promises pleasure. But this maxim cannot be accepted as a universal law, he says, for the following reason. It is motivated by self-love. But self-love is the basic feeling for supporting life. If this maxim becomes a law of nature, it will transform self-love into a universal force of self-destruction, thereby introducing a contradiction into the entire system of nature. Since such a contradictory system of nature cannot sustain itself, the maxim of suicide cannot become a universal law of nature. Therefore the maxim in question cannot be endorsed by the categorical imperative. So Kant brands suicide as immoral. But his reasoning is invalid. It would be valid if the maxim were to commend suicide for every case of self-love. But the maxim in question commends suicide only for those tragic cases when life becomes truly unbearable. If such a selective use of suicide is adopted as a universal law, it can enhance the vitality of nature instead of destroying it.

Kant's second example is a case of false promise. Suppose that I have an urgent need to borrow money. But my financial condition is so bad that I can secure a loan only by making a false promise for its repayment. My maxim is to borrow money on a false promise. Kant says that this maxim cannot become a universal law of nature, either, because it contradicts itself. If it were to become a universal law, every promise would be known to be false. In such a world, it would be impossible to secure a loan on a false promise. As a universal law, the maxim will destroy itself and extinguish the institution of making and keeping promises. This is its self-contradiction. Therefore it cannot be adopted as a moral rule. Again, Kant's reasoning is faulty. The universal adoption of this maxim cannot produce such a disastrous consequence. It does not commend lying for every occasion of making a promise but only for special cases where there is no other way to secure a loan. But Kant does not leave the maxim in such a narrow scope. In fact, he expands its scope to all cases of lying beyond the domain of promise-making. In his infamous short essay, 'On a Supposed Right to Lie because of Philanthropic Concerns', he holds that it is morally wrong to lie even when it may appear morally justified. Suppose that a helpless girl knocks on your door and tells you that she is being chased by an assailant. She asks for your help and protection. So you hide her in your house. But the assailant soon appears and asks whether you have seen the girl. Should you lie to the assailant or tell him the truth? Most people would regard it as grossly immoral to tell him the truth. But Kant categorically states that it is our duty not to lie even in this case.

It is a truism that moral rules should be universal. But Kant clearly misunderstands their universality. He takes it to mean that there can be no exceptions for a moral rule under any circumstances. But all moral rules are subject to exceptions because no rule can ever correctly cover all possible circumstances. For the illustration of this point, let us use the legal distinction between rules and principles. The rules are specific; their examples are the rules against lying or stealing. The principles are general; their examples are the principles of justice or equality. Rules can be criticized and justified in terms of principles because the former are derived from the latter. We have to make an exception to a rule when it cannot be applied without violating one of our principles. We cannot tell the truth about the hidden girl to the assailant without aiding the wrongdoer at the expense of his victim. That would surely go against our moral principles. Whereas moral principles have broad ranges of application, moral rules are generally enclosed within the implicitly accepted scopes. Unlike moral rules, there may be no exception for moral principles, especially the highest one. This is the fundamental difference of universality between rules and principles. One may insist on the absolute universality of principles, but not on that of rules. Kant can allow no exception for the categorical imperative because it is his highest moral principle. But he cannot do the same for moral rules. Nor does he give any reason for allowing no exceptions. He simply assumes that it is required by the universality of moral rules. This assumption only reflects his poor understanding of the universality of moral laws.

Kant's third example involves the question whether it is our duty to develop natural talents or neglect them. He invites us to suppose that we are living in a place like the South Sea Islands, whose rich natural resources make it possible to live in comfort without developing natural talents. Under those fortunate circumstances, he admits, we can live with the maxim of neglecting our talent as a universal law. Although a system of nature can exist under such a law, he says, no rational being can will that it should become a universal law. He has used the formal test of consistency in rejecting the maxims of the first two cases. But this test cannot work for the third case because it can eliminate neither the maxim of neglecting natural talents, nor that of developing them. Both maxims can become the laws of nature. So Kant has to use a substantive test and calls it the test of rational choice: The maxim of developing natural talents will be chosen by the rational person over the maxim of neglecting them. What is the reason for this rational choice? Kant says that a rational being wills the development of natural talents because it is useful 'for all sorts of possible purposes' (GMM 423). This rational choice is based on the instrumental argument for fulfilling the purposes of inclination. Therefore it is a prudential and consequential argument, which belongs to the hypothetical imperative rather than the categorical imperative. With the third case, Kant has transformed the categorical imperative into a hypothetical one because he cannot handle this case with the principle of formal rationality. This clearly exposes the vacuity of his ethical formalism.

Kant's fourth example concerns the maxim of helping others in need. It is opposed to the maxim of not helping others. He says that neither of them can be rejected by the formal test of self-contradiction. The two competing maxims of this case can be equally accepted as universal laws of nature. Under the maxim of self-reliance and repudiating help from others, Kant says, the human race can certainly exist and even fare better than in a state where everyone is engaged in mutual help. Hence he again has to appeal to substantive rationality: We would rationally choose the maxim of helping others rather than the maxim of not helping others in need for the following reason. By not adopting it, we would deprive ourselves of all hope of aid on those occasions when we badly need help from others (GMM 423). This argument is again consequential, instrumental, and prudential. Its substantive ground is the importance of securing valuable help from others in the future. The maxim can be expressed in a hypothetical imperative: if you would like to receive help from others in the future, then you ought to operate on the maxim of helping others in need. No wonder, John Stuart Mill complains that Kant always appeals to the consequences of adopting moral maxims (*Utilitarianism*, ch. 1). Indeed, Kant's consequential arguments again turn his categorical imperative into a hypothetical one. What is even more confusing is that the formula of universal law is not a single formula because it operates with two forms of testing maxims: formal and substantive. The formula of universal law contains two notions of rationality: formal and substantive rationality. It is not one formula, but two in one. Kant uses it as a formal generative principle in the first two cases and as a substantive generative principle in the last two cases. So there are two versions of the formula of universal law: formal and substantive.

FORMAL AND SUBSTANTIVE RATIONALITY

Given the two versions of the formula of universal law, Kant's concept of rational autonomy is compatible only with the formal version because it relies only on the formal criterion of self-consistency. But the substantive version transforms rational autonomy into rational heteronomy because it has to appeal to substantive criteria. Probably for this reason, a number of loyal Kant scholars have argued that the formal criterion of contradiction operates not only in the first two cases, but also in the last two. By this argument, they have maintained that the two versions of the formula of universal law are reducible to one formal version. This unitary view is their attempt to defend Kant's concept of rational autonomy and to protect the integrity of the formula of universal law as one consistent generative principle of moral maxims. Let us now look at some examples of this loyal attempt for Kant's defence.

Although the last two cases do not involve the logical contradiction of maxims, H. J. Paton says, they involve the contradiction in the will because it can universalize the bad maxims only by contradicting itself.[2] Onora O'Neill restates Paton's view by dividing Kant's formal criterion into two types: the contradiction in conception and the contradiction in the will.[3] The contradiction in conception operates in the first two cases, and the contradiction in the will in the last two cases. Bruce Aune has advanced a similar argument with his idea of consistent willing. The formula of universal law demands consistency in the choice of rational will. He holds that Kant uses this one formal principle of consistency in all four cases. But he recognizes two types of inconsistent volition: (1) to will a maxim whose universalization is practically impossible and (2) to will a maxim the consequence of whose universalization is inconsistent with the other objects of rational desire.[4] Christine Korsgaard calls (2) practical contradiction and recognizes two other formal criteria: logical contradiction and teleological contradiction.[5] She holds that logical contradiction governs the first case, practical contradiction the second case, and teleological contradiction the last two cases. If these interpretations are right, there are three versions of the formula of universal law rather than the two versions I have proposed. But those three versions can still be aligned with the distinction between formal and substantive rationality. Logical contradiction alone belongs to formal rationality; practical and teleological rationality belong to substantive rationality.

Let us go over the four cases again to determine whether these three types of contradiction are really used in Kant's account of the formula of universal law. We have already seen that the maxim of suicide does not involve any logical contradiction. Even if it is in conflict with self-love, that does not mean that it contradicts itself. Moreover, self-love does not demand the continuation of one's life under all possible conditions. Suppose that you are trapped in a pain-racked body in a terminal disease and that even painkillers cannot alleviate your pain. If there is no other way of escaping from this terrible condition than suicide, you would surely consider killing yourself for the sake of self-love. We have also seen that a selective use of lying can produce no practical contradiction and that to refrain from lying in some special cases would be highly immoral and irresponsible. The third case surely concerns natural teleology because natural talent is given by nature. But is there a teleological contradiction in neglecting natural talent? Natural teleology means that it develops with its own power for its own goal. To block this course of natural development may be called teleological contradiction. But I am not blocking it by neglecting my natural talent. On the contrary, I am leaving nature to take its course.

O'Neill says that neglecting one's talents creates a contradiction in the will for the following reason.[6] Rational people should develop their talents because they want to engage in many kinds of activities and because those activities require developed talents and skills. The maxim of neglecting one's talents undercuts the intention of engaging in those activities. Therefore the will that adopts this maxim is incoherent because it wills certain ends but refuses to prepare the means necessary for their fulfilment. This is a contradiction in instrumental rationality. By this criterion, however, we can find no fault with the imaginary person of the

South Sea Islands. To engage in the activities of O'Neill's description is not his end because he has chosen to have a carefree life. It would indeed be incoherent for the carefree islander to adopt the maxim of enslaving himself to developing all his talents, which he will never use. So the contradiction in the will is never involved in the choice of maxims in this case.

O'Neill says that Kant's fourth example also involves contradiction in the will. Kant indeed describes it as a case of conflict. A will that adopts the maxim of not helping others in need is in conflict with itself because it denies itself the help from others when it needs it. But this argument can be inverted. The adoption of the other maxim also creates a contradiction in the will because it assumes the duty of helping others, which conflicts with the desire to be free of that sort of trouble. Since both maxims create some conflict in the will, both maxims should be rejected if the contradiction in the will is the only formal criterion for the adoption of maxims. Bruce Aune believes that the rational will should choose the maxim of mutual assistance because it is more beneficial for oneself than the other maxim. If the rational will were to choose the less beneficial maxim, it would go against its own well-being. That is a contradiction in the will because it is not in harmony with itself. In fact, this is Kant's own argument for choosing the maxim of beneficence. But which maxim is more beneficial is a question of prudence and consequence, which assigns only instrumental value to maxims. This again transforms the categorical imperative into a hypothetical one. Even more important, it is impossible to say that the maxim of beneficence is more useful for everyone. Which of the two maxims is more useful for an individual depends on her hierarchy of values and her circumstances. If she is a sworn champion of rugged individualism, who looks upon aid from others with contempt, she can choose the maxim of non-beneficence without any conflict in her will. She can do the same if her fortunate circumstances allow her to do without anyone's help. These decisions cannot belong to formal rationality because they involve desires and circumstances. Therefore, the conflict in the will is not a formal criterion. Kant stresses the formal notion of contradiction and gives the impression that the formula of universal law is a formal principle. But that is only his pretence for covering up the substantive content he injects in the application of this allegedly formal moral principle.

I do not want to give you the wrong impression that the formal version of the formula of universal law is a truly formal principle, whereas its substantive version is a formal principle only in disguise. In both cases, Kant has produced moral rules by illicitly injecting substantive content in the application of his formal principle. The generation of substantive moral rules from purely formal principle is as impossible as the transformation of formal categories into substantive ones, which we noted in the last chapter. Both of them require the impossible operation of transubstantivation. In short, Kant's claim of ethical formalism is vacuous not because it can produce no moral maxims, but because it can produce too many. As Hegel says, there can be no maxim that cannot pass the formal test of self-consistency.[7] The only maxim that can fail this simple test is an outright self-contradictory rule such as 'I will lie and will not lie under any conditions'. But no one would even consider it as a maxim. There is no point even in testing it because it nullifies itself. Some maxims may hide contradictions, but Kant's examples do not belong to this sort of maxims. Therefore, the formula of universal law can never function as the generative principle for moral rules because its formal test can never discriminate the immoral maxims from the moral ones.

THE EXISTENCE OF THE CATEGORICAL IMPERATIVE

After explaining the formula of universal law with four examples, Kant makes the startling admission that he has not yet given a proof for the existence of the categorical imperative that does not depend on the incentives of inclination (GMM 425). This admission is startling because it follows his demonstration of how the categorical imperative can function as the formal procedure for generating all moral laws. But his demonstration has failed to show the independence of the categorical imperative from the incentives of inclination, because he has used those incentives overtly and covertly in his own application of the formula of universal law. That is surely a reason to doubt the existence of the categorical imperative. But there is another reason for the doubt. If the categorical imperative is the ultimate source of all moral laws, why had nobody ever heard of it until Kant's announcement? In the first section of the *Groundwork*, he informally introduces the first formula of the categorical imperative and says that it agrees with the practical judgements of ordinary human reason (GMM 402). In his discussion of the universal moral law, he chiefly stresses the commonsense understanding of justice against seeking one's advantages at the expense of others. This conception of moral laws is not any different from the Christian notion of moral laws inscribed in everyone's heart, or the laws of conscience. Only toward the end of his informal discussion does Kant mention moral legislation. But he never brings up his radical theory of rational autonomy and its formal rationality until the second section of the *Goundwork*, where he announces the categorical imperative by its own name. The title of the second section is 'Transition from Popular Morality to Metaphysics of Morals'. This may indicate that the categorical imperative is meant to be Kant's own metaphysical account of popular morality.

Surely, it is beyond ordinary moral consciousness that every rational human being is a moral legislator. That is why nobody had ever heard of rational autonomy for moral legislation and the categorical imperative as its formal procedure. Hence Kant has every reason to question the existence of the categorical imperative. Just before his explanation of the formula of universal law, he says that we do not have the advantage of its reality given in experience and hence we have to investigate its possibility (GMM 420). 'The possibility of the categorical imperative' can have two meanings. One of them is its metaphysical possibility, the other is its practical possibility. He will explain its metaphysical possibility by the postulate of freedom (GMM 454). By using the four examples, he may be demonstrating its practical possibility, that is, how it can function as the generative moral principle. In that case, he is proposing the categorical imperative as a new foundation for moral legislation to replace the old foundations. The latter have subscribed to the heteronomy of practical reason; the former advocates its absolute autonomy for the first time in history. This is why the *Groundwork* is his Copernican revolution in ethics.

Kant may be presenting the categorical imperative as his own invention for the implementation of rational autonomy. Since the concept of rational autonomy is also his own invention, he may feel the need to show the right procedure for its implementation. On the other hand, he may be claiming that the categorical imperative is dictated by rational autonomy and that he has only discovered it by his metaphysical analysis. Should we take him for the inventor of the categorical imperative or its discoverer? This is the most baffling question about Kant's relationship to the categorical imperative, and I have not been able to answer it to my own satisfaction. His startling admission that he has not given the proof for the existence of the categorical imperative may very well be his moment of honesty and sobriety, in which he has realized that even he is not sure of its existence. If he has discovered it, there should be no reason for him to worry about its existence because its discovery presupposes its existence. But he cannot have the same assurance if he has invented it. So he may have thought of the need to prove its existence. But he does not proceed to produce the proof. Instead he talks about how not to do it. He says that the existence of the categorical imperative cannot be proven by empirical means such as human nature or inclination because its sublimity and dignity far transcend the empirical domain.

Since the categorical imperative is binding on all rational beings, Kant says, the proof of its existence should be connected to the concept of rational will. If he can show that connection, he can produce positive proof for the existence of the categorical imperative. He was concerned with its negative proof when he stressed its independence from the incentives of inclination. With this preliminary, he goes into an extended discussion on the nature of the will. He singles out its two properties: (1) its capacity to determine itself in conformity with certain laws and (2) the ends as the ground of its self-determination. These two items are required for the exercise of rational autonomy, and they stand in the relation of form and content. The first of these two items has been fully discussed in the formula of universal law. So he now concentrates on the second item. It appears that he is now moving from the form to the content of the categorical imperative. But he does not say so. He recognizes two kinds of ends: subjective and objective (GMM 428). The subjective ends are private purposes and projects. They belong to inclination and have only conditional value. There can be no universal principles or practical laws governing them. They belong not to the categorical imperative, but only to hypothetical imperatives.

Kant says that only a rational being can be an objective end because its existence is an end itself. Hence it must not be used as a means. Such a being has absolute value. Kant distinguishes between persons and things. A person is an absolute and objective end that has absolute value. A thing has only a relative value. A person has dignity; a thing has price. Unlike things, persons cannot be used as mere means for the satisfaction of inclination. They command respect because they are the agents of rational will. Kant attributes the absolute value of persons to their rational will. They can never command such value and respect by their inclinations, which they share with mere things and brute animals. This is Kant's argument that an animal cannot be an objective end and can be used as a mere means. When a mother cat raises a litter of kittens, she has an end as objective as a human mother does. One need not be a Buddhist to recognize that animals are also objective ends, although this does not automatically entail that we have the duty to treat them as such. They have feelings, knowledge, and purposes. They know how to distinguish their children from the children of others and their friends from their foes. They have purposes in seeking food and rearing their children and experience feelings in every phase of their existence. They have all the emotive and cognitive requirements for being ends in themselves. But they are only things by Kant's standard because they have no rational will. If his version of rationalism can recognize only rational beings as objective ends, it is clearly irrational.

This extended discussion began with the problem of proving the existence of the categorical imperative. But Kant never connects it to that problem. Instead he uses it to introduce the second formula of the categorical imperative. If there is to be a supreme practical principle for the human will, namely the categorical imperative, he says, it must be based on the objective end of rational will (GMM 429). If the categorical imperative is based on the objective end of rational will, he can say, it cannot infringe upon the autonomy of rational will. Then he can take this as positive proof for the existence of the categorical imperative. But Kant never bothers to connect this point to the problem of proof. Instead, he restates the categorical imperative in terms of the objective end: *Act in such a way that you always treat humanity never as a means, but always as an end.* This is the second formula, which is also known as the formula of humanity. Let us now see how the concept of ends is used in this formula. We should never forget the distinction between subjective and objective ends. The latter have absolute value and belong to the categorical imperative; the former have only relative value and belong to hypothetical imperatives. We need this reminder because Kant himself may forget it.

In his explanation of the second formula, Kant uses the same four examples he used for the explanation of the first formula. He says that the maxim of suicide is wrong because it amounts to the use of oneself as a mere means for escaping from painful circumstances. A human being is not a thing to be used as a means. But suicide does not use the whole self, but only the empirical self, which has no absolute value by Kant's own standard. If the empirical self and inclination have only relative value, they should be used like any other things. Suppose that you are kept alive by a tyrant, who takes pleasure in torturing you day and night. He is using your body as his instrument of torture. Now suppose that there is no other way of terminating this torture but suicide. It would be hard to label such a suicide as an abuse of your body. Kant extends his discussion to all other forms of abusing one's body and stresses respecting and protecting its integrity. He does not realize that he has foreclosed such respect for human bodies by consigning them to the empirical domain, where they can have no dignity but only price, that is, instrumental value. If only the rational will has absolute value, it is entitled to use its body as mere means. Kant says that a deceitful promise is wrong because it uses another person as a mere means. By the same logic, we have no right to lie even to those who are intent on assaulting innocent people or endangering our national security. Thus the second formula generates the same problem as the first formula.

The third and the fourth examples are even tougher for the formula of humanity. Kant admits that to neglect the development of talents is not to use a human being as mere means, but claims that it is not in harmony with the formula of humanity. Human beings should develop their talents for greater perfection for the sake of the end that belongs to nature. This is the way to advance the ends of humanity (GMM 430). Kant is now appealing to the perfection of natural talents and the fulfilment of natural ends. This is the ethics of perfection that he has branded as a heteronomy of practical reason. In the fourth example, he again appeals to the natural end of all human beings, namely, happiness. He admits that we can subsist without contributing to each other's happiness. But that would be only a negative, not a positive agreement with the principle of humanity as an end in itself. He says that a positive agreement can be achieved only when everyone tries to further the private ends of others as far as possible (GMM 430). The second formula of the categorical imperative turns out to be the ethics of private ends, which he has consigned to the domain of relative values and hypothetical imperatives.

After these four examples, Kant again insists that the principle of humanity as an end in itself has borrowed nothing from experience because it must arise solely from pure reason (GMM 431). He says that the principle has excluded all interests from inclination. Therefore it can stand as the unconditional moral law. He may assert this as his proof for the existence of the categorical imperative that is free of inclination. But he cannot make this claim because he has expanded the concept of end to cover all natural ends and private interests. He has seriously compromised the autonomy of rational will in his application of the formula of humanity to the four sample cases. But he still insists that the principle of humanity has shown that the categorical imperative arises solely from pure reason because it is based on its own objective end. Strangely, he also says that there is no way to prove that there are practical propositions that command categorically (GMM 431). So he finally concedes that the existence of the categorical imperative cannot be proven.

Kant connects the formula of humanity to the kingdom of ends, which is a community of rational beings. This leads to the third formula of the categorical imperative: *Act on the maxims of a member who makes universal laws for a possible kingdom of ends* (GMM 439). He explains the relation of the three formulas to one another. But his account of their relation is twofold: (1) the thesis of equivalence and (2) the thesis of progression. The thesis of equivalence means that the three formulas are equivalent to one another because each of them produces the same result. The thesis of progression means that there is a progression in the sequence of the three formulas. He states the thesis of equivalence: Three formulas express the same moral law (GMM 436). He has indeed tried to show that the first and the second formulas produce exactly the same result by going over the same four examples. Then he talks about the difference between the three formulas:

The first formula gives the form of moral law, the second formula gives its matter in the domain of ends, and the third formula brings all moral beings together in a kingdom of ends. He describes the succession of these three formulas as the progression from the category of unity (the form of the will) through the plurality of its matter (the ends) to the totality or completeness of its system of ends (GMM 436).

In the thesis of progression, Kant describes the relation of the first two formulas as that of form and matter. In that case, it goes against the grain of his philosophy to say that the first two formulas are equivalent. In his philosophy, form and matter are two components of one object. They are neither equivalent nor interchangeable. They are complementary; they need each other. In fact, the first and the second formulas cannot produce the same result although Kant has tried to generate the same maxims from them. If the formula of universal law is strictly restricted to the form of moral maxims, as we have noted, it can endorse all maxims which are free of self-contradiction, even the obviously immoral maxims for lying, stealing, and killing. It is equally obvious that most of these immoral maxims are prohibited by the formula of humanity. If form and matter are complements to each other, the two formulas should be taken as two complementary features of all moral maxims. One of them provides their form, that is, their universality; the other provides their content. Neither of them can operate singly as the generative principle of all moral maxims because they have to operate jointly like two hands for clapping. These two stages of form and content can be followed by the third formula in the progression of the categorical imperative. The third formula advances moral legislation from the context of individual choice to the context of social choice. The first two formulas are sufficient for the context of individual choice, but not for the context of social choice. The latter context must coordinate the individual choices. For example, it is inadvisable for all individuals to make their own traffic rules. To participate in the life of social coordination and cooperation is to be a member of the kingdom of ends. The three formulas can mark the three stages in the realization of the categorical imperative.

The thesis of progression is incompatible with the thesis of equivalence. If each of the three formulas is equivalent with one another, there can be no progression from one to the others. If they are equivalent, they should be logically independent of each other. That is the impression that Kant gave in his explanation of the first two formulas by using the four sample cases. So I suspect that the thesis of progression must have been his afterthought. But this afterthought has the virtue of bringing together the three formulas into a coherent scheme of moral legislation. On the other hand, such coherence is missing from the thesis of equivalence. Kant has yet to explain why the categorical imperative can be stated in so many different ways, especially the relation between the first two formulas. The first formula is a principle of formal rationality, but the second formula is a principle of substantive rationality. The principle of formal rationality was adopted for the sake of rational autonomy, which he regarded as incompatible with any principle of substantive rationality. He will repeat this point in the second *Critique* (33–4). Hence the first two formulas cannot be accepted as two alternative expressions of rational autonomy and its categorical imperative.

RATIONAL AUTONOMY AND MORAL LEGISLATION

The third section of the *Groundwork* is entitled 'Transition from a Metaphysics of Morals to a Critique of Pure Practical Reason'. This is the reversal of the procedure advocated in the first *Critique*, where a critique of pure reason was said to be a propaedeutic for the metaphysics of morals. This reversal may be explained by the subtitle: 'The Concept of Freedom is the Key for an Explanation of the Autonomy of the Will'. Since Kant has used the concept of rational autonomy as the metaphysical foundation for his moral theory in the second section of the *Groundwork*, he has to explain this metaphysical foundation by a critique of practical reason. He is going to take the concept of freedom as the key for this explanation. Indeed, the concept of freedom is the central topic of the third section of the *Groundwork*. He begins the discussion by describing the will as a kind of causality, which is free of alien determination. This is only a negative concept of freedom. But freedom is not lawless. Its causality is in accordance with its own immutable laws. This is the positive concept of freedom.

The distinction between the negative and the positive concept of freedom can be described as the distinction between freedom from empirical forces and the freedom to act on one's own power. The latter is to be governed by one's own law in exercising freedom. Kant says that the positive concept of freedom is none other than the concept of autonomy. Then he specifically mentions the first formula of the categorical imperative (but not the other formulas) as the expression of the concept of autonomy. He reaffirms the formula of universal law as the principle of moral legislation under the autonomy of rational will. Thus his discussion of positive freedom is concerned with the problem of moral legislation. With this preliminary, he considers the relation between the formula of universal law and the concept of autonomy. 'If, therefore, freedom of the will is presupposed,' he points out, 'morality together with its principle [the formula of universal law] follows from it by mere analysis of its concept' (GMM 477). To put it another way, the relation of the moral principle to the concept of autonomy is analytic. But he says that the principle of morality itself is a synthetic proposition: 'But the principle of morality – that an absolutely good will is that whose maxim can always contain itself regarded as a universal law – is nevertheless always a synthetic proposition; for, by analysis of the concept of an absolutely good will that property of its maxim cannot be discovered' (GMM 447, tr. Gregor).

The principle of morality (the formula of universal law) is said to be synthetic because it cannot be discovered by the analysis of the concept of an absolutely good will. But this is not the same as to say that the principle of morality itself is synthetic. Its synthetic character cannot be established by its relation to the concept of an absolutely good will. The analytic and synthetic relations obtain between the subject and predicate within a proposition, not in the relation of the proposition to something outside itself. Kant is misusing his own analytic/synthetic distinction. He is confusing two issues: (1) whether the moral principle is analytic or synthetic, and (2) whether its relation to the concept of autonomy is analytic or synthetic. The second question should be settled by his earlier assertion that the moral principle follows analytically from the concept of freedom of the will. In that case, the same principle should also follow analytically from the concept of an absolutely good will because such a will is a free rational will. Therefore, their relation must be analytic, too. But Kant says it is synthetic. This is the sticky problem of the quoted passage.

Most commentators have evaded this problem by taking (1) as Kant's only contention because he will again call the categorical imperative a synthetic proposition later (GMM 454). But they regard (1) as a misapplication of the analytic/synthetic distinction. Since Kant has made the distinction in terms of the subject–predicate relation, they hold, it is inapplicable to imperatives because they are not descriptive propositions with subjects and predicates. But imperatives are also composed of subjects and predicates although their subjects are often suppressed. 'You ought to do what you ought to do' is an analytic command; 'You ought to love your neighbour' is a synthetic command. Since an analytic imperative is trivial, Kant takes it as a truism that all imperatives are synthetic, whether categorical or hypothetical. Therefore he is not really concerned with the synthetic character of the moral principle, but with its synthetic relation to the concept of autonomy.

No doubt, the categorical imperative follows from the concept of autonomy because the former is the way the latter is exercised. But the concept of autonomy alone cannot dictate the content of the moral principle because the latter is not contained in the former. Hence the formulation of the categorical imperative, which states its content, does not follow analytically from the concept of autonomy. Their relation is synthetic. We can make their relation analytic by the following formulation of the categorical imperative: *Act only in accordance with the moral laws of your own making*. This analytical formula cannot determine what kind of moral laws ought to be adopted by practical reason. But those laws require some content, which cannot be derived analytically from the concept of rational autonomy. How can practical reason provide the content for the categorical imperative without compromising its own autonomy? This is the basic question for Kant's theory of moral legislation, although he never states it openly. But he has left sufficient textual evidence for his struggle to resolve this problem in his effort to explain the formulations of the categorical imperative. So I propose to examine this evidence to determine the contour of his thought process, which lies behind those formulations.

When Kant informally introduces the categorical imperative in the first section of the *Groundwork*, he says that a moral law is the sort of law that can determine the rational will which is free of all natural impulses (GMM 402). This follows from the concept of rational autonomy because it is the freedom of practical reason from natural impulses. He says that such a rational law of freedom can be accepted and respected as a universal law for its own sake. This consideration leads to his first formulation of the categorical imperative. The autonomy of the will lies in its conformity with this type of law because it is not dictated by inclination. Then Kant considers two opposite maxims for moral rules: the maxim to lie and the maxim not to lie. He recognizes that either of them can be chosen for a rule of prudence. Since that is not a moral choice, he considers the possibility of adopting these two maxims as universal laws apart from selfish reasons. He says that the maxim to lie cannot be adopted as a moral law because it would destroy itself as soon as it was made a universal law. Hence this maxim must be rejected, but the maxim not to lie can be accepted because it does not destroy itself by becoming a universal rule. This is his formal procedure for selecting and adopting moral rules, which can avoid the problem of choosing maxims on the basis of their content.

Before formally presenting the categorical imperative in the second section of the *Groundwork*, Kant says that we have to investigate its possibility. But he wants to postpone it to the last section of the *Groundwork* because it will require a special and difficult toil (GMM 420). As we noted, he indeed takes on this special and difficult toil in the last section of the *Groundwork*. But he does not completely ignore this problem in the second section of the *Groundwork*. He wants to determine whether the mere concept of a categorical imperative can provide its formulation. To that end, he compares a categorical imperative with a hypothetical imperative. Whereas a hypothetical imperative is governed by its condition, he says, a categorical imperative is free of all conditions. It is impossible to know what is contained in a hypothetical imperative until its condition is given. But this is not the case with a categorical imperative, according to Kant; we can immediately know what it contains because it is free of conditions. He says that a categorical imperative contains nothing but the universality of a law as such (GMM 421). Therefore, he says, there is only a single categorical imperative. With this preliminary, he formally presents the formula of universal law. He does not say that this is one of the various ways of formulating the categorical imperative.

Instead, he calls it the one and only categorical imperative, from which all imperatives of duty can be derived. Then he compares the universal moral laws with the universal laws of nature. Just as pure understanding prescribes a priori laws for nature, pure practical reason prescribes moral laws for human beings. So he reformulates the categorical imperative in analogy to the laws of nature: *Act as if the maxim of your action were to become through your will a universal law of nature.* Hence this is not another formula of the categorical imperative although it has been regarded as one. It is only a corollary of the first formula in the analogy of moral laws to natural laws.

This analogy can set up the Copernican revolution in ethics as the counterpart to the Copernican revolution in epistemology. The two revolutions could be perfectly matched when Kant's Platonic ethics was in place. Just as pure understanding derives a priori natural laws from the categories, so pure reason derives a priori moral laws from the Ideas of reason. But this perfect parallel breaks down with his rejection of Platonic Ideas as the foundation of moral laws. Practical reason is now deprived of a priori resources for making laws, although they are still available for pure understanding. Kant has to explain how practical reason can make moral laws without using the pure concepts or Ideas of reason. Without such an explanation, the categorical imperative would be only an empty shell of moral command. When Kant explains the operation of the categorical imperative with four examples, he first uses the formal criterion he used in the first section of the *Groundwork*. But the formal criterion of logical consistency can set only the minimum requirement for all laws because self-contradictory laws can never be implemented. By stretching and twisting the formal criterion, Kant tries to manage the first two cases. Even by this devious manoeuvre, he cannot resolve the last two cases by the formal test. But he refuses to abandon the formal criterion. Instead he expands it from the contradiction in conception to the contradiction in the will, as we noted earlier. Since these two criteria are said to involve contradictions, they may appear to be two forms of one formal criterion. But they are two radically different criteria. One is formal; the other is substantive. With these two criteria, the first formula of the categorical imperative ceases to be a single principle. It becomes two principles in one.

The fatal defect of the first formula is its indeterminacy. The formula of universal law is not firmly fixed; its allegedly formal criterion is anything but formal in the normal sense. In Kant's hand, it stretches over from the self-contradiction of a maxim to the self-contradiction of a will. Since it operates like a rubber band, it is impossible to be certain what maxims can or cannot pass its test. This makes the categorical imperative highly indeterminate in terms of its content. This problem of indeterminacy can be avoided only by restricting the formal criterion to its purely formal function. Then it becomes vacuous and cannot handle the problem of content for moral laws. There is no reason to assume that these problems of the first formula could have escaped Kant's attention, if they can be detected by his critics. In that case, he could not be satisfied with the first formulation of the categorical imperative and its formal criterion. He may have decided to cope with this problem by finding a substantive criterion for choosing moral maxims in the objective ends of rational will. I am basing this conjecture on the transition from his presentation of the first formula to his presentation of the second formula. After discussing the first formula, he calls it the canon for morally appraising all actions. Some maxims cannot become universal laws because they cannot even be thought without contradiction. Although other maxims can be thought without contradiction, they cannot be chosen as universal laws by a rational will without contradicting itself (GMM 424). This summation expresses Kant's claim that the first formula contains a universal 'canon' for choosing and rejecting all moral maxims.

If Kant had been fully assured of the first formula as a universal canon, he would not have bothered with the second formula because another universal canon would be gratuitous. After his summation of the first formula, he says nothing about another formula of the categorical imperative. Instead, he makes the startling admission that he has not yet given a proof for its existence. For this proof, ostensibly, he tries to connect the categorical imperative to the concept of a rational will and its object, which serves as the objective ground for its self-determination (GMM 426–7). This assertion makes no sense without presupposing that the first formula can provide no objective ground for the self-determination of a rational will. If it could, the second formula would be gratuitous. On the other hand, if the second formula can provide the objective ground in question, it can also prove the autonomy of the will because it will be seeking its own end by following the second formula. For these reasons, the second formula and its substantive criterion can overcome the fatal deficiency of the first formula and its formal criterion. This is my account of why Kant did not stop with the first formula, but moved on to the second one.

If he had been fully satisfied with the first formulation and its formal criterion, he would not have made the effort to secure a substantive criterion in the second formulation. The third formulation is not another formula for the categorical imperative, but only a further elaboration of the second formula. When rational beings make laws that treat all of them as ends in themselves, they legislate for a kingdom of ends. This is the third formula. Hence Kant treats it as a corollary of the second formula (GMM 433). So there are only two really functioning formulas for the categorical imperative. One of them is presented as formal, and the other as substantive. When he writes the *Critique of Practical Reason*, he will retain only the first formula of the categorical imperative and drop all others as we will see later. But he will transform it from a formal to a substantive principle. If he had been fully satisfied with the multiple formulations of the categorical imperative as proposed in the *Groundwork*, he would have retained them all without any change in the second *Critique*.

The end of rational will is surely fit to be the content and matter of moral laws. The rational self can be autonomous in treating itself as an end in itself. Hence the principle of treating all human beings as ends in themselves seems to follow from the concept of autonomy. But human beings have not only rational but also empirical ends, and Kant tries to cover them all under the second formula of the categorical imperative, thereby turning it into a hypothetical imperative in some cases. If this formula were restricted to rational ends, it would follow analytically from the concept of rational autonomy. But as soon as it is extended to empirical ends, it also becomes highly indeterminate because different empirical ends can present different moral problems as manifested in Kant's own four cases. To help a drug addict get some cocaine cannot have the same moral significance as to help a victim of a traffic accident. Thus, the second formula of the categorical imperative has turned out to be as indeterminate as the first formula because of the content of moral laws. When Kant talks about different formulas, he gives the impression that the categorical imperative is open-ended for its formulation. In fact, it is indeterminate on the two levels of formulation and interpretation (application). It can be given more than one formulation, and each of them can be given more than one interpretation. This is the indeterminacy in Kant's theory of moral legislation, which shows up as the synthetic relation between the moral principle and the concept of rational autonomy.

Is there any normative constraint for controlling this indeterminacy or any guideline for making moral laws? This is the central question for Kant's doctrine of rational autonomy and moral legislation. If moral legislation is to be governed by the concept of freedom alone, the former can be as indeterminate and uncontrollable as the latter. He must settle this problem of indeterminacy in moral legislation for the completion of his moral theory. I propose that he is trying to do this in the last section of the *Groundwork* and that his intent is revealed in its subtitle: *The Concept of Freedom is the Key for an Explanation of the Autonomy of the Will.* His intent can become clearer if 'the Autonomy of the Will' is read as the autonomy of the will in moral legislation. After mentioning the synthetic relation between the concept of an absolutely good will and the formula of universal law, Kant proposes the positive concept of freedom as the third term for explaining their synthetic relation. The remainder of the third section of the *Groundwork* is supposed to be this explanation. Although the concept of freedom can explain the problem of indeterminacy in moral legislation, it cannot offer its resolution. In fact, he never brings his extended discussion of freedom to bear upon the problem of indeterminacy and its resolution. He says that freedom is presupposed for rational will because reason is the author of its own principles independent of foreign influences (GMM 448). This statement combines positive and negative freedom. Positive freedom is to be the author of its own principle; negative freedom is to be independent of foreign influences. So stated, the two freedoms may appear to be independent of each other. But positive freedom creates moral laws not only to gain negative freedom from inclination, but to govern them in the practical domain.

Why should pure reason care to make any laws for governing inclinations and take any interest in affairs of the empirical self?

This is the question of motivation for moral legislation, which Kant never brings up for discussion. I will show its importance by using what the Stoics said about their motivation for virtue. They wished to protect their rational life from desires and passions by the virtue of *apatheia*, the Stoic virtue of being indifferent to passions. Kant agrees with the Stoics when he recognizes no positive moral value for inclination. But he also backs off from the Stoic position when he recognizes our need for happiness and admits it as an essential element in the concept of the highest good. But the recognition of this need may be no more than the surrender of rational self to the demands of empirical self. A truly rational self may ignore and suppress the empirical self, as the Stoics taught. If we follow this line of thought, we have to say that the rational self should make laws only for the suppression and control of inclination. But this is not the motivation of the rational self for making moral laws on Kant's theory. What then is the motivation of practical reason in moral legislation? Although Kant does not directly face this question, he offers an answer in his statement that the word 'ought' of the categorical imperative stands for the word 'would' of rational will (GMM 449). The categorical imperative is a command only for the empirical self against its inclination. But it expresses what the rational self would do willingly. In that case, the problem of moral legislation is to formalize what practical reason would seek for social order. In ethical Platonism, this question can be settled by the Idea of Justice. But the noumenal world without Platonic Ideas can offer no guideline for this question. Although it is still called the intelligible world, it is the Lockean substratum of total darkness that can shed no light on moral legislation. Karl Ameriks astutely points out that Kant had better show that the intelligible world constitutes a realm of laws.[8] But Kant claims it only as a realm of freedom in the *Groundwork*.

Kant says that the idea of freedom makes possible the categorical imperative because the moral law (the law of the intelligible world) is contained in the idea of freedom (GMM 454). But he never explains how the moral law is contained in the idea of freedom. In all probability, he is only repeating what he said at the beginning of section 3 of the *Groundwork*: the moral principle follows from the concept of freedom. But we have noted that their relation is not analytic but synthetic because the concept of freedom alone cannot spell out moral laws. If the moral law were inscribed in the concept of freedom, it would be possible to derive the moral law analytically from the concept of autonomy (or freedom). But Kant never claims to have derived the various formulations of the categorical imperative from the concept of freedom. The fact that the categorical imperative can be given different formulations can attest to the indeterminacy of moral law. Moral law may be indeterminate because it is a product of freedom, which may be inherently indeterminate. But Kant has not faced the problem of how to derive determinate moral laws from the indeterminate concept of freedom. He will tackle this problem in the *Critique of Practical Reason*, not squarely but only obliquely.

In the second *Critique*, Kant gives the formula of universal law as the fundamental law of pure practical reason, but does not even mention the categorical imperative. A couple of times, he mentions the categorical command, which is compatible with any moral laws because all moral laws are categorical commands. He says, 'The will is thought as independent of empirical conditions and hence, as a pure will, is determined *by the mere form of law*, and this determining ground is regarded as the supreme condition of all maxims' (C_2 31, tr. Mary Gregor). Maxims have no special connection to the categorical imperative; they were essential even for his Platonic ethics of the first *Critique*. He marvels at the strange fact that the will can be determined by the mere form of law. This is the lingering residue from his ethical formalism, which he will soon discard for ethical Platonism. The form of law cannot determine its content. Kant then says that the formal principle 'forces itself upon us of itself'. If so, he does not have to explain why the fundamental moral law takes the formula of universal law because it is not his choice. Hence he has no freedom for its alternative formulations. He calls it 'the formal determining ground of the will' (C_2 32). Thus he resolves the indeterminacy of moral legislation by restricting the freedom of moral legislation to a single formula.

Kant again stresses that the formal principle can guarantee rational autonomy because it is solely concerned with the lawful form and does not depend on the material condition (C_2 33–4). Here again he associates the formal principle with rational autonomy. But he does not even mention the second formulation of the categorical imperative, which was concerned with the matter of moral law. He restates the content of the second formula as a by-product of the respect for moral law (C_2 76–8). By using only the formula of universal law, he may give the impression that he is purifying and perfecting his ethical formalism. On the contrary, he abandons it by transforming the formula of universal law from a formal into a substantive principle. He calls it the fundamental law of a supersensible nature, which is called the archetypal world in distinction from the ectypal world (C_2 43). In the *Groundwork*, he never associated the formula of universal law with the supersensible world because it was supposedly made by the rational will. But he now calls it the fundamental law of a supersensible nature. Such a law cannot be made or unmade by the rational self because it belongs to the supersensible world that is eternal. He equates the supersensible nature with the archetypal nature (*natura archetypa*). 'Archetypes' is his favourite icon for Platonic Ideas.

When Kant explains the application of his fundamental moral principle, he never uses the formal criterion of consistency. For the endorsement of a moral maxim, he appeals to the familiar test of whether it can be accepted as a universal law of nature. But he appeals not to the natural order of phenomena (*natura ectypa*), but to the natural order of archetypes (*natura archetypa*). He says, 'Therefore, this law must be the idea of a supersensuous nature, a nature not empirically given yet possible through freedom' (C_2 44, tr. Beck). In 'Of the Typic of the Pure Practical Judgement', he explains this point more fully. Given any proposed maxim, you should ask yourself whether you would be willing to be in a social order where the maxim is perfectly realized as its law of nature (C_2 69). The test of maxims uses an ideal type of nature that does not really exist in the empirical world. In the *Groundwork*, Kant did not even mention the distinction between these two natural orders because he recognized only the empirical natural order in his application of the formula of the universal law of nature. He admitted that the two opposed maxims of helping others and not helping others could equally become universal laws of nature. But now he can say that only one of them can become a universal law of the ideal natural order. Thus he is replacing the empirical natural order with the Platonic ideal natural order for moral legislation. When he uses the formula of universal laws of nature, he gives the impression that he is still operating with the categorical imperative of the *Groundwork*. But he is refashioning it with Platonic Idealism. We have earlier noted that Kant wrote the second *Critique* in order to meet his critics' demand for the explanation of his Copernican revolution in the *Groundwork*. But Kant is repudiating his own revolution instead of defending and justifying it. This is the irony of his presumed explanation.

Beside Platonic archetypes, Kant employs a few Ideas of his own such as the Idea of a person, the Idea of respect, the Idea of moral interest, etc. These Platonic Ideas constitute the intelligible matrix for the autonomy of rational will and its moral legislation, which could not be provided by 'the intelligible world' of Lockean substrata. Therefore the will is not determined by the mere form of law as Kant says, but by the law that embodies Platonic Ideas. Thus he reinstates his ethical Platonism. But this drastic reversal of his moral theory has never been noticed because it was performed so surreptitiously. This mystery is especially notable in Kant's handling of the question why moral laws should be expressed as universal laws. In the *Groundwork*, he just presented it as a formula of the categorical imperative, without explaining it. In the second *Critique*, however, he changes his tune and explains the universality of the moral principle in terms of justice. He says that its universality forces us to subject our happiness and advantages to the sense of justice and punishment (C_2 37). If the formula of universal law is dictated by the sense of justice, its universality is no longer an unexplainable mystery. It is the mark of legislation guided by the transcendent Ideas of the intelligible world.

Kant had to abandon his ethical formalism because he could not cope with its theoretical absurdities. Let us count a few of them. First, he could not explain why there were so many ways of formulating the categorical imperative. He presented them as ad hoc procedures for choosing moral maxims, but never articulated the general principle governing all those procedures. Second, his criterion of formal consistency was anything but formal or logical because he stretched and twisted it to allow his formal principle to have all sorts of substantive content. Third, he used the concept of an end to cover both subjective and objective ends in the formula of humanity, thereby turning the categorical imperative into a hypothetical one. Fourth, he tried to explain the relation of the first two formulas as the form and matter of moral law and yet made the logically impossible claim that they are equivalent and independent of each other. Fifth, he dictated the unholy union of formal principles with empirical content, thereby endangering the autonomy of rational will. Most important of all, it was impossible to know exactly what duties were dictated by the categorical imperative because of the indeterminacy in its formulation and interpretation.

All these absurd consequences have arisen from one basic problem of his ethical formalism: how to get substantive moral laws out of his empty formalism. This legislative operation is logically impossible because it requires the generation of substantive content from the logical form. In its nature, this operation is similar to Kant's attempt to generate the substantive categories (the rules of synthesis) from the formal ones (the forms of judgement). As we noted in the last chapter, he tried to pass it off as a legitimate conceptual transformation by his dubious double function theory of categories. He now tries to accomplish the impossible formal moral legislation by smuggling in substantive content through his devious applications of the allegedly formal principle. Those tricky maneuvers have eventually trapped him in a tangle of absurdities. But he would never acknowledge those absurdities. Nor would he openly renounce his formalist enterprise altogether. Instead, he quietly saves himself by filling the empty husk of his ethical formalism with the ideal content from the Platonic archetypal world.

THE DIALECTIC OF PRACTICAL REASON

Kant opens the Dialectic of Practical Reason with the concept of the highest good, which was introduced in the Canon of Pure Reason of the first *Critique*. The highest good is the complete good. Although the moral good is absolute, Kant says, it is not complete and whole for rational beings because they also need the natural good of happiness. But those two types of good should be proportionate with each other. Therefore, the highest good consists of three parts: (1) virtue (the moral good), (2) happiness (the natural good), and (3) their exact proportion. The last of these three parts is demanded by pure reason. Kant repeatedly says that morality (or virtue) is the worthiness to be happy. But the worthiness is not always rewarded with happiness. The virtuous often suffer, while the wicked often prosper. There appears to be no necessary connection between worthiness and happiness in this world. In that case, how can virtue and happiness be combined in the concept of the highest good? This is the dialectical problem of practical reason. Kant says that the relation between virtue and happiness should be either analytic or synthetic. If their relation is analytic, they are necessarily connected with each other. If their relation is synthetic, they are associated only accidentally. He notes that their relation was regarded as analytic by the Stoics and the Epicureans (C_2 111). The Stoics believed that happiness consists in the consciousness of one's virtue. Hence virtue and happiness are identical. Therefore their relation is analytic. The Epicureans believed that virtue is the cause of happiness. If one has virtue, one can be assured of happiness as its effect. Therefore their relation is again analytic. But Kant rejects both of these ancient views.

Kant holds that there can be no necessary connection between morality and happiness because they belong to two separate and independent domains. Morality is dictated by pure reason; happiness is governed by the natural world. Therefore, their relation is synthetic and contingent. If so, we cannot realize the highest good by our moral efforts alone. Unlike morality, happiness is not under the control of rational will. It is governed by the laws of nature. Therefore there is no way to realize both components of the highest good. It is an impossible ideal. But the moral law commands us to promote the highest good (C_2 114). Practical reason is demanding the impossible. This is the antinomy of practical reason. What is surprising is Kant's claim that the moral law commands us to promote the highest good. He never made this point in his discussion of the highest good in the Canon of Pure Reason or in the *Groundwork*. Never before has he claimed the promotion of the highest good as our duty. But he is now making this claim to set up the antinomy of practical reason. In the first *Critique*, he set up the cosmological antinomies by using the contradiction between thesis and antithesis. But he does not use this format for the antinomy of practical reason. To be sure, he says that the self-contradictions of pure practical reason generate the dialectic of practical reason (C_2 109), but he never spells out those contradictions. He has only argued that the relation between the two components of the highest good is synthetic. If so, the two components cannot contradict each other because they are independent of each other. For these reasons, some commentators have questioned Kant's notion of practical antinomy.[9] But we can make out something like an antinomy. If the promotion of the highest good is a command of practical reason, it is necessary deontically. But it is practically impossible to secure happiness commensurate with morality for everyone in this world. To be sure, there is no logical contradiction between these two sentences. But there is a practical conflict between the two. It may be called a practical antinomy, not only because it takes place in the world of practice, but because it is the conflict between the deontic necessity of a moral command and its practical impossibility. We can take this as our charitable understanding of Kant's antinomy of practical reason.

Kant resolves his antinomy with two postulates: the immortality of the soul and the existence of God. The first requirement for the realization of the highest good is moral perfection because it is the foundation of the highest good. Kant holds that an endless progress is required for moral perfection (C_2 122). Such a progress is not possible in this world, but only in the eternal world on the condition of immortality. This is the first postulate. Kant's argument should not be taken for a proof of immortality. It is only a postulate or a hypothesis, which is beyond proof and disproof. A proof is an item of knowledge; a postulate is an item of belief. The exact apportionment of happiness to virtue is not a part of moral perfection. Nor can it be handled by human beings. It requires the infinite wisdom and power of God. The highest good can be realized only in the kingdom of God. This is a design argument not for this world, but for the other world. But it is again not a proof, but a postulate. It is strange that Kant has to use two postulates to resolve one antinomy. In truth, he has two antinomies. One is the antinomy of moral perfection, and the other is the antinomy of harmony between morality and happiness. The first antinomy is the conflict between the necessity of moral perfection dictated by practical reason and its practical impossibility in this world. Since moral perfection is impossible in this world, Kant should say, it can be resolved only by the postulate of immortality. The second antinomy is the conflict between the necessity of harmony between morality and happiness and its practical impossibility in this world. This antinomy is resolved by the postulate of the existence of God. Kant has derived not one but two antinomies from the concept of the highest good.

The resolution of the first antinomy makes the other world a perpetual moral purgatory. The resolution of the second antinomy makes the other world a perfectly just world. Although this world is morally imperfect and unjust, the other world must be perfect and just. This is the upshot of Kant's moral theology. Bertrand Russell objects to it on the ground that there is no reason to expect the other world to be better than this world.[10] This is a valid criticism on the condition that we know nothing about the noumenal world. But the noumenal world can be understood in either the Lockean or the Platonic model, as I pointed out in the last chapter. In the Lockean model, the other world is inaccessible and unintelligible. Therefore Kant has no right to assume that it is any better than this world. In the Platonic model, however, the noumenal world is supposed to be intelligible and perfectly rational. It is the home of rational will. Only as members of the intelligible world are human beings supposed to have their freedom and moral commands. So I propose that this sort of rational world is presupposed for Kant's moral theology.

There are more important issues in Kant's moral theology than Russell's objection. They concern his basic premise, the concept of the highest good. Its first element is the moral good, which is usually assumed to be dictated by the categorical imperative. This is a mistaken assumption. The moral antinomy cannot be established by the force of the categorical imperative because it entails a tangle of theoretical absurdities. We have noted that we cannot even be certain what duties are dictated by the categorical imperative. Such a precarious moral principle cannot sustain a dialectical conflict of practical reason. Fortunately, Kant has abandoned the categorical imperative and refurbished his moral principle in the Analytic of the second *Critique*. So this new moral principle must be assumed to be the premise for the concept of the highest good. If morality and happiness are two independent goods, why should they be proportionate with each other? Kant never explains this point beyond saying that morality is worthiness to be happy. I suppose that he is implicitly appealing to our sense of justice. To be worthy means to deserve. If virtue deserves happiness, it is unjust for virtue to be denied happiness. In the Canon of Pure Reason, Kant used the concept of the highest good as the principle of justice. In an ideal community, everyone will do their duty and be rewarded accordingly, and that will secure the apportionment of happiness to morality (A809/B837). Thus the concept of the highest good is dictated by the Idea of Justice. This is the only way to reconcile the duty to promote the highest good with the concept of rational autonomy, which categorically excludes happiness from moral consideration. Happiness is now accepted not in its own right but as the requirement of justice.

Although Kant talks about the duty to promote the highest good, he never explains how this duty has arisen. He does not say that the concept of the highest good is the determining ground of the moral will. He only says that we have the duty to promote the highest good because it is the ultimate end of practical reason. He simply derives this duty from the concept of the highest good. Many commentators have pointed out the impossibility of fulfilling this duty. In their view, it is impossible to gauge the virtue of others correctly, or to secure the right amount of happiness for it. Kant may say that the impossibility of fulfilling this duty is the heart of his antinomy of practical reason. But to dictate an impossible duty goes against his fundamental moral principle because the maxim of an impossible duty cannot be accepted as a universal law. Hence an impossible duty can never be a duty for any rational being. Thus Kant has never succeeded in establishing his antinomy of practical reason. When Kant derives the impossible duty from the highest good, he gravely misunderstands the nature of Ideas. Normative Ideas are the objects of aspiration, but not the source of obligation. They neither command nor chastise anyone. The concept of the highest good is a normative ideal for the aspiration of all rational beings. This is quite different from regarding it as the source of our duty. Can Kant still sustain his antinomy on the concept of the highest good as an ideal of practical reason? In the Canon of Pure Reason, he entertained the possibility of realizing the highest good in an ideal community. But no normative ideals can ever be fully realized, if Plato is right. Kant's antinomy cannot be sustained on the mere difficulty of realizing a normative ideal or on the impossibility of its perfect realization. Neither of them can produce a practical antinomy, although both of them can pose serious existential problems. But these problems are not antinomies.

For the sake of argument, let us suppose that Kant's antinomy is real, and consider how his postulate can resolve it. In his philosophy, the moral imperative and duty are necessary only for human beings, who are composed of rational will and inclination. The categorical imperative is the command that the rational self issues to the empirical self. The problem of moral struggle arises for human beings because they are saddled with their empirical selves. When human beings die in the phenomenal world and go to the noumenal world, do they still retain their empirical selves? If the empirical selves belong to the phenomenal world as Kant says, they cannot be retained in the noumenal world. In the intelligible world of noumena, human beings should be purely rational beings. They can no longer have any moral problems because they are free of temptations and inclinations. There can be no need for making any progress for moral perfection, let alone an endless progress. Moreover, no progress can take place in the noumenal world because it is situated beyond space and time. Where there is no time, there can be no progress. Kant's talk about moral progress and perfection can make sense only if human existence in the noumenal world is the continuation of its existence in the phenomenal world. In his essay, 'The End of All Things', Kant imagines the other world as a continuation of this world. But that is incompatible with his theory of noumena. Thus his resolution of the moral antinomy makes no sense in the context of his own transcendental idealism. It is no more than his moral adaptation of the Christian dogma for the redemption of humanity in the other world.

RELIGION OF PRACTICAL REASON

Kant reshaped his conception of religion in terms of his moral theory. Let us go over its basic features. He believes that God does not stand as a power that has its own laws and commands different from the moral law and its dictates. What God demands from ethical subjects is nothing other than what is dictated by moral reason. To do the will of God is to perform the duties of the moral imperative. There is no way to please God other than to be morally perfect. To be religious is to be moral; to be moral is to be religious. Morality and religion are functionally identical, and their functional identity is expressed in Kant's statement that religion and God are internal to morality. He admits that his internalism goes against the traditional view that morality and religion are external to each other. In general, the traditional religions portray God as a powerful being, whose will is independent of our will, whose commands can override even our moral dictates and whose favour can be sought by special rituals and devotions. Kant rejects such externalism as a religious delusion (R 168–70). He calls it the anthropomorphic misconception of God and his relation to us, that is, the error of understanding God as someone like a powerful human being who demands our service and devotion. This misconception lies behind the religions of *cultus externus*. These religions impose on their devotees a set of obligations or observances that consist of prayers, rituals, services, and various prohibitions. Furthermore, the gods of these religions are assumed to be pleased or displeased by the performance or non-performance of these religious duties. Most of these religions have specially ordained experts called priests, ministers, or shamans, who have the power of officiating and facilitating the performance of religious duties.

Cultus externus, Kant insists, makes no sense to anyone who correctly understands the nature of God as the most perfect being, that is, omniscient, omnipotent, and, above all, morally perfect. It makes no sense to render any service to such a being because he is in need of nothing and can derive no benefit from our services. Even the praise of his perfection cannot add anything to his perfection, any more than flattery can to his honour. God does not need our prayers to find out what we need. Nor can he be moved by our supplication because his mind is governed only by moral dictates. The *cultus externus* can never fulfil the religious function of moving or pleasing the true God by human beings. Kant uses the label 'natural religion' to designate his view of religion, because it can be fully comprehended by the natural power of human reason, that is, without the aid of supernatural revelation. Natural religion is opposed to supernatural or revealed religion (R 155). The latter stands on the authority of external revelation through prophets, but the former stands on the authority of internal revelation by pure reason. Kant's idea of natural religion may appear to reduce religion to morality. But he insists that natural religion retains all the essential features of traditional religions. In his view, those features are the moral attributes and

functions of the supreme being, as the holy law-giver, the benevo-
lent ruler, and the just judge. Any other attributes of God such as
omniscience, omnipotence, and omnipresence are only supplemen-
tary to his moral attributes; they are the requisite conditions for
discharging his moral functions. Kant says that Christianity is the
only moral religion, while the others are servile religions. The
central function of servile religions is to curry favour from the
supernatural powers; they place human beings in a servile relation
to those powers. This servile relation has been transformed into a
moral one by Jesus of Nazareth. Jesus transformed the old law of
Moses, the rules for external observance, into the new law, the
rules for internal disposition. Kant finds Jesus's moral interpretation of religious life most conspicuously in the Sermon on the
Mount, and he reads its concluding remark – 'Therefore be
perfect, as your heavenly Father is!' – as his exhortation for moral
perfection (R 159–60).

Kant gives a moral interpretation of Christian dogmas. The
dogma of original sin explains our innate propensity to do evil,
which is to flout the maxims of duty and to succumb to the maxims
of inclination. Kant regards it as a superstition to believe that this
propensity was generated by Adam's fall from grace and then
passed on to his posterity. On the contrary, this propensity is the
radical evil innate in human nature (R 29). No doubt, the original
human nature is said to be good. This good principle is the
freedom to obey the moral law, which is opposed to the evil principle or disposition. The radical evil does not come from the animal
nature of human beings because the animal nature is morally
neutral. The radical evil makes its appearance only with the
consciousness of moral law. It is the perpetual propensity to incorporate our inclination into moral maxims. This is the source of
guilt, which can be overcome only by the revolution of heart that
turns against inclination and its temptation for the sake of moral
law. Salvation from the radical evil lies only in moral perfection
(R 83). It cannot be achieved by the miraculous power of an
external god. The theistic miracles are incompatible with the principle of rationality; they can only paralyse human reason (R 86).

Moral perfection and salvation is the ultimate end of creation
(R 60). This ideal of moral perfection is embodied in the Son of
God. Kant interprets the incarnation of God in Christ not as a
miracle of the supernatural order but as the manifestation of a

moral ideal. As moral agents, he says, all of us have the ideal of a morally perfect human being. Such an ideal, if ever realized in this world, can be called an incarnate God. Kant calls the ideal of moral perfection the archetype of moral life. But this archetype, he insists, cannot be identified with Jesus Christ himself. He is only an instance or example, while the archetype resides only in pure reason (R 61-3). The relation of archetype and example is misrepresented in the traditional dogma of the incarnation, which exalts Jesus as a member of the Holy Trinity. He regards the dogma of the Trinity as theoretically incomprehensible and practically unserviceable. If the Son of God is so exalted as to stand above all human temptations and struggles, he is too remote from our existence to serve as a useful model. The value of the Son of God as our practical model lies in his essential identity with all human beings, and every human being who strives to achieve moral perfection can be called a son of God, a man well-pleasing to God. By incarnating the ideal of moral perfection, the Son of God brings the kingdom of God to the earth.

Kant interprets the kingdom of God as an ethical common-wealth. It is the community of virtue founded on moral law. It is analogous to the political community of a state. Their common aim is to get out of the lawless state of nature, but they adopt different types of law. The political community employs the laws of coercion; the ethical community allows only the laws of freedom. The latter is realized in the form of a church. But the church can be visible or invisible. The visible church is an actual union of human beings as an ethical community. Its members participate in its ethical life, helping and caring for one another. The invisible church is the ideal union of all human beings, which cannot be an object of experience. Every visible church has its own particular history, but the invisible church does not because it is the universal one. Every visible church has its own ecclesiastical dogmas, rituals, and scriptures. But they are only incidental vehicles for propagating one purely rational faith. There is a gradual transition from the diversity of ecclesiastical faith to the unity of rational faith (R 115). The churches of different ecclesiastic faiths may fight against one another for the preservation of their particular faiths. This is the church militant. But when they flower into one unchanging and all-unifying church, they will become the church triumphant. This transition initiates the history of the universal Church, and Kant locates this moment of triumph in the birth of Christianity from Judaism (R 127). When this ethical community is fully realized, the kingdom of God will be finally established on earth. The ultimate end of this movement is the moral perfection of not only individuals, but the entire human race. It will be the great cosmic revolution that will establish one universal ethical community for all human beings (R 134). This is the ultimate end of creation and the redemption of humanity from the evil principle. At this point, Kant fully embraces the spirit of the Enlightenment and believes that the moral destiny of humanity can be fully realized in the phenomenal world, whereas in the first two *Critiques* he had placed his hope for its full realization in the noumenal world. But this drastic change in his historical outlook had already taken place in the third *Critique*, which was published two years earlier than *Religion within the Boundaries of Mere Reason*, as we will see in the next chapter.

THE IMMANENT IDEAS

Kant finally published the *Metaphysics of Morals* twelve years after laying its foundation in the *Groundwork*. Let us now see how much the earlier work is really used for the later work. It contains two parts: Metaphysical Principles of Justice and Metaphysical Principles of Virtue. The first part is political and legal philosophy; the second part is virtue ethics. The relation of these two parts is based on Kant's distinction between internal and external freedom. Internal freedom is the freedom of moral will; external freedom is political and social freedom. This distinction roughly corresponds to the traditional distinction between the domain of ethics and the domain of politics, which was never recognized in the *Groundwork*. Therefore the *Metaphysics of Morals* is written in a more traditional style than the *Groundwork*, which has been called Kant's Copernican revolution in ethics. In the later work, Kant fully affirms the old ethic of perfection and employs two Platonic Ideas he had cited in the Transcendental Dialectic of the first *Critique*. The Idea of Justice (or the republican constitution) is the basis for the Metaphysical Principles of Justice; the Idea of Virtue is the basis for the Metaphysical Principles of Virtue. Most amazing of all, Kant does not even mention the demarcation between the phenomenal and the noumenal worlds. Platonic Ideas do not constitute a separate world although they are supersensible entities.

In the Metaphysical Principles of Justice, Kant states the principle of justice: *Every action is just [right] that in itself or in its maxim is such that the freedom of the will of each can coexist together with the freedom of everyone in accordance with a universal law* (MM 230, tr. Ladd). In the formulation of this principle, Kant does not use the formulas of the categorical imperative. Even the use of the word 'maxim' shows no special connection with the *Groundwork*, because he had already used it in the first *Critique*. The function of a universal law is to secure the equality of freedom. The universality of law is appreciated for its substantive function rather than its formal function. Kant had made this change already in the second *Critique*, as we noted earlier. Equality of freedom means the equality of rights; the concept of external freedom is interchangeable with the concept of rights. Kant says that the principle of innate freedom is the source of all rights (MM 237). The principle of innate freedom is the innate right to external freedom under universal laws. It contains the right to equality, independence from others, sovereignty over oneself, and liberty to do anything without harming others. The innate right eventually expands to the property right of acquisition and disposition. All these rights belong to private law insofar as they do not interfere with the same rights of others. Hence they require no legislation. In this regard, private law is different from public law, which is an expression of the collective will and belongs to a civil society (MM 311). The constitution of a civil society is the collective action of a community. Kant accepts the theory of social contract and identifies the state as the general united will, thereby officially installing Rousseau's theory of general will as the basis for his theory of public law (MM 313–15).

The ultimate end of a civil society is to secure equality and justice for all its citizens. Kant says that the well-being of a state should not be confused with the well-being or happiness of its citizens. He identifies the well-being of a state with its justice (MM 318). Kant's theory of justice is his elaboration of the Platonic Idea of Justice, that is, the Idea of a Republican Constitution. His surreptitious return to ethical Platonism in the second *Critique* comes into full bloom in a parade of Ideas in the *Metaphysics of Morals*. Time and again, he appeals to the Ideas of pure reason. The original community of possession is an Idea; so is the concept of private (intelligible) possession in distinction from the empirical concept of physical possession (MM 250–5). The concept of civil society that limits the individual will in accordance with the general will is also an Idea of reason, because the concept of general will is an Idea (MM 306). The concept of a civil state is the Idea of what a state ought to be according to the pure principles of justice. This Idea serves as an internal standard for every actual union of human beings in a commonwealth (MM 313). The original contract, by which individuals can get out of the state of nature, is not a historical or empirical concept, but an Idea of reason (MM 315). So is the concept of an ideal state, which Kant identifies with a republican constitution (MM 341). The rational ideal of human community takes its final form in the Idea of a peaceful universal community of all nations (MM 352).

Where does Kant get all these Ideas? It is unlikely that he plucks them out of Platonic Heaven. These Ideas of social institution are too deeply embedded in the phenomenal world. They are immanent rather than transcendent. So I propose that practical reason generates these Ideas by articulating the transcendent Idea of Justice. In that case, the function of practical reason has changed from the *Groundwork*, where it was charged with the task of making moral laws by rational choice without appealing to transcendent Ideas. There Kant complained that the concept of perfection was too indeterminate (GMM 443). By this statement, he meant that transcendent Ideas were too indeterminate. He is now making them more determinate by generating a series of immanent Ideas for social institutions ranging from the original contract for a civil society to private and public laws of an ideal state. His theory of justice is a procession of Ideas and their descent from Platonic Heaven to the phenomenal world. He never mentions the distinction between the empirical and the intelligible worlds, which served as the framework for all his previous ethical theories. Instead, he talks about the distinction between the empirical and the intelligible normative concepts such as the empirical possession and the intelligible possession in private law (MM 249). The intelligible normative concepts are framed in terms of immanent Ideas.

In the Metaphysical Principles of Virtue, Kant defines ethical duties as those ends that are at the same time duties, and recognizes two duties of this kind: the perfection of oneself and the happiness of others (MM 385). This is a remarkable turnabout from his position in the *Groundwork*, where he categorically rejected happiness as the ground of moral theory. Because ethical duties involve the ends of action, Kant says, their maxims are different from the maxims of legal duties, which do not involve the ends of action. He calls the latter the formal maxims and the former the material maxims. The formal maxims are end-independent; the material maxims are end-dependent. A formal maxim is valid if and only if it can be accepted as a universal law for governing the domain of external freedom, regardless of the end of its action. The question of whether it can be accepted as a universal law is not decided by any of the formulas of the categorical imperative. It is decided by the principle of justice, which requires the equality and harmony of all individuals in the exercise of their freedom. The question of what sort of ends are pursued does not enter into this decision. A material maxim is valid if and only if it is linked to an end that is at the same time a duty. The question of what sort of ends are pursued is central for the acceptance of a material maxim. Hence the theory of virtue is chiefly his examination of what sorts of end are ethical duties.

Kant divides the duty of perfecting oneself into perfect and imperfect duties to oneself (MM 421–7). Perfect duties to oneself are further divided into those duties to oneself as an animal being and those duties to oneself as a moral being. The first perfect duty to oneself as an animal being is to preserve one's animal nature. Kant says that this duty forbids suicide, wanton self-abuse, and self-stupefaction through immoderate use of food and drink. He mentions neither the maxim nor its universal form. Suicide is wrong not because of its maxim but because it goes against the duty of preserving one's natural being and because it destroys the natural basis of oneself as a moral being (MM 422–3). He shows no trace of formalistic argument from the *Groundwork*. This is also true of his discussion of the duty to oneself as a moral being (MM 429–37). He says that this duty is opposed to the vices of lying, avarice, and false humility (servility). He condemns lying as a vice, not because of any maxims, but because it obliterates the dignity of a liar as a human being and because it goes against the natural purpose of communication. He is advocating the ethics of perfection, which he rejected in the *Groundwork*. What is even more remarkable is that his idea of perfection includes not only moral but natural ends, which were difficult to incorporate into the categorical imperative in the *Groundwork*. He no longer maintains a rigorous separation between natural and moral orders, or between natural and moral persons, because both of them can belong to the ideal order. Now he admits moral dispositions as an essential element in the moral character of a person because they are included in moral perfection. They constitute the moral virtue of a person (MM 383). In the *Groundwork*, he recognized rational will as the only moral virtue and relegated all dispositions to the empirical domain. He never recognized their moral value.

Kant divides the duties to others into the duties of love and the duties of respect. He endorses the maxim of benevolence as a universal law and links its universality to the universal idea of humanity. He says that this maxim is dictated by the idea of needy rational beings, who are united by nature in one dwelling place for mutual aid (MM 453). He is appealing to the Idea of a Community. The community in question is not even a civil society, but a natural community. But this natural community must belong not to *natura ectypa*, but to *natura archetypa* because it is an Idea. He says that the duty of respect is based on the dignity of human beings. Because of their dignity, they should never be used as mere means. We should never despise or mock other people, nor should we ever slander or abuse them. Pride is also a vice, which goes against one's proper esteem of others, because it amounts to the demand of special esteem from others, which goes against the equal dignity of all human beings. The duty of respect is far more important than the duty of love. The omission of the latter is only a lack of virtue; the omission of the former is a vice. Let us consider the relation of human dignity to moral law. In the second *Critique*, Kant derived the respect for persons from the respect for moral law. Human beings have dignity because they can obey moral law. This is the primacy of moral law over the dignity of human beings, which has raised the troublesome question of whether immoral or amoral human beings (remorseless sinners, idiots, and children) have any dignity. But this question is now forestalled by his assertion of human dignity without basing it on moral law. The concept of human dignity now stands as one of the substantive Ideas for the formulation of ethical duties.

There is one serious defect in Kant's ethics of ends: he never demonstrates the existence of obligatory ends. Without giving any reason, he simply names two such ends: the perfection of oneself and the happiness of others. But we can link them to the concept of the highest good. John Silber refines it as the conjunction of the natural good and the moral good.[11] He equates the natural good with happiness. But the concept of happiness is ambiguous. It can be empirically defined as the feeling of pleasure or normatively defined as doing well. A drug addict can achieve happiness by the former definition, but not by the latter. The realization of natural ends may well be the best definition of happiness in its normative sense. If the concept of the highest good is defined in terms of natural and moral ends, it is the ground for the duty of achieving natural and moral perfection. Happiness is no longer linked to morality as its reward. For my own self, I have to seek both natural and moral perfection. For others, I can only help them seek their natural perfection, not their moral perfection because the latter is beyond my control. Thus, the Metaphysical Principles of Virtue advocates an ethics of perfection, which Kant had categorically rejected in the *Groundwork*.

Kant's new ethics of perfection even includes natural perfection. In the *Groundwork*, he never entertained the idea of natural end or perfection for ethical consideration. This remarkable change in his attitude to the natural world had taken place in the *Critique of Judgement*, seven years before the publication of the *Metaphysics of Morals*, when he recognized natural teleology as a fundamental principle of the phenomenal world, as we will see in the next chapter. With the inclusion of natural good in its own right rather than only as a reward for morality, his concept of the highest good becomes complete. It can now provide the axiological hierarchy for ranking all human ends, which is presupposed by his discussion of obligatory ends. For example, to demean oneself for social advancement is bad because it is to sacrifice the higher end of human dignity for the lower end of material gain. The question of priority is also important for determining our duties to others. Though we have the duty to promote their happiness, Kant says, we should not do so when it can be done only at the expense of their moral virtue. We should respect the moral good of others as higher than their natural good. Thus the concept of the highest good determines not only the obligatory ends but also their relative rankings. This is the ultimate Idea of reason, which Kant once identified as the Idea of the necessary unity of all possible ends (A328/B385). Thus the role of Ideas is as important for his theory of virtue as it is for his theory of justice.

I have shown that the Ideas of practical reason function as the foundation for both parts of the *Metaphysics of Morals*. I have gone against the firmly established tradition of reading this text as an application of the foundation laid out in the *Groundwork*. The titles of these two works have led Kant scholars to assume that the *Metaphysics of Morals* is a systematic application of the categorical imperative. They rarely recognize that Kant had already dropped the categorical imperative in the second *Critique*. Mary Gregor holds that he derives all duties of justice and virtue from the categorical imperative.[12] Let us see whether this sort of derivation takes place in the *Metaphysics of Morals*. We have already noted a few obstacles to deriving the duties of virtue from the categorical imperative. First, the ethics of perfection is incompatible with the categorical imperative and its rational autonomy because it is a heteronomous ethics. Second, happiness as the ground of duty is also incompatible with the categorical imperative. Third, Kant seldom uses either the formula of universal law or the formula of humanity for the derivation of ethical duties.

The duties of justice may appear to have some relation to the categorical imperative because it requires a universal law. Some scholars maintain that the principle of justice follows directly from the formula of universal law.[13] But there is an important difference between the two. The universal laws given by the formula of universal law are the maxims of action. But the principle of justice does not provide the maxims of action; it secures the freedom and equality of all citizens. Its universal laws function as the legal framework for distributing and protecting their freedom equally. Mary Gregor holds that the principle of justice is similar to the formula of humanity because the principle of justice fixes absolute limits to our freedom.[14] Again, there is an important difference between the two. The formula of humanity is not a principle of freedom or its limits. It only dictates respect for persons as ends in themselves. The respect in question may function as the limits to our freedom. But the principle of justice sets the limits to our freedom not for the respect of persons, but for the sake of freedom itself, that is, for its legitimate exercise. Kant counts the respect of persons not as a duty of justice, but as a duty of virtue because it is an obligatory end, whereas the principle of justice involves no ends. There is no way to link the *Metaphysics of Morals* to the *Groundwork*.

Shortly after the *Groundwork* and years prior to the *Metaphysics of Morals*, Kant forswore ethical formalism in the second *Critique* as we have already seen. In the *Metaphysics of Morals*, Kant did not merely reaffirm his ethical Platonism, but constructed immanent Ideas by articulating the transcendent Platonic Ideas for their application to the phenomenal world. By the power of these immanent Ideas, he laid the foundation for the German Idealism of Hegel and Schelling. But this Platonic revolution has gone unnoticed by most scholars. Many of them have spared no effort to defend the categorical imperative out of their fidelity to their revered master. They have succeeded in selling the categorical imperative as the heart of his moral philosophy and the *Groundwork* as its best exposition. This is the gravest misfortune that has overtaken his moral philosophy. The categorical imperative was the flicker of his fatally ill-conceived theory that flared up only once in his long career. He never retained it after the *Groundwork*. But its magnification by Kant scholars has totally blinded our eyes to the recurrent Platonic themes in his ethical writings.

John Rawls was one of the few astute scholars to recognize the futility and triviality of Kant's formalism. In his Kantian interpretation of his own theory of justice, he says:

> It is a mistake, I believe, to emphasize the place of generality and universality in Kant's ethics. That moral principles are general and universal is hardly new with him; and as we have seen these conditions do not in any case take us very far. It is impossible to construct a moral theory on so slender a basis, and therefore to limit the discussion of Kant's doctrine to these notions is to reduce it to triviality. The real force of his view lies elsewhere.[15]

Rawls is talking about the formula of universal law: to take it as the heart of Kant's moral theory is to reduce it to triviality. He says, 'The real force of his view lies elsewhere.' He has dismissed the categorical imperative as trivial and found his inspiration in Kant's theory of justice. This was his secret for becoming one of the most productive Kantians in the past century, while the loyal followers of Kant were blithely advocating his ethical formalism. But even Rawls failed to realize that Kant's theory of justice was not his own invention but his adaptation of Plato's theory for the liberal ethos of modern Europe. So Rawls never recognized the ultimate source of inspiration for his own theory of justice. Thus he mistook himself for a Kantian because he never came around to appreciate the Platonic legacy in Kant's normative theory, probably the only thing worth saving in his entire philosophy.

CHAPTER 3

BEYOND THEORY AND PRACTICE

(AESTHETICS, TELEOLOGY, AND HISTORY)

In the last chapter, we noted that Kant wrote the second *Critique* against his original plan of writing only one *Critique of Pure Reason* because he had changed his mind about the foundation of his normative theory. By the time he was completing the *Critique of Practical Reason*, he again believed that he was completing his Critical enterprise. He announces its completion in the conclusion of the second *Critique*, where he makes his moving observation about two wonders, 'the starry heaven above me and the moral law within me', the two things for ever-increasing admiration and reverence (C_2 161–2). The first wonder is located in the external world, and the second wonder in the inner self. These two wonders represent the two worlds of phenomena and noumena, the domain of theoretical reason and the domain of practical reason. They are the objects of inquiry in the two *Critiques*. In the conclusion of the second *Critique*, he is summing up his accomplishment not only in that volume but for his entire Critical Philosophy. Hence it reads like the final coda for the Critical programme as a whole. But two years later he published another *Critique*, the third and last one. It is called the *Critique of Judgement*. What is his excuse for writing this piece? In the Introduction to this volume, he reaffirms the division of philosophy into two domains of nature and freedom. If this is correct, the first two *Critiques* should have covered the entire philosophy, leaving no room for another *Critique*.

Kant makes a special plea for writing the *Critique of Judgement*. He now claims to see an enormous chasm between the phenomenal and the noumenal world and proposes to use the faculty of judgement to bridge this chasm. This faculty can establish the

144

ground of unity and mediation between the two worlds, he says, because it lies between the understanding and reason. This special plea comes as a huge surprise for those familiar with his previous works. Never before had he even mentioned the chasm between the two worlds. But he now says that the chasm blocks the influence of the noumenal world on the phenomenal world. As we noted in the last chapter, Kant has only proved that we are free in the noumenal world, but he has never shown that the noumenal freedom can break into the phenomenal world. He is now concerned with this practical problem of freedom and calls it the problem of mediation. But he never bothers to explain how the new faculty of judgement performs the function of mediation in any part of the third *Critique*. After mentioning it in the Introduction, he simply drops it for the remainder of the book.

The new faculty of judgement is equally surprising. In the first *Critique*, Kant presented the understanding as the faculty of judgement. He said, 'Now we can reduce all acts of the understanding to judgements, and the *understanding* may therefore be represented as a *faculty of judgement*' (A69/B94, tr. Kemp Smith). But he says that the new faculty of judgement performs a different function from that of the old one. He distinguishes two types of judgement, determinative and reflective (C_3 179–80). They are two ways of relating a particular (object) to a universal (concept). If the universal is given, judgement only subsumes the particular under it. This is the role of determinative judgement, which belongs to the understanding. On the other hand, if only the particular is given, judgement has to find a suitable universal for it. This is reflective judgement presumably because it requires reflection. Kant says that reflective judgement ascends from the particular to the universal, while determinative judgement descends from the universal to the particular. In the First Introduction to the third *Critique*, Kant explains this functional difference by using the categories and the concepts of reflection of the first *Critique* (C_3 211'–12'). The understanding begins with its pure concepts and makes judgements by subsuming empirical intuitions under them. The reflective judgement begins with empirical intuitions and forms empirical concepts on the basis of those intuitions. According to this view, all empirical judgements must be reflective. But that goes against Kant's general thesis in the third *Critique* that all reflective judgements are governed by a priori principles. Probably for this reason, Kant drops this characterization of reflective judgement in the Second Introduction to the third *Critique*. In its place, he tries to describe reflective judgements in terms of their content: the transcendental principle of purposiveness. 'Being purposive' is different from 'being purposeful'. The latter means an intentional purpose; the former has nothing to do with intention. To say that something is purposive means that it appears to have a purpose although it does not belong to an intentional agent.

Kant recognizes two types of purposiveness: formal and real. A beautiful flower pleases our aesthetic sensitivity. This function of the flower appears to be designed for our pleasure. This is its formal purposiveness. Compare the beautiful flower with a healthy heart. The latter has a real purpose; it performs a biological function for the body. Its function also appears to be designed for the body, but not for us the observers. This is its real purposiveness. The formal purposiveness is subjective; the real purposiveness is objective. Both of them concern the mereological relation of parts and whole. In an organic entity, its parts and whole sustain each other for the development of their common life. This is their teleology. A similar functional relation of parts and whole also obtains in a watch, but it is an external relation mechanically arranged by its maker. The teleology of an organic entity is internal to its nature. Kant believes that the internal relation of parts and whole is equally essential for appreciating beautiful objects although their relation is not fully teleological. In the relation of parts and whole, both a beautiful object and a living thing look like the products of a purposeful design.

The concepts of function and purpose involve values. For this reason, Kant associates reflective judgement with the notion of estimation and appraisal. When someone says that her cat is beautiful, it can be taken as a description and/or as an appraisal. So is the statement about a healthy heart. Fact and value mingle in reflective judgement. Hence it may be said to lie somewhere between the understanding and reason because the understanding is the faculty of descriptive judgement and reason is the faculty of evaluative judgement. But aesthetics and teleology cannot be accounted for by the first two *Critiques*. Biology is not one of the natural sciences that can be explained by the understanding and its categories. Those sciences are governed by the causal principle alone. There is no room for the concepts of living and dead and for the organic function of plants and animals in the first *Critique*. The second *Critique* involves the question of value, but it is restricted to moral value. To be sure, Kant discusses the value of happiness and desires in connection with moral value, but he never considers aesthetic values in his practical philosophy. He now recognizes the importance of both aesthetic and teleological judgements in human experience. By lumping them together under the new label of reflective judgement, he has set out to remedy the two serious omissions from his first two *Critiques*. He recognizes two types of aesthetic experience, the beautiful and the sublime, and divides his Critique of Aesthetic Judgement into the Analytic of the Beautiful and the Analytic of the Sublime. We will consider these two Analytics in sequence.

THE ANALYTIC OF THE BEAUTIFUL

Aesthetic judgement is also called the judgement of taste. It is always a singular judgement, for example, 'This rose is beautiful'. The general statement 'The roses are beautiful' cannot qualify as an aesthetic judgement because it should be free of all general and determinate concepts. Even the singular judgement 'This rose is beautiful' loses its purity as an aesthetic judgement because of the word 'rose' unless it is used only for the referential function of the subject of the proposition. To make it a purely aesthetic judgement, we should say, 'This is beautiful'. It should be free of all concepts. The word 'beautiful' does not represent a concept of beauty, according to Kant. It expresses the feeling of pleasure. To put it another way, 'This is beautiful' does not describe an object or a fact, but expresses the feeling of a subject. He reduces the property of being beautiful to the subjective feeling, which is free of all concepts. It is called the non-conceptuality of aesthetic feeling or judgement. It is a big mystery that feeling can make a judgement without using a concept. This is an emotive theory of judgement that contravenes the common notion of judgement. But there is an even bigger mystery in Kant's theory. If a judgement is made by feeling, it is bound to be subjective and empirical. But Kant insists that aesthetic judgements are objective because they are governed by an a priori principle. He will talk about these aesthetic mysteries in the Analytic of the Beautiful by using the four forms of aesthetic judgement: Quality, Quantity,

Relation, and Modality. They are called the four Moments. He has reduced the twelve judgement-forms of the first *Critique* to these four headings. Let us now look into these four Moments.

As to its Quality, Kant says, an aesthetic judgement is devoid of all interest. This is supposed to differentiate aesthetic judgement from the judgement of the agreeable and the moral judgement. The judgement of the agreeable is governed by the empirical interest of inclination, and the moral judgement by the rational interest of practical reason. Kant says that the pleasure of aesthetic judgement is neither the gratification of appetites nor the esteem for moral goodness. Therefore it is free of all interests. This is his doctrine of aesthetic disinterest. This doctrine is so contrary to our aesthetic experience that it has never been taken seriously. If aesthetic experience is pleasurable as Kant says, how can we have no interest in it? Pleasure and pain are bound to be matters of interest for all sentient beings. Kant equates the disinterest of aesthetic judgement with its indifference to the existence of its objects (C₃ 205). This is clearly counter-intuitive. We can never be indifferent to the existence of beautiful or ugly objects. The obvious truth is that aesthetic judgements are matters of aesthetic interest. But Kant allows no room for aesthetic interests by his argument of elimination. He recognizes no other human interest beside the empirical interest of inclination and the rational interest of practical reason. By this poor argument of elimination, he shuts his eyes to the very existence of aesthetic interests.

Kant admits only social interest in the beautiful. He says that someone abandoned on some desolate island would not even look for flowers and that we develop interest in beautiful things only by socialization (C₃ 297). This is again counter-intuitive. But he also lists the beautiful together with the agreeable and the good as three objects of liking (C₃ 210). If the beautiful is an object of liking, it must be an object of interest. But what does disinterest have to do with the quality of aesthetic judgement? In the first *Critique*, he said that the quality of judgements is determined by the nature of predicates (A72/B97). The predicate in an aesthetic judgement ('This is beautiful') is 'being beautiful'. Kant may be trying to clarify the nature of this predicate by saying that it does not describe a property of an object, but only expresses a subjective feeling. This is to define beauty not in terms of objective properties, but in terms of aesthetic feeling. Then he has to distinguish aesthetic feeling from other feelings, but he cannot do it by saying that aesthetic feeling is the feeling of beauty because that will give a circular definition of beauty. This circularity can be avoided if aesthetic feeling can be defined as the feeling connected to no interest because all other feelings are connected to some interests. But that is impossible because there can be no feeling without any interest. Thus Kant's attempt to define beauty in terms of the feeling of disinterest is abortive.

The Second Moment of aesthetic judgement is its Quantity, its universality. But its universality is different from the universality of a universal judgement because aesthetic judgement is always singular. Its universality means its universal validity, which is supposed to follow from the First Moment of aesthetic judgement. That is, because aesthetic judgement is free of all interests, it cannot be influenced by private interests. Therefore it must hold for everyone. This is Kant's argument for the Second Moment. But we have discredited his doctrine of disinterest. For the sake of argument, let us grant that aesthetic judgement is free of all interests. In that case, it is a free-floating judgement, which can have no binding force. On the other hand, the universality of a judgement means its binding power on everyone. Therefore the disinterest of aesthetic judgement cannot ground its universality. Kant seems to feel that he needs more than disinterest to account for its universality. Because aesthetic judgement is free from all private interests, he says, it describes the beautiful as if beauty were a characteristic of the object (C₃ 211). His assertion means that aesthetic judgement is projecting beauty as the property of an object because it is free of all private interests. But he does not explain how aesthetic judgement makes this projection out of disinterest. If it has no interest whatsoever, it should make no projection at all. If it has the freedom from all interests, it should be able to make any projection it wants to. It is impossible to predict what must or can come out of disinterest.

Kant's argument for the universality of aesthetic judgement is not limited to its disinterest. He compares the judgement of the agreeable with that of the beautiful. Whereas the former can vary from one person to another ('Everyone has his own taste'), he says, the latter must be universal (C₃ 212). If someone says, 'This poem is beautiful *for me*', he says, that would be ridiculous because that person does not even know what it means to make an aesthetic judgement. When one makes an aesthetic judgement, Kant believes, that person is demanding an agreement from all others. An aesthetic judgement is made not merely for oneself, but for all others. This argument is based on his idea of what it means to make an aesthetic judgement. But I do not know how many people share this idea with him. Even if all human beings share it with him, that alone cannot prove the universality of aesthetic judgement because its universality cannot be secured by their intention alone. When a religious person says that God exists, she surely intends that her statement is universal. But her intention has no influence whatsoever on the universality of her statement.

Kant then says that the universality of aesthetic judgement does not stand on concepts of the objects, that is, there is no objective ground for its universality because beauty is not an objective property. The subjective feeling of beauty is the basis for the universality of aesthetic judgement (C_3 215). This is the paradoxical feature of Kant's view. How can subjective feelings establish the universality of aesthetic judgement? This is the most difficult question for his aesthetic theory. He says that concepts are inadmissible for aesthetic judgement because they destroy the sense of beauty (C_3 215). In aesthetic judgement, it is not the concepts but the feeling that speaks with 'a universal voice' (C_3 216). This universal voice is the ground of universality, Kant says. In this regard, aesthetic feeling is radically different from other feelings. Feelings in general are assumed to be private and particular, but aesthetic feeling is now claimed to be universal. How and where does aesthetic feeling derive its universal voice? Kant may be answering this question when he says that the universal voice is only an Idea. But what sort of Idea is it? It must be the Platonic Idea of Beauty. If aesthetic feeling is governed by this Idea, it must be universal. Although a person may be unsure of making a judgement of taste in conformity with 'this Idea', Kant says, it is the object of his contemplation (C_3 216).

In the next section (§9), Kant just drops the Idea from his discussion and takes on the question of whether the feeling of pleasure precedes or succeeds the judgement. In the judgement of the agreeable, he says, the feeling of pleasure precedes the judgement. In the judgement of taste, on the other hand, the feeling of pleasure succeeds the judgement. The feeling of pleasure is the cause of judgement for the agreeable, but is the effect of judgement for the beautiful. This is obviously true for the agreeable. When I bite into a delicious apple, I taste the pleasure of its sweetness. That is the cause of my judgement, 'The apple is sweet'. But it is unlikely that an aesthetic judgement produces pleasure as its effect. When I am struck by a beautiful sunset, I can feel the aesthetic pleasure of the scene as immediately as the sweetness of an apple. My aesthetic judgement of the scene appears to follow the aesthetic pleasure just as my judgement on the apple follows my pleasure of tasting its sweetness. Therefore, both the judgement of taste and the judgement of the agreeable appear to be alike in being dictated by the feeling of pleasure. If they are produced by the pleasure of feeling, the judgement of taste cannot be free any more than the judgement of the agreeable. So Kant tries to make his case for their difference with his theory of free play for cognitive powers in aesthetic judgement.

In determinative judgement, the operation of imagination and understanding is not free because it is governed by determinate concepts. Their operation is free in aesthetic judgement because it involves no determinate concepts. Kant says that the subjective pleasure of aesthetic judgement is produced by the harmony of their free play (C_3 218). The pleasure arises from the quickening of imagination and understanding by their free play and reciprocal harmony. When I see a sunset, there are many ways of appreciating its beauty although it may strike me as immediately as the delicious taste of an apple. I can reflect on the relation of parts and whole in a beautiful sunset in various ways. The more I reflect on their relation, the deeper my appreciation of its beauty can become. Kant associates aesthetic pleasure with contemplation (C_3 222). Aesthetic reflection is contemplative. Without such reflection and contemplation, Kant may say, my pleasure of being struck by a sunset may not be any different from my pleasure of biting into a sweet apple. At most, the immediate pleasure of a sunset is no more than a stimulus for aesthetic reflection, if it is to be an aesthetic experience. Our aesthetic reflection can become even more complicated when we read a novel or listen to a sonata. But there are no fixed rules for conducting our aesthetic reflection. This free play of imagination and understanding produces the pleasurable feeling of making aesthetic judgements. Therefore, aesthetic pleasure can be described as the pleasure concomitant to aesthetic judgement. Even if aesthetic judgement and pleasure take place simultaneously, the pleasure is still an effect of the judgement. But Kant unwisely mixes up the pleasure of free play with the pleasure of communication with others. The free play of my imagination and understanding does not depend on my communication with others. I may gain some additional pleasure by communicating my aesthetic pleasure with others, but this additional pleasure is not aesthetic, but social.

The Third Moment handles the relation of aesthetic judgement to its object. The free play of cognitive faculties cannot produce pleasure by reflecting on an ugly object. But Kant cannot say that aesthetic pleasure is derived from a beautiful object because he does not recognize beauty as a property of an object. So he says that a judgement of taste is based on the form of purposiveness of an object (C_3 221). We have already noted that the word 'purposive' refers to the harmonious unity of parts in a whole, their mereological relation. Such a harmonious order appears to be designed for a purpose. When the harmonious order is a living entity, its purposiveness expresses a real purpose. When it is not living, its purposiveness has no real purpose. It has only the form of purposiveness without its content, which is also called the purposiveness without purpose or formal purposiveness. The aesthetic feeling of pleasure is derived from the formal purposiveness of an object. It is as though the harmonious order of a beautiful object were designed for the harmony of cognitive faculties. This may be called the subjective purposiveness of aesthetic objects in distinction from the objective purposiveness of organic entities. The objective purposiveness is a real function that serves the well-being of organic entities, for example, the function of a heart. The subjective purposiveness does not serve such an organic function, but only the affective function of occasioning the harmonious free play of cognitive powers for aesthetic pleasure. If the form of purposiveness provides the occasion for aesthetic pleasure, the object of aesthetic judgement plays a causal role. In that case, the causal relation of aesthetic qualities should be analogous to the causal relation of secondary qualities. Although secondary qualities are subjective, they represent some objective properties. Therefore Kant must admit some objective properties of the object for occasioning aesthetic pleasure. This is the objection by Karl Ameriks.[1]

Kant can meet this objection by naming the objective properties that constitute the formal or subjective purposiveness. If he can do it, he can give the definition of beauty in terms of objective properties. We have already noted that Kant cannot define beauty in terms of feeling because he has not found a way to discriminate aesthetic feeling from other feelings. He is now trying to define aesthetic feeling in terms of the formal or subjective purposiveness of an aesthetic object. But this attempt can become successful only if he can define the subjective purposiveness in terms of objective properties and meet Ameriks's objection. But this seems impossible for the following reasons. The properties of subjective purposiveness cannot be reduced to any physical properties like the vibrations of light and air that produce colours and sounds, because those properties belong to the relation of parts in a whole. Kant is trying to capture this mereological relation by using the form of purposiveness because the relation of parts and whole is a sort of form. But not all mereological relations produce aesthetic pleasure. Kant says that many flowers, birds, and crustaceans deliver aesthetic pleasure when they are viewed without knowing the natural teleology of their forms, that is, their objective purposiveness (C_3 290). But there are some flowers, birds, and crustaceans that are not beautiful, and yet each of them has its own mereological form. So he has to find a way to discriminate the pleasurable mereological forms from the displeasurable ones.

Objectively speaking, there is no difference between the form of a beautiful crustacean and that of an ugly one because both of them have a well-defined mereological order. But one of them has the subjective purposiveness, and the other does not. How can we determine which one does and which one does not? There is no way to make this determination except by appealing to our sense of pleasure. This is another way of saying that the formal purposiveness is not objective but subjective. In Kant's own words, it belongs not to objects, but to their representation by our cognitive faculties (C_3 221). For this reason, there is no way to define the formal purposiveness of an aesthetic object in terms of its objective properties. Consequently, there is no way to discriminate aesthetic feeling from other feelings in terms of aesthetic objects. Thus aesthetic feeling that defines beauty remains undefined even after it is connected to the formal purposiveness of an object. In short, Kant has not yet given a definition of beauty. This is surprising because the examination of aesthetic judgement in the Analytic of the Beautiful is meant to deliver a clear definition of beauty.

If Kant resorts to the subjective test of feeling in determining whether or not an object has a purposive form, he faces the danger of downgrading aesthetic judgement to the empirical level. Its empirical reduction would obliterate the distinction between the judgement of taste and the judgement of the agreeable. To avoid this danger is the most difficult feature of the Analytic of the Beautiful. Aesthetic judgement is bound to be empirical if it is based on feeling because feelings are empirical by their nature. Probably to ward off this empirical danger, Kant distinguishes pure from empirical aesthetic judgements. Aesthetic judgements are empirical if they contain empirical elements such as the sensation of charms and emotions. They are pure if they are solely concerned with the form of purposiveness. This has been known as Kant's aesthetic formalism. In the appraisal of art works, his formalism locates their beauty in their design and composition. He acknowledges that the empirical elements such as colours and tones are a matter of aesthetic judgement though they do not belong to its form. But he says that most people believe that those empirical elements are beautiful in their own right, when they talk about beautiful tones or colours. They are making empirical aesthetic judgements, which are distinctly different from pure aesthetic judgements (C_3 224). In his view, it is prejudicial even to say that the beauty of an object can be enhanced by such empirical elements as tones and colours.

Kant's aesthetic formalism, however, is open for widely different interpretations. The most extreme version is to restrict the form of beauty to its spatiotemporal form and separate it from the empirical factors for the sake of its purity. This has turned Kant's formalism into a laughing stock for making a scarecrow out of the sensuous feeling of beauty. But such a reduction of aesthetic form to the spatiotemporal form is already blocked by Kant's own theory of aesthetic judgement. Time and again, he has said that it cannot be based on determinate concepts. The spatiotemporal relations are governed by determinate concepts. Therefore, the aesthetic form must be much richer and broader than the spatiotemporal form. The former should include all sorts of symbolic relation and association. But Kant never tries to define the aesthetic form in such a rich and broad sense. Probably, he cannot do it. The definition of aesthetic form will involve the same difficulties that we encountered in the definition of the purposive form of an aesthetic object because these two are one and the same.

Whereas the spatiotemporal forms are rigid and determinate, the aesthetic form is flexible and indeterminate. A painting can be described purely in terms of its spatial form, but that cannot capture the aesthetic form that governs its design. Likewise, a musical composition can be described purely in terms of notes and sounds, but that cannot capture the aesthetic form that expresses its thematic development. The rigid and determinate spatiotemporal forms cannot provide any occasion for aesthetic reflection, but the flexible and indeterminate aesthetic forms can do it. Our aesthetic judgement is largely our reflection on aesthetic forms. Does the idea of aesthetic form apply to the objects of natural beauty as well as works of art? Kant would give an affirmative answer to this question. He would say that we should appreciate the beauty of those natural objects as though they were designed just like works of art. That is what is meant by saying that natural beauty lies in the form of purposiveness.

The idea of aesthetic form has one more advantage. It forestalls the separation of forms from their content because there can be no aesthetic forms without empirical content. But the empirical content must always be subservient to aesthetic forms. This is closely related to Kant's distinction between free and subservient beauty (C_3 229). Free beauty is autonomous. It solely stands on the pure aesthetic pleasure that arises from the formal properties of objects that occasion the free interplay of cognitive faculties. But beauty can become subservient to a determinate concept, which can set its own standard of perfection. Subservient beauty is manifested by the beauty of horses, human bodies, and church buildings. Even in our aesthetic judgement of these objects, our feelings are influenced by our conception of their perfection. Our idea of a beautiful church is different from our idea of a beautiful train station because our sense of beauty is subordinated to our concepts of church and train station. Free beauty is experienced in the beauty of flowers, birds, and crustaceans. When we appreciate their beauty, we may not even connect it to their biological functions because we know nothing about them. If we do, their beauty becomes subservient. Free beauty is based on pure aesthetic judgement, which is compromised neither by determinate concepts nor by empirical factors. But even pure and free beauty is not free of all rational concepts. On the contrary, Kant says, it is based on the Ideal of Beauty (C_3 232). It is an indeterminate Idea of a maximum or perfection, which cannot be defined in determinate terms. It can only be exemplified by concrete instances. This Ideal is the Idea that Kant introduced as the universal voice in the Second Moment. Now he calls it the archetype of taste and says that this archetype rests on an indeterminate Idea of reason.

If there is the archetype of beauty, it can solve all Kant's problems of defining beauty, aesthetic form, and aesthetic feeling. They can be easily defined in reference to the Ideal of Beauty. Why then does he not use it? This is the biggest mystery of the Analytic of the Beautiful. Instead of using the Ideal of Beauty, Kant talks about the difficulty of using it in aesthetic judgement. For such use, the Idea must be fixed rather than vague. It can be fixed only by a concept of objective purposivenss, the opposite concept of subjective purposiveness. The beauty that is appreciated by this sort of determinate Idea should belong not to the pure judgement of taste, but to the object of partly intellectual judgement. In short, the Idea of Beauty cannot be admitted in aesthetic judgement without compromising its purity. As a matter of fact, Kant says, an ideal of beautiful flowers, beautiful trees, or beautiful gardens is unthinkable, and even the ideal of their beauty based on their determinate purposes is equally inconceivable (C_3 233). He admits only one object, for which we can have the ideal of perfection. That is the moral perfection of human beings (C_3 235). That is the real and highest purposiveness. Thus he introduces the Idea of Beauty in the last section of the Third Moment only to deny its relevance for the judgement of taste.

Kant ends the Third Moment by saying that 'a judging by an ideal of beauty is not a mere judgement of taste' (C_3 236). This is the strange feature of the Third Moment. But it is understandable because the acceptance of the Idea of Beauty is incompatible with his aesthetic formalism, whose intent is to locate beauty not in the object but in the subjective feeling. The admission of the Idea of Beauty would locate beauty in the object. If the Idea of Beauty is exemplified in a beautiful object, its beauty should be its objective property. In Kant's own words, its purposiveness would be not subjective but objective. In that case, the aesthetic form of the object can be described by the simple predicate of 'being beautiful' rather than the cumbersome predicate of 'being purposive without purpose', which is dictated by Kant's decision to deny the existence of beauty as an objective property. As we will see later, he will eventually endorse the Platonic Idea of Beauty as the fountainhead of all beauty, natural or artificial. But for the moment, he is resisting the Idea of Beauty for the sake of aesthetic formalism.

The Fourth Moment of aesthetic judgement is its necessity, that is, it is necessarily valid. But its necessity cannot be explained by a priori concepts or intuitions. Kant says that its necessity means exemplary validity. But the concept of exemplary validity is highly complicated. He describes it as a necessity of the assent of everyone to a judgement that is regarded as an example of a universal rule that cannot be stated (C_3 237). When someone makes an aesthetic judgement, he says, that person offers it as an example of an ideal standard and has the right to demand that it be accepted by all others because everyone shares the same ideal standard. If there were no such objective principle or standard governing aesthetic judgement, it would have no necessity and be as contingent as the empirical taste of sense. Kant's introduction of an ideal standard is the most dramatic development in the Analytic of the Beautiful. So far, he has tried to secure the universality and objectivity of aesthetic judgements without using any standards. He has appealed only to the free interplay of cognitive faculties and its feelings. As we have already noted, this looks like an impossible task. He may have realized that there is no way to accomplish this impossible task without employing some ideal standard. But where is this ideal standard and what is it like? Amazingly, Kant identifies the ideal standard as a subjective principle, which determines only by feeling rather than by concepts (C_3 238). So he is still stuck with subjective feeling.

So our earlier question of how subjective feeling can make objective judgements becomes our new question of how subjective feeling can function as an ideal standard. The following appears to be Kant's answer to this new question. He says that aesthetic feeling is a special feeling shared by everyone. Therefore, he calls it a common sense, that is, common to everyone. He emphatically distinguishes this special common sense from common sense in the ordinary sense and describes the former by the Latin phrase, *sensus communis aestheticus*. In order to avoid confusion, let us call it aesthetic common sense. If it is the subjective feeling for making aesthetic judgements, it is just another label for the free interplay of cognitive powers. Hence this label is misleading because their free interplay is much more than a mere feeling. The feeling of aesthetic pleasure is only an outcome of the free interplay. Paul Guyer says that Kant gives three definitions of common sense: (1) as a principle, (2) as a feeling, and (3) as a faculty.[2] But these three definitions are different descriptions of the same aesthetic feeling. Aesthetic feeling is the principle of aesthetic judgements and the faculty for making them. Kant says that aesthetic common sense must be presupposed to account for the exemplary necessity of aesthetic judgement.

Kant has yet to explain how aesthetic common sense can account for the exemplary necessity of aesthetic judgement. To this end, he examines the operation of aesthetic common sense in §21. He describes it as the attunement of cognitive powers with the object and their harmony with each other. But his description is ambiguous enough to be taken on two levels: perceptual and aesthetic. If it is taken on the perceptual level, it is no different from the cooperation of imagination and understanding in the synthesis of the manifold intuition, as advocated in the Transcendental Deduction of the first *Critique*. But Kant does not stop there. He says that the attunement of cognitive powers varies in proportion, depending on objects (C_3 238). He never mentioned this sort of variation in the Transcendental Deduction. He goes on to say that there must be one attunement most conducive for the quickening of mental powers. He is talking about the stimulation of imagination and understanding for aesthetic judgements. He finally says that feeling is the only way to determine the most conducive attunement of cognitive powers. He is presumably referring to aesthetic feeling. If so, feeling is the final judge for determining the quality of the attunement of cognitive faculties. It is the final arbiter of aesthetic common sense. This is to take Kant's description of cognitive powers and their attunement on the aesthetic level. He has also described the cooperation between imagination and understanding on the perceptual level. Their cooperation is cognitive on the perceptual level, but affective on the aesthetic level. It produces perceptual knowledge in one case and the pleasure of feeling in the other.

There are two ways of understanding the relation between cognitive and aesthetic judgements. One is to place them on the same level, where they are exclusive of each other. If a judgement is cognitive, it cannot be aesthetic; if it is aesthetic, it cannot be cognitive. This view has been fostered by Kant's repeated emphasis on their difference. Time and again, he has said that concepts are inadmissible for aesthetic judgement because they destroy the sense of beauty. However, if concepts are not involved in aesthetic judgement, there is no way to explain the cooperation of imagination with the understanding. Without using concepts, moreover, it would be impossible to tell the beauty of a bird from the beauty of a horse. The cognitive distinction between a bird and a horse must be the precondition for the appreciation of their beauty. Therefore the relation of cognitive and aesthetic judgement should be understood as vertical rather than horizontal. The free play of imagination takes place not by getting rid of concepts, but by going beyond cognitive judgement. Aesthetic judgement supervenes on cognitive judgement. The harmony between imagination and understanding takes different forms for cognitive and aesthetic judgements. When the imagination is used for cognition, Kant says, it is subject to the restriction of the understanding. But the imagination is free from this restriction in aesthetic judgement (C_3 316–17). In cognitive judgement, the harmony of cognitive powers is achieved by the subordination of imagination to understanding. In aesthetic judgement, it is achieved by silencing the understanding and allowing the imagination its total freedom, which in turn produces the aesthetic feeling of pleasure. That establishes the aesthetic autonomy of imagination and the nonconceptuality of its aesthetic judgement.

In §21, Kant begins with the cognitive harmony of faculties on the perceptual level and then moves on to their harmony on the aesthetic level because the former is the basis for the latter. When he talks about their aesthetic harmony, he recognizes the gradation and variation of attunement, which is unlikely for their cognitive harmony. But it is inevitable if aesthetic judgement is the free play of imagination and if its feeling is unconstrained by the concepts of understanding. We have already considered this possibility in the Second Moment, where Kant introduces the free interplay of imagination and understanding. In the end, the ultimate free play belongs to the imagination. That spells a troublesome consequence for the necessity of aesthetic judgement. The free play of imagination and its feeling can issue in any number of different aesthetic judgements on the same object.[3] The multiplicity and diversity of aesthetic judgements can perhaps be controlled by ranking them in accordance with some aesthetic standard or principle. But this principle is supposed to be the feeling of imagination, the final arbiter of aesthetic common sense. How is it possible for the feeling of imagination to function as the aesthetic standard or principle and yet maintain the necessity and universality of aesthetic judgement? This is the most critical question for Kant's theory of aesthetic judgement and its aesthetic common sense.

In the last section of the Fourth Moment, Kant brings back the ideal standard. He says, 'This indeterminate norm of a common sense is presupposed by us' (C_3 239). 'This indeterminate norm of a common sense' is an ambiguous expression. It can mean the indeterminate norm that belongs to a common sense, or the indeterminate norm that is called a common sense. The former reading takes 'of' as the indication of possessive relation; the latter reading takes it as the indication of appositive relation as in 'the City of New York'. Kant himself is not sure which is the right way to take it. He asks whether such a common sense exists as a constitutive principle of aesthetic judgement or as a regulative principle of reason. If the common sense generates its own standard, it is a constitutive principle. If it only follows the Idea of reason, it is only a regulative principle. Then he rephrases the same question as whether taste is a natural and original faculty or only the idea of an ability yet to be acquired and therefore artificial. If taste is a constitutive principle, it is a natural and original faculty. On the other hand, if it is only a regulative principle, it is an ability to be acquired and exercised in accordance with the Idea of reason. Kant cannot decide whether aesthetic common sense is an original or acquired ability, a constitutive or regulative principle. That is, he cannot tell whether aesthetic common sense prescribes its own normative standard or derives it from the domain of Ideas. With this uncertainty, he concludes the Fourth Moment.

This uncertainty reveals a drastic change in Kant's position on the Ideal of Beauty. At the end of the Third Moment, he introduced it only to deny its relevance for aesthetic judgement. He was resisting its lure because it was incompatible with his aesthetic formalism. He is now recognizing the possibility of its support for the aesthetic common sense. He is weakening his resistance to the Ideal of Beauty because he begins to see more clearly its indispensability for aesthetic experience. But he can accept the Ideal only by abandoning his aesthetic formalism for the sake of aesthetic Platonism. So there is a tension between the two aesthetic theories. In aesthetic formalism, the autonomy of aesthetic common sense is total and absolute. But it has to be subordinated to the Idea of Beauty in aesthetic Platonism. This tension is analogous to the tension between Kant's ethical formalism and his ethical Platonism. As we have seen in the last chapter, practical reason has total autonomy for moral legislation in his ethical formalism. But it does not have such autonomy in his ethical Platonism because it derives moral laws from the transcendent Ideas. But total autonomy is not a total bliss because it is absolutely devoid of substantive standard. It is totally vacuous like a blank cheque. This was the reason why Kant had to abandon ethical formalism, as we noted in the last chapter. Now he is driven into the vacuous emotive trap of aesthetic formalism. He now realizes that the totally free feeling of aesthetic pleasure is too nebulous to provide the solid foundation for the objectivity and universality of aesthetic judgements.

In the General Comment on the Analytic of the Beautiful, Kant mulls over the tension between freedom and lawfulness in aesthetic judgement. He says that it is a contradiction to say that the imagination is free and yet lawful (C_3 241). This is the first time that Kant mentions the lawfulness of aesthetic judgement. Evidently he has seen its importance after stressing the freedom of imagination. He then says that the law is given by the understanding alone. If the imagination is compelled to follow a law of the understanding, it cannot be free. Therefore, Kant says, the free play of imagination must be lawful without a law. That is indeed a contradiction, which reflects the tension embedded in the two alternative ways of understanding the free play of cognitive powers. Their interplay has absolute freedom in aesthetic formalism, but only constrained freedom in aesthetic Platonism. The latter is governed by Platonic Ideas, but the former is free of this Platonic constraint. There was the same tension between the total autonomy of Kant's ethical formalism and the constrained autonomy (or heteronomy) of his ethical Platonism. Although he does not mention the Idea of Beauty by name, it is on his mind when he talks about the 'indeterminate norm of a common sense', which was considered in §22. But he makes no attempt to resolve the tension before concluding the Analytic of the Beautiful. Probably, he has no idea how to do it because he is firmly trapped in his aesthetic formalism.

THE ANALYTIC OF THE SUBLIME

When Kant moves into the Analytic of the Sublime, his exposition shows two radical changes. First, he abandons the format of Four Moments, the hallmark of his formalism. Second, he brings the Ideas of reason to the forefront, the foundation of his normative Platonism. In the opening paragraph, he says that we refer both the beautiful and the sublime to indeterminate concepts. He is now willing to use the indeterminate concepts for his account of not only the sublime, but also the beautiful. The use of indeterminate concepts for the account of the beautiful is the repudiation of aesthetic formalism in the Analytic of the Beautiful, which stressed the non-conceptuality of aesthetic judgements. The beautiful exhibits an indeterminate concept of the understanding, Kant says, while the sublime exhibits an indeterminate concept of reason (C_3 244). The distinction between the beautiful and the sublime corresponds to the demarcation between the understanding and reason. The beauty of nature is contained within the boundary of perceptual experience; the sublime is the experience of its majesty that breaks open all finite boundaries. Whereas the experience of beauty involves the harmony of imagination and understanding, the experience of the sublime derives from the discrepancy between sensibility and the Ideas of reason (C_3 257).

Kant divides the sublime into the mathematically sublime and the dynamically sublime. This distinction follows the distinction between the mathematical and the dynamical categories in the first *Critique*. The mathematically sublime exhibits the majesty of nature in terms of its immense magnitude, for example, a soaring mountain or a boundless ocean. The dynamically sublime displays its majesty in terms of its awesome power, for example, lightning and thunder. But these natural scenes and events are not truly sublime in themselves. So Kant says that sublimity must not be sought in nature, but in our Ideas (C_3 250). The natural scenes and events can only evoke the sense of sublimity by stimulating the imagination to be in tune with the Idea of infinity (C_3 255). Whereas the beautiful produces the feeling of pleasure and comfort, the sublime induces the feeling of terror and respect. In order for the mind to be attuned to the feeling of the sublime, Kant says, it must be receptive to Ideas and culture is required to gain such receptivity. But he insists that cultural training cannot create the sensitivity to the sublime. It can only refine the receptivity of common sense (C_3 265).

This remark echoes back to Kant's question in the Fourth Moment of the Analytic of the Beautiful, whether aesthetic common sense is an original and natural faculty or an ability acquired by training in the domain of Ideas. He is now giving his answer to this question: It is a natural faculty that can be developed by training. Although the feeling of the sublime is rooted in the trained sensibility, Kant still insists that the judgement of the sublime is necessary because it is based on an a priori principle (C_3 266). But he does not identify this a priori principle. It is obviously the Idea of reason that is involved in the experience of the sublime. By presupposing the Idea of reason, it is so much easier to make a case for the necessity and universality of aesthetic judgements even in the domain of feeling, namely, the feeling of sublimity. In fact, he does not even argue for it as he did for the necessity and universality of aesthetic judgement in the Analytic of the Beautiful, where he tried to do it without the Idea of reason. So he argued for the universality and necessity of aesthetic feeling by using the feeling itself as its own principle and standard. That was as senseless as it is to pick up oneself by one's own bootstraps. This is the basic difference between his aesthetic formalism and aesthetic Platonism.

By the power of the sublime, Kant says, the imagination expands its scope beyond the sensible world and feels out for the supersensible world of Ideas. Hence the feeling for the sublime is very much like the feeling for moral law (C_3 268, 271). But he never identifies the two. The feeling of the sublime is only an analogue to the feeling of moral law. The Ideas of reason radiate pervasively throughout the Analytic of the Sublime and defuse Kant's aesthetic formalism of the Analytic of the Beautiful. The form of purposiveness is not even mentioned in his account of the sublime. But Henry Allison says that the purposive forms are none other than the expression of aesthetic ideas.[4] In support of this claim, he cites Kant's own statement, 'that cipher through which nature speaks to us figuratively in its beautiful forms' (C_3 301). But 'the beautiful forms' are not the same as 'the purposive forms' in Kant's lexicon. The expression 'the beautiful forms' assigns the property of being beautiful to the forms. But the expression 'the purposive form' does not assign the property of being beautiful to the forms, but only the property of being purposive. The latter property occasions the aesthetic feeling of pleasure. Kant never says that the aesthetic feeling is produced by beautiful forms because he cannot say it without presupposing the existence of the property of being beautiful in the object. His theory of the beautiful is to locate beauty not in the object, but in the subjective feeling. 'The purposive form' is the counterpart of aesthetic formalism to 'the beautiful form' of aesthetic Platonism. By the time he uses the expression 'the beautiful forms', Kant is already moving out of aesthetic formalism into aesthetic Platonism.

Kant's aesthetic Platonism becomes full blown in his theory of fine arts. The creative activity of artistic genius is guided by aesthetic Ideas. In his discussion of fine arts, he says that beauty (whether of nature or of art) may be called the expression of aesthetic Ideas (C_3 320). He is redefining beauty in terms of aesthetic Ideas, thereby extending his aesthetic Platonism from the domain of sublimity to that of beauty. He is abandoning the formalist definition of beauty in terms of purposive forms. If beauty expresses aesthetic Ideas, it cannot be a mere subjective feeling but must be an objective property because whatever expresses or reflects an Idea is objective. What is intentionally created by artists cannot be subjective any more than what is intentionally done in our moral acts can be subjective. In the Analytic of the Beautiful, to be sure, Kant talks about Ideas three times but he never connects them to his aesthetic formalism. In the Second Moment, he tries to connect an Idea not to the purposive form, but to the universality of aesthetic judgement. In the last section of the Third Moment, he introduces the Ideal of Beauty only to deny its relevance for aesthetic judgement. In the last section of the Fourth Moment, he considers the ideal standard of beauty for aesthetic common sense, but ends his discussion by expressing his uncertainty over its role. He tries to adhere to his aesthetic formalism by suppressing the Ideas of reason throughout the Analytic of the Beautiful. Thus the Analytic of the Beautiful is controlled by aesthetic formalism, and the Analytic of the Sublime by aesthetic Platonism. But these two aesthetic theories cannot be unified in one theory because they are diametrically opposed as the subjective and the objective theory of the same phenomena. Their opposition most clearly shows up in the Deduction of Pure Aesthetic Judgements.

Kant says that the Deduction is limited to the beautiful; it does not cover the sublime. He explains why this has to be the case. The beautiful belongs to the form of purposiveness, but the sublime is formless and unpurposive (C$_3$ 279–80). If the sublime is formless, its nature cannot be explicated by aesthetic formalism. As we have seen, our sense of sublimity involves the Ideas of reason. Kant says that the analysis of the sublime has already shown its a priori foundation, namely, the Ideas of reason. Therefore, he says, its analysis is the exposition of aesthetic judgement for the sublime and also its deduction. And its exposition is relatively simple, too. But such a simple procedure is not available for the deduction of aesthetic judgements for the beautiful because it does not employ the Ideas of reason. So Kant has to give complicated arguments in Sections 31 through 40, where he appears to restate his aesthetic formalism of the Analytic of the Beautiful. But his restatement diverges from the Four Moments on the question of standards for aesthetic judgement. In the Four Moments, he mentioned the Idea of Beauty three times. In the Deduction of Aesthetic Judgements, he does not mention it even once. He tries his best to keep his aesthetic formalism from getting contaminated by aesthetic Platonism.

Kant insists on the harmonious interplay of imagination and understanding as the only a priori foundation for aesthetic judgement. In §35, Kant brings back the paradox of freedom and lawfulness in aesthetic judgement that was discussed in the General Comment on the Four Moments. This paradox could be resolved by appealing to the Idea of Beauty, as we noted earlier. But Kant eliminates the paradox instead of resolving it. He had created the paradox by assigning both freedom and lawfulness to the imagination. He now changes their assignment by giving freedom to the imagination and lawfulness to the understanding. In §21, he recognized the variation and gradation of the proportion between imagination and understanding, the obvious source for the indeterminacy of aesthetic judgements. But he removes it by talking about 'the proportion between these cognitive powers' minus its variation and gradation. Thus he secures the universality of aesthetic judgement by placing a straightjacket on the interplay of imagination and understanding. Nor does he say anything about how the proportion of cognitive powers is determined. In §22, he talked about the indeterminate and ideal standard embedded in aesthetic common sense and wondered whether it was constitutive or regulative. In §40, he restates his view of aesthetic common sense, but says nothing about its indeterminate standard. He only stresses the communicability of common sense. Thus, he has purged his aesthetic formalism of all traces of aesthetic Platonism and removed all elements of indeterminacy from the supposedly free interplay of cognitive powers, thereby securing the uniformity of aesthetic judgements.

Kant's transcendental deduction of aesthetic judgement turns out to be a transcendental reduction of multiplicity to uniformity. Probably, there is no other way to secure the necessity and universality of aesthetic judgements within the framework of his aesthetic formalism because it is a formalism without forms. It is solely based on the feeling of aesthetic pleasure. In the Analytic of the Beautiful, Kant has tried to establish his aesthetic formalism by transforming the feeling of aesthetic pleasure into the forms of aesthetic judgement. This transformation is the opposite process to that of transforming formal functions into substantive ones, which was demonstrated in Kant's alleged conversion of formal categories into substantive ones. But these two operations are two different versions of the same Kantian transubstantivation. One of them converts formal properties and functions into substantive ones; the other converts substantive properties and functions into formal ones. The latter is designed to provide emotive forms for aesthetic feelings; the former is designed to provide conceptual forms for sensory perceptions. But both operations turn out to be abortive because they are logically impossible to execute.

Kant defines fine art as the activity of aesthetic freedom. Its free creative act is much like the free play of imagination in aesthetic judgement. Neither of them can be governed by definite rules. Kant assigns the creative power of aesthetic freedom to genius and calls fine art the art of genius. The artistic genius is the agent, through which nature gives the rule to art. But the rule is indeterminate and inimitable; its originality cannot be duplicated. In this regard, Kant says, a great artist like Homer is different from a great scientist like Newton. The latter's work can be described in determinate rules and concepts. Kant says that the artistic genius derives the creative spirit from aesthetic Ideas. He defines the aesthetic Idea as the imagery of the imagination that prompts much thought for artistic production (C_3 314). An aesthetic Idea is the opposite of a rational Idea. No concept can be adequate for the former; no intuition can be adequate for the latter. This is a remarkable change in Kant's conception of Ideas. In the first two *Critiques*, he had recognized only purely rational Ideas. But the aesthetic Ideas are accessible to sensibility, and the formation of these Ideas belongs to artistic imagination. A poet creates an aesthetic Idea by providing imagery to rational ideas of invisible entities such as the realm of redemption and damnation, eternity and creation, virtues and vices, etc. The poetic imagery is too rich to be described in concepts, and its richness prompts and expands the poetic imagination (C_3 315). None of these things can be reduced to a set of determinate rules. But the absence of rules can also create trivia and anarchy. The originality of art depends on the originality of aesthetic Ideas. These Ideas are the thematic Ideas of artworks. They are indispensable not only for the production of artworks, but also for their appreciation. Kant says that we cannot talk about the aesthetic themes of music and poetry without reference to aesthetic Ideas (C_3 328).

Because aesthetic Ideas belong to the imagination of artistic genius, they are not transcendent but immanent. The immanent aesthetic Ideas are created by articulating the transcendent Idea of Beauty for the phenomenal world. Seven years after the third *Critique*, Kant extended the construction of immanent Ideas to the ethical domain in the *Metaphysics of Morals*, where he paraded a battery of immanent ethical Ideas ranging from the Idea of social contract to the Idea of a republican constitution as we noted in the last chapter. Those immanent Ideas are created by articulating the transcendent Idea of Justice for the phenomenal world. The construction of these ethical Ideas is analogous to the construction of aesthetic Ideas. Both of them are the descent of Platonic Ideas to the phenomenal world.

THE DIALECTIC OF AESTHETIC JUDGEMENT

Kant recognizes only one antinomy in the Dialectic of Aesthetic Judgement.

(1) Thesis: A judgement of taste is not based on concepts.
(2) Antithesis: A judgement of taste is based on concepts.

Kant notes that the concepts involved in this dispute can be taken to be determinate or indeterminate. The thesis is true if it is formulated in terms of determinate concepts, but false if it is formulated in terms of indeterminate concepts. The converse is the case for the antithesis. Thus the antinomy arises from the ambiguity of the word 'concepts'. By clarifying this ambiguity, Kant resolves the antinomy: Aesthetic judgements do employ concepts, but only indeterminate ones. But the antinomy and its resolution make sense only in the context of aesthetic Platonism, which accepts indeterminate concepts. They make no sense in the context of aesthetic formalism, which accepts no concepts whatsoever, determinate or indeterminate. In the context of aesthetic formalism, which stresses the non-conceptuality of aesthetic judgement, it makes no sense to argue whether or not a judgement of taste is based on concepts. Hence neither the thesis nor the antithesis of the aesthetic antinomy can be stated in the language of aesthetic formalism. Nor can it make any sense of Kant's resolution of the antinomy because it is equally incompatible with the non-conceptuality of aesthetic judgements. But most commentators have tried to understand the antinomy and its resolution in the context of aesthetic formalism as expounded in the Analytic of the Beautiful, because they have never recognized Kant's aesthetic Platonism. Amazingly, however, none of them has ever said that the aesthetic antinomy and its resolution make no sense because they are formulated in terms of concepts. None of them has ever pointed out their incompatibility with the non-conceptuality of aesthetic judgements.

Most commentators have respectfully accepted Kant's formulation of the aesthetic antinomy and his resolution. But they have complained about one thing. After resolving his antinomy in terms of indeterminate concepts, Kant says that those indeterminate concepts are connected to the supersensible because no intuition can determine them (C_3 340). He even calls it the supersensible substrate of humanity. Most commentators have felt simply paralysed by this move to the supersensible world because Kant has never mentioned the supersensible in the Analytic of the Beautiful. Since the supersensible makes no sense, many scholars have tried to understand Kant's resolution of the antinomy without the supersensible. For example, Paul Guyer has bravely suggested that the concept of the supersensible substrate be substituted by the concept of the harmony of cognitive faculties. Because their harmony cannot be specified by any rule, he says, the concept of their harmony can meet the requirement of being an indeterminate concept.[5] He duly concedes that their harmony belongs not to the supersensible, but to the sensible world. Even then, the concept of their harmony cannot be an indeterminate concept employed in aesthetic judgements. To be sure, aesthetic judgements are made by the free interplay and harmony of imagination and understanding. But they are not based on the concept of their harmony. Moreover, the word 'concept' is used in its plural form ('concepts') in the formulation of the thesis and the antithesis. But the concept of the harmony of cognitive faculties is a single concept. These are the obvious objections to Guyer's proposal.

Henry Allison tries to improve upon Guyer's proposal by replacing the concept of the harmony of cognitive faculties with the concept of the beautiful. Since the feeling of beauty arises from the harmony of cognitive faculties, to replace the concept of their harmony with the concept of the beautiful can be regarded as a refinement of Guyer's proposal. Allison says that the concept of the beautiful is the indeterminate concept required for the resolution of the antinomy and that this indeterminate concept can be counted as a concept of the supersensible. But there are a few obstacles to this contention. First, the concept of the beautiful is only one concept, but Kant talks about more than one concept in the antinomy and in its resolution. Second, he has never said that aesthetic judgements are based on the concept of the beautiful in the Analytic of the Beautiful. His project is to explain the nature of beauty by the subjective feeling of purposive forms. This is the central point of his aesthetic formalism. Fully aware of this point, Allison identifies the concept of the beautiful with the form of purposiveness.[6] However, the form of purposiveness is not a concept but a form of feeling. Third, as long as we stay within the bounds of Kant's aesthetic formalism, we cannot say that the concept of the beautiful is an Idea of reason because he assigns the beautiful to the domain of understanding. But Allison says, 'The concept [of the beautiful] can likewise lay claim to being an idea of reason, or at least involve such an idea.'[7] But he presents no textual support for this view.

Kant calls the beautiful an indeterminate concept of the understanding and the sublime an indeterminate concept of reason (C_3 244). Neither Allison nor Guyer can find the adequate indeterminate concepts for the resolution of the aesthetic antinomy because both of them are trapped in Kant's aesthetic formalism. But those indeterminate concepts abound in his aesthetic Platonism. Those indeterminate concepts are aesthetic Ideas. As we noted earlier, the aesthetic Ideas are created by articulating the transcendent Idea of Beauty for the phenomenal world. The transcendent Idea is one supersensible concept, but there are many aesthetic Ideas. The formulation of the antinomy does not directly involve the former, but only the latter. The indeterminate concepts that are directly involved in the formulation of the antinomy are stated in the plural (It is the dispute whether or not a judgement of taste is based on *concepts*), because they are aesthetic Ideas. But all of them can be traced back to one supersensible concept, the transcendent Idea of Beauty. This is the supersensible substrate of all beautiful objects. But Kant calls it the supersensible substrate of a judging subject and humanity as well (C_3 340). He may be referring to the noumenal substrate of a judging subject and human beings because human beings have access to the transcendent Ideas as noumenal beings.

It is impossible even to imagine that Kant has formulated the aesthetic antinomy and its resolution in terms of aesthetic Ideas as long as one takes the Analytic of the Beautiful as the foundation of his aesthetic theory. But the Analytic of the Beautiful is only the first part of Kant's aesthetics; it is succeeded by the Analytic of the Sublime and Kant's theory of fine arts. These succeeding parts have paraded a series of aesthetic Ideas, thereby replacing aesthetic formalism with aesthetic Platonism. We have noted that Kant even redefines beauty (whether of nature or of art) in terms of aesthetic Ideas (C_3 320). Once this textual development is recognized, it is impossible not to think of aesthetic Ideas in reading the antinomy and its resolution. For those who cannot keep up with the textual development, Kant provides a gentle reminder in the Comment that follows the resolution of the antinomy, where he gives an extended discussion of aesthetic Ideas. Given this sequence of his expositions, it is most natural to identify the indeterminate concepts with aesthetic Ideas. By virtue of these Ideas, it is possible to have meaningful disputes on the beauty of artworks and nature. Without an appeal to these Ideas, all aesthetic disputes would be pointless. Kant has in mind the kind of disputes we have on the beauty of literary works and musical compositions. But these disputes cannot be clearly settled because they are based on indeterminate thematic Ideas. Kant notes this point by adding parenthetical statements to the antinomy. In support of the thesis, he says that aesthetic disputes cannot be resolved by proofs because they are not based on concepts. In support of the antithesis, he says that aesthetic disputes are still meaningful because they are based on concepts. These remarks make no sense unless they are placed in the context of aesthetic Ideas.

After the resolution of the antinomy, Kant again stresses the difference of aesthetic Ideas from rational Ideas. He also says that to recognize the role of aesthetic Ideas is what distinguishes rationalist aesthetics from empiricist aesthetics. He divides rationalist aesthetics into the realist and the idealist camps (C_3 347). The realist camp holds that the aesthetic Ideas are exemplified in the objective properties of nature. The idealist camp rejects this realist position and holds that those Ideas are only the subjective principles for aesthetic judgement. Kant aligns himself with the idealist camp for the following reason. Nature has no intention of producing beautiful objects. They are in fact produced by its mechanical operation. Because the beauty of nature lies in purposiveness without purpose, it is not objective but subjective. The same is true of the works of fine art (C_3 350). Kant talks as though he were crawling back to his aesthetic formalism. But that is implausible. If fine art is the expression of aesthetic Ideas by artistic genius, it is purposive with a real purpose. The beauty of artwork must be its objective property created by an artist.

Kant is confusing two issues: (1) whether or not beauty is created intentionally by nature and (2) whether beauty is a subjective feeling or an objective property. The debate between the two rationalist camps concerns (2), but Kant has taken it as (1). No rationalists have ever maintained that natural beauty is objective because it is created intentionally by nature. Question (1) has nothing to do with Question (2). The question whether something is objectively beautiful or not cannot be determined by asking whether it has been created intentionally or accidentally. A great number of things are ugly although they are created with the intention of creating beauty. There are also a great number of beautiful things that are created accidentally. Kant's faulty argument reflects his inability to make a clean break with his aesthetic formalism and subjectivism even after admitting the function of aesthetic Ideas. But those Ideas cannot be contained in the domain of subjective feeling.

NATURAL TELEOLOGY

Although the beauty of nature may be only its subjective purposiveness, its teleology is its objective purposiveness. But the natural purposiveness is different from what Kant calls the intellectual (intentional) purposiveness. When human beings act for a purpose, their purpose can be expressed in a concept. But the natural purpose cannot be conceptual because it is mindless. It can be either intrinsic or extrinsic. When grass becomes food for cattle and the latter feed predatory animals, this food chain is governed by extrinsic purposiveness. The intrinsic purposiveness governs the mutual relation of parts of an organism. It has been known as the final cause. This is the principle governing the life of an organism, which cannot be fully explained by the mechanical laws. Kant says that such an organic entity is both the cause and effect of itself (C_3 370). This is the classical conception of *causa sui* that has been used for the definition of God. In mechanical causation, a cause is never the same as its effect. But the *causa sui* is its own cause and effect. Kant explains it by taking a tree as an example. It has the power of self-organization and self-development, whereas a mechanical object such as a car or watch is an inert object designed by an external agent. Since the power of self-organization cannot be explained by the blind mechanism, Kant attributes it to Ideas.

He begins his analysis of teleological judgement by recounting Plato's story in the *Phaedo* of Socrates' conversion (C_3 363). Socrates was impressed with Anaxagoras' view that all things in nature were ordered not by dead matter but by the living mind. From this Socrates concluded that the mind could do this only by virtue of Ideas. Kant takes this as the essence of Plato's theory of Ideas. He says, 'For the concept of natural purposes leads reason into an order of things that is wholly different from that of a mere natural mechanism, which we no longer find adequate when we deal with such natural products. And hence the possibility of such a product is to be based on an idea' (C_3 377, tr. Pluhar). Thus the Ideas of reason again become important for Kant's teleology, as they were for his aesthetics. But he insists that the teleological Ideas are only subjective. He stresses the difference between physics and biology. Physics is the science of mechanical causation that studies the objective forces of nature and their operation. But the science of biology is not restricted to mechanical causation; it can give a teleological explanation of organisms. But it does not describe the objective forces of nature, whereas the mechanical explanation does. The teleological explanation solely belongs to our subjective way of understanding natural phenomena. This is the tension between mechanism and teleology, which generates the dialectic of teleological judgement.

Kant presents the antinomy of teleological judgement as the conflict of two maxims of reflective judgement (C_3 387).

(1) The first maxim of reflective judgement is the thesis: All production of material things and their forms must be understood in terms of merely mechanical laws.
(2) The second maxim of reflective judgement is the antithesis: Some products of material nature cannot be understood in terms of merely mechanical laws (that is, they require a different causal law, namely, of final causes).

Kant says that these maxims are the subjective rules that function as regulative principles rather than as constitutive ones. If the maxims are converted to constitutive principles, he says, they will read as follows:

(3) Thesis: All production of material things is governed by mechanical laws.
(4) Antithesis: Some production of material things is not governed by mechanical laws.

Because these two propositions are objective, Kant says, they contradict each other. They can make a true antinomy. But he says that there is no contradiction in the conflict of two maxims. So there are two pairs of antinomies for teleological judgements. For their distinction, let us call (1) and (2) the subjective antinomy of teleology and (3) and (4) the objective antinomy of teleology. The subjective antinomy is the conflict of subjective maxims; the objective antinomy is the conflict of objective principles. This distinction is important for understanding Kant's teleological theory as a whole. There is no contradiction in the subjective antinomy, he says, because the opposed maxims are not meant to be two rules of exclusion. The first maxim says that we should try to understand all things in terms of mechanical laws as far as possible. The phrase, 'as far as possible', should have been attached to the thesis to avoid its miscomprehension. When our mechanical explanation fails, Kant says, the second maxim allows us to understand natural phenomena in terms of final causes. Hence the two maxims are complementary. So he resolves the subjective antinomy by reconciling the two maxims with each other. But the same kind of reconciliation cannot be given to the objective antinomy because it is an outright contradiction.

The formulation of these antinomies, however, has presented some serious problems for attentive scholars. What is meant by 'mechanical laws'? In general, this expression has been taken as equivalent to 'causal laws' or even to the causal principle. This has been the natural response induced by Kant's own usage of 'mechanism' as just another name for the causal principle in the first two *Critiques*. But their presumed semantic equivalence makes the teleological antinomy incompatible with Kant's conception of causal laws or principle. In the first *Critique*, he treated the causal principle not as regulative but as constitutive. In the formulation of the teleological antinomy, he treats mechanical laws as regulative and reduces them to a subjective maxim. On this ground some attentive scholars have rejected the identification of mechanical laws with the causal laws or principle. Peter McLaughlin gives the most cogent argument for this rejection.[8] In the formulation of the teleological antinomy, he holds, Kant gives 'mechanism' a different meaning from that of the causal principle. Whereas the latter governs the temporal relation of events in their causal relation, the former governs the relation of parts and whole. Unlike the causal relation, the relation of parts and whole is not the temporal relation of succession because parts and whole operate simultaneously. Mechanism is the thesis that the nature of a whole is determined by the nature of its parts or their properties. Consider the function of a watch. It is completely determined by the operation of its parts. We can give a mechanical explanation of a watch, but not of a plant or animal. Kant says that it is absurd to attempt a mechanical explanation of organisms or to hope for another Newton for the science of biology (C_3 400). So there are two ways of understanding natural phenomena: mechanistic and organismic.

In §71, Kant discusses the peculiar relation of these two ways to human intelligence. He notes that they are not on a par for our intelligibility. The organismic understanding cannot give the same kind of intelligible explanation as the mechanistic understanding can. So Kant compares the human understanding with another possible form of understanding. The latter is supposed to be intuitive, whereas the former is discursive. But the intuitive understanding is not the same as the intuitive intellect that he talked about in the first *Critique*. The intuitive intellect is supposed to have intellectual intuition whereas our intuition is sensible. That is not the difference between the intuitive understanding and our discursive understanding. Kant imagines that the intuitive understanding operates in the opposite manner to our discursive understanding. Whereas the latter understands a whole in terms of its parts, the former understands parts in terms of their whole. He says that the discursive understanding uses a universal analytically. Its concept can be called an analytic universal; it is achieved by the analysis of a whole to its parts. On the other hand, the intuitive understanding is supposed to use a universal synthetically. Its concept may be called a synthetic universal.

But the expression 'synthetic universal' cannot capture the idea in question because a synthetic universal is liable to be construed as a universal generated by the synthesis of analytic universals, the reverse side of mechanism. A better expression may be 'an organismic universal' or 'a holistic (wholistic) universal', the concept of a whole that cannot be fully described by its parts. The concept of an analytic universal may also be better expressed as a mechanistic universal or as an atomistic universal because atomism is generally opposed to holism (or wholism). The antonym of 'holism' should be 'mereism'. 'Holism' is derived from the Greek word *holos* (whole); 'mereism' refers to the Greek word *meros* (part). I am introducing these technical terms to elucidate Kant's central point that the two types of understanding are opposite in the direction of their investigation. The intuitive understanding is holistic; our discursive understanding is mereistic. The latter understands the whole in terms of its parts; the former understands the parts in terms of their whole. The direction of their understanding is the direction of their explanation.

Kant says that the mechanical explanation is the peculiarity of our human understanding, that is, it is much more intelligible for us than the organismic explanation. Hence mechanism is the mark of true science for us whereas the opposite should be the case for the intuitive understanding. This is Kant's psychological account of our bias for mechanistic science. McLaughlin questions this psychological account. He believes that the mechanical peculiarity of our understanding has been shaped by the development of modern science, especially physics.[9] Its method has been known as the analytic-synthetic method. This is the scientific method of dividing a whole into parts and of explaining the nature of the whole by the properties of its parts and their interactions. In fact, I believe, Kant's own theory of analysis and synthesis that we noted in the first chapter is derived from this scientific tradition. From this arises his favourite expression, that we can understand only those things we can put together. What we can put together is the product of our synthesis, which is the reversal of mechanical analysis. The mechanical method is best exemplified by particle physics in its continuous division of matter into ever smaller particles and their isolation for the study of their properties. The method of mechanical analysis is the method of isolation.

McLaughlin does not notice that what Kant calls the method of intuitive understanding has also been an important feature of modern science, namely, biological and social sciences. The cells of an organism cannot be studied by isolating them from one another because they cannot function as cells in isolation. They can function only when they are linked with one another in an intricate network. This is especially true of neurons. A single isolated neuron is no longer a neuron. The study of cells and neurons requires the method of connection. They have to be connected with millions of others if they are to be observed in their organic function. There lies the practical difficulty of neuroscience and cellular biology, which is exactly the opposite to the practical difficulty of building huge accelerators for detecting infinitely small particles and measuring their imperceptible properties. Some biologists may even claim that they are studying cells and neurons by the purely mechanical method. But that is impossible because the purely mechanical method cannot be used without killing the objects of their study. An isolated cell can be studied only insofar as it is kept alive in an organic environment.

Does the study of a living organism require a basically different method from the method of studying dead matter? Consider the peculiar phenomenon of protein folding. In mechanical terms, all protein molecules are just chains of amino acids. But this mechanical account cannot explain their biological functions, which are determined by their shapes. The chains of amino acids coil and fold themselves into specific three-dimensional shapes, which are associated with specific biological functions. But we do not know the mechanical laws governing this process of coiling and folding. So we can say that the phenomenon of protein folding can be understood only functionally (or holistically), but not mechanically (or mereistically). Even the distinction between the living and the dead cannot be satisfactorily stated in mechanical terms because they are indistinguishable on the mechanical level. The phenomenon of life consists not in the mechanical relation of parts, but in their holistic relation. Hence we can intuitively distinguish the living from the dead by looking at the operation of a living organism as a whole even when we know nothing about the mechanical operation of its parts. The concept of living has its own intelligibility, which is clearly different from the concept of mechanical intelligibility. Hence the former may be irreducible to the latter.

These two ways of understanding constitute the debate in Kant's teleological antinomy. As he says, this antinomy can be stated as the conflict of two methodological views or the conflict of two ontological views. By treating the antinomy only as methodological, he avoids the ontological issue of whether organic entities are ultimately reducible to dead matter. But he takes up this issue in the last section of the Critique of Teleological Judgements before its Appendix. Although we should try to extend the mechanistic account of living things as far as we can, he holds, the organic entities can never be fully reduced to mechanical parts. Nor is it possible to substitute the concept of natural purposes for the mechanistic analysis and explanation. Kant regards the two principles of mechanism and organicism as equally indispensable for the understanding of biological phenomena. He proposes that the relation of these two principles be understood in an analogy to an engineer's design of a machine. The design begins with an idea and then it is realized by assembling materials in accordance with that idea. Those materials are the matter of the design; the initial idea is its form. The matter is subordinated to the form by mechanical laws (C_3 414). The form and matter of the design are united in the mind of the engineer. By this analogy, Kant proposes that the two principles of mechanism and teleology in nature are united in the supersensible mind. This is Kant's resolution of the teleological antinomy on the ontological level, although he does not call it so.

Kant's handling of teleology is unsatisfactory. He has resolved the antinomy as the conflict of two maxims. But the maxims are subjective rules. If the two principles of mechanism and teleology are only subjective maxims, even mechanistic science should be understood only as a subjective science together with biology. I am not sure whether Kant would endorse this implication. The basic model of physics and chemistry is mechanistic. Chemistry explains the structure and function of a molecule in terms of its constituent atoms; nuclear physics explains the structure and function of an atom in terms of sub-atomic particles. Since these sciences are governed by the subjective maxim of mechanistic analysis, would Kant say that they are only our subjective way of looking at natural phenomena? How does the subjectivity of scientific maxims affect the objectivity of scientific investigation? Kant has not taken up this question. He also says that the natural purpose is an Idea. In his philosophy, an Idea is usually taken to be objective. But he says that the Idea of natural purpose only appears to be constitutive but regulative because it belongs to reflective judgement (C_3 405). In that case, teleological judgement should be as subjective as aesthetic judgement. We have extensively examined his struggle to generate the objectivity (universality and necessity) of aesthetic judgements from the subjective feeling of aesthetic pleasure. When he realized the futility of this struggle, he turned to the transcendent Idea of Beauty. He may have to do the same for teleological judgements.

Kant opens his examination of teleological judgement by accepting the Idea of natural purpose as his premise, but still insists that it is not constitutive but only regulative. Does it mean that the concept of natural purpose is only our subjective way of looking at natural phenomena? This leads to the most critical question concerning reflective judgement in general: Is it subjective or objective? If aesthetic judgement is subjective, there can be no objective distinction between the beautiful and the ugly things. If it is objective, then the distinction between the beautiful and the ugly is objective. Kant evades the choice between these two positions even when he advocates aesthetic Platonism. As we noted earlier, he divides aesthetic rationalism into the realistic camp and the idealistic camp. By this division, he can say that aesthetic properties are not real but only ideal, that is, they are objective only for those who have the Idea of Beauty and aesthetic Ideas. He may take the same evasive position about teleological properties. But he holds that only the mechanical explanation is intelligible for us and the teleological explanation is not intelligible. We have already noted that this is his bias for mechanism, which can be justified only by his mereistic conception of intelligibility. Because of this preconception, he cannot fully appreciate the holistic approach of biological sciences.

Although Kant favours the mechanistic reduction of teleology, he is also convinced that the reduction can never be completed. This is really his resolution of what we earlier called the objective antinomy of teleological judgements. But he gives no reason for this resolution. He only says that there can be no Newton of biology. This assertion can be taken mechanistically or holistically. Taken mechanistically, it means that no one can ever figure out all the mechanical laws governing the phenomenon of life because those laws are too complicated for human intelligence. This is an untenable assertion because it is an empirical question whether it is possible or impossible to achieve a complete reduction of biology to mechanism. It can be settled only by the development of empirical science. But Kant's assertion can be taken in the holistic perspective: Even when all the mechanical laws governing life are discovered, it will still be impossible to explain why life emerges from the operation of those laws. Because the phenomenon of life consists in holistic connections as we noted earlier, it cannot be explained by its reduction to mechanical relations.

Probably, Kant is preoccupied with this holistic view because he goes on to consider a few traditional theories on the emergence of life from matter in §72. The strongest of them is hylozoism, the view that matter is not dead but alive and its living force can account for the natural purpose. But Kant dismisses it on the ground that we cannot even think of living matter and that the concept of living matter is self-contradictory because the essential character of matter is lifelessness (C_3 394). He then adds that we have no a priori insight into whether living matter is possible. In that case, we have no a priori insight into its impossibility, either. Therefore, it is only his metaphysical dogma that the essential character of matter is lifelessness.

In one regard, the hypothesis of living matter is better for the union of mechanism and teleology than the hypothesis of the supersensible. The former is an empirical hypothesis; the latter is a transcendent one. Kant inherited the latter hypothesis from Leibniz. As we already noted, Kant opens his Critique of Teleological Judgement by quoting Plato's story of Socrates' conversion from mechanism to teleology in the *Phaedo*. In all probability, Kant had got it from Leibniz. As a staunch Platonist, Leibniz was so impressed with the story that he inserted it as a note in his *Discourse on Metaphysics*. On many occasions, he cites this story to support his teleological view of nature against the Cartesians and their mechanistic view. But he does not reject mechanism. Instead he advocates its subordination to teleology as an essential feature of the pre-established harmony. This was his adaptation of teleological Platonism. Kant is accepting this Leibnizian version of teleological Platonism when he appeals to the supersensible for the resolution of the teleological antinomy. He also reinstates the Leibnizian pre-established harmony for the reconciliation of mechanism and teleology just as he did for the reconciliation of freedom and determinism.

NATURAL TELEOLOGY IN HUMAN HISTORY

In the Appendix to the Critique of Teleological Judgement, Kant raises the question of what is the ultimate purpose of nature as a whole. He locates it in the realization of the highest good as he had defined it in his moral theory. Since it can be realized only by human beings, he says, humankind is the ultimate purpose of nature as a whole (C_3 427). Human beings deserve this special station because of their rationality and morality. In the second *Critique*, he said that the highest good could be fully realized only in the eternal world of noumena. Now he is preaching that its realization is the ultimate purpose of nature. Thus he has entertained two ways for the realization of the highest good: noumenal and phenomenal. The postulate of immortality is necessary for the noumenal realization of the highest good, but not for its phenomenal realization. The former is Kant's retention of Christian legacy; the latter is his adoption of secular ethos, especially the spirit of progress that has been fostered by the Enlightenment and the French Revolution. In the secular mood, he tries to understand humankind as the children of Mother Nature and its historical development under the aegis of her providence.

In the chain of natural desires for happiness, Kant says, humanity is only a link no different from other animals even in the food chain. Human beings are special only for their ability and will to set their own goals. Only for this reason, they hold the title of lord of nature. As the lord of nature, they must not be subject to nature's purposes, but pursue their own purpose independent of nature. Such a purpose is to develop culture beyond nature (C_3 431). Kant divides culture into the culture of skill and the culture of discipline. The culture of skill is only for the promotion of happiness; the culture of discipline is for the liberation of the will from the despotism of desires and other natural chains, which make it impossible to pursue our own independent goals. Hence to develop the culture of discipline is the ultimate purpose of nature for humanity. But the culture of discipline is not a weapon against nature, because it is the development of natural endowment that enables humanity to transcend Mother Nature just the way children grow up and become independent of their mothers. This is the natural teleology for humanity as the children of Mother Nature.

The culture of discipline is what Kant called practical freedom ('the will's independence of coercion through sensuous impulses') in the first *Critique* (A534/B562). He has been impressed with Rousseau's idea that human beings can become truly human by subjugating their natural instinct and appetite, transcending the domain of nature, and establishing the domain of culture. Rousseau had adopted this idea of culture from Plato's teaching that human beings can become divine by transforming their beastly passions into virtues. 'The culture of discipline' is just another name for the culture of virtue as propounded by Plato for his ideal state in the *Republic*. Kant believes that the culture of discipline will enable humanity to establish their sovereignty over natural impulses and institute a civil society for the liberty and equality of all citizens. This will take human beings out of the state of nature, where the unconstrained freedom of each destroys the freedom of all. Civil society thus established by the force of reason will eventually spread and rule the whole world. Kant regards this as the final purpose of creation (C_3 435). He will reaffirm this conception of human destiny three years later in *Religion within the Boundaries of Mere Reason*, as we have seen in the last chapter. But he had published this idea six years earlier than the third *Critique*, in the *Idea for a Universal History from a Cosmopolitan Point of View* (1784). In this essay, he presents the Idea as the driving force for human history, as its title indicates. In the first *Critique*, he had said that history was the domain of practical reason just as nature was the object of theoretical reason (A807/B835). Now he tries to situate history in the matrix of nature, that is, how human culture evolves out of the chaotic state of nature. Although the human world appears to be chaotic, he says, we can discern its slow but steady evolution (KGS 8:17). In support of this view, he proposes nine theses for the following outline of human history.

It is Nature's purpose that human natural capacities be fully developed not in any individual but in the whole race. Nature intends that human beings use their capacities to work out their own way of securing their well-being. To this end, Nature has used the clever device of mutual antagonism or the unsocial sociability of human beings. These expressions of 'purpose' and 'intention' are Kant's way of talking about the natural purposiveness as defined in the Critique of Teleological Judgement. If human beings were not driven by their heartless competitive vanity and their insatiable desire for possession, he holds, all their excellent capacities would remain dormant. Through competition and antagonism, human beings conquer their inclination to indolence, awaken all their powers, and take the momentous step on a long journey from barbarism to culture. The development of human capacities, however, requires a social order with the greatest possible freedom. Such a social order is a perfectly just constitution in which mutual opposition between its members becomes consistent with freedom and justice. Hence, Kant says, to design a just civic constitution is the highest problem that Nature assigns to the human race. Such a civic constitution establishes a commonwealth. The passions that can be destructive in wild freedom can do the most good if they can be tamed in a civic union. But the commonwealth of individuals cannot be secured without securing peace and harmony among different nations. The same antagonism that sets individuals against each other also drives different nations into hostile relations. It will take a league of nations to secure peace and harmony among the sovereign states. Thus, the ultimate purpose of Nature is to lead humankind from the state of individual rivalry to the state of international harmony.

Five years after the third *Critique*, Kant restates and expands his conception of human destiny in *Perpetual Peace* (1795). For the evolution of humankind, he says, Nature has used the device of war. Humankind begins in the state of nature, which is a state of war, and scatters itself to the four corners of the world by a ceaseless war. But Kant says that war has also produced the legal order on three levels: civil law, the law of nations, and the law of world citizenship (KGS 8:365). He claims that these legal orders are the work of Nature. She produces them whether human beings will or not. How does Nature accomplish such a feat? Nature does this by placing different groups of people close to each other in antagonistic relations. Since they have to form themselves into states for their defence, war compels them to submit to public laws. War is the mother of political order. Of all political orders, Kant says, the republican constitution is the only fitting one for the rights of individuals. But it is the most difficult one to establish and even more difficult to preserve because of selfish human inclinations. Although many have said that a republic would have to be a nation of angels, Kant says, here again Nature comes to the aid of humankind by organizing the state in such a way that the power of selfish inclinations is contained by their mutual opposition (KGS 8:366). The republican constitution requires not virtuous people but an effective social order that balances selfish inclinations against each other for public benefits. Such a social order can be designed even for a race of devils if we know the mechanism of Nature.

Although a good constitution is not to be expected from morality, Kant says a good moral condition is to be expected only under a good constitution (KGS 8:366). Nature designs and produces a political order as a precondition for morality. This is only a figure of speech for talking about natural teleology, which is unconscious and unintentional. But this figure of speech can be justified as follows. As children of Nature, all human beings are born with their natural instinct for selfishness, which leads them into the state of perpetual war. But Mother Nature has also endowed them with intelligence and they have been driven to develop it to cope with the problem of war. They have eventually gained the ingenuity to move out of the state of war and to build a civil society for an orderly exercise of their freedom, thereby laying the ground for the flowering of culture. But a civil society restricted within the boundary of a single state is liable to be destroyed by the war of competing states. Therefore humankind is destined to extend the peaceful union of warring individuals to a similar union of warring states. This chain of events has been initiated by Mother Nature and her generous endowment. Therefore Kant can say that human history is the work of Mother Nature. She has not only given birth to humankind, but given it the power to realize the highest good.

It is about time for us to face the question that was raised at the beginning of this chapter: How does reflective judgement function as the mediator between Kant's two worlds of phenomena and noumena? As I have already said, he never provides a satisfactory account of its mediation. As Ernst Cassirer correctly notes, Kant does not give us 'even a hint' for understanding the mediation in question.[10] Therefore it has become the object of an endless guessing game. So I had better warn you against expecting too much from this guessing game. Let us first note that this question contains three questions. Since there are two types of reflective judgement, how does each of them mediate between the two worlds? This involves two questions because the mediation by aesthetic judgement need not be the same as the mediation by teleological judgement. This leads to the third question: How can these two types of reflective judgement explain the mediation required for morality? This question is Kant's most urgent problem for his entire philosophy, as he says in the Introduction to the last *Critique*. In his translator's Introduction to the last *Critique*,

Werner Pluhar explains the mediation in question as follows. Kant had asserted the existence of two supersensibles in the first two *Critiques*, creating the chasm between phenomena and noumena. These two supersensibles are to be mediated by the supersensible of the third *Critique* through the concept of purposiveness.[11] This account is off target. Two supersensibles cannot be mediated by a third one. What requires mediation is not the separation of two supersensibles from one another, but the separation of the sensible from the supersensible. But Pluhar is not the only one who has tried to use the supersensible for mediation. In fact, it has almost been the standard approach in this guessing game. For another example, Francis Coleman says that the supersensible is the *tertium quid* that harmonizes the dictates of nature with the command of morality.[12] This is again off target. The *tertium quid* must be associated not with the supersensible, but with reflective judgement.

Henry Allison has given a more thoughtful account of mediation than most. But his account is restricted to the role of aesthetic judgement.[13] He begins with the formal isomorphism between aesthetic judgement and moral experience. Both of them point to the supersensible. Kant regards natural beauty as a symbol of the moral good. On the basis of these facts, Allison says that the cultivation of aesthetic sensitivity prepares and facilitates our moral transition from the phenomenal to the noumenal world. This transition is the mediation between the two worlds. Allison is solely concerned with the problem of mediation for morality; he never talks about the mediation performed by aesthetic judgement itself. The role of aesthetic judgement is cited only as a propaedeutic for the transition to the supersensible world. Probably, Allison assumes that aesthetic judgement makes the same transition. In the Introduction to the third *Critique*, Kant indeed talks about the transition from the sensible to the supersensible. But he is more concerned with the influence of the supersensible on the sensible world, that is, how moral laws can be realized in the phenomenal world (C_3 176). This is the transition from the intelligible to the sensible world.

Henry Allison has considered only the transition from phenomena to noumena, but not the transition from noumena to phenomena. But Kant is concerned with the two-way transition. One is the upward transition from phenomena to noumena; the other is the downward transition from noumena to phenomena. The upward transition is for the recognition of moral law; the downward transition is for its realization. How does aesthetic judgement make these two transitions? There is no simple answer to this question because Kant has espoused two aesthetic theories, aesthetic formalism and aesthetic Platonism. In aesthetic formalism, reflective judgements are made by the subjective feeling directly induced by the free interplay of imagination and understanding. There is no need for mediation because their free interplay involves no supersensible world. But Kant's aesthetic Platonism presents the problem of mediation because the ultimate foundation of all aesthetic judgements is the Idea of Beauty that belongs to the noumenal world. This Idea is so transcendent and so abstract that it is not readily applicable to the phenomenal world. This is the chasm between phenomena and noumena. To fill this chasm, imagination and understanding construct aesthetic Ideas by articulating the transcendent Idea of Beauty in terms of sensible imagery. This is the way of artistic genius and its inspiration. In Platonic language, this is the descent of Ideas from Platonic Heaven to the natural world. In Kantian language, it is the mediation between phenomena and noumena, which is performed by the immanent aesthetic Ideas. This mediatory transition is made not only by human beings, but also by nature itself. As we noted earlier, Kant calls natural beauty the expression of aesthetic Ideas.

The same sort of two-way mediation takes place in teleological judgements. Kant says that natural purpose is a supersensible Idea that cannot be found in the blind mechanism of nature (C_3 377). Human beings make the upward transition for recognizing this Idea and the downward transition for realizing it in the natural world. But this mediation is made not only by human beings but also by natural teleology. On the highest level, there may be only one Idea of natural purpose. In the *Timaeus* (39e), Plato recognizes only one Idea of Life. But every species is governed by its own Idea of natural purpose. On this level, the multiplicity of teleological Ideas may correspond to the multiplicity of aesthetic Ideas. We may assume that the particular Ideas of natural purpose are generated by the articulation and specification of the transcendent Idea of Life, just as the particular aesthetic Ideas are generated by the articulation and specification of the transcendent Idea of Beauty. In the phenomenal world, the Ideas of Life are usually conjoined with the Ideas of Beauty.

When Kant names the objects of natural beauty, they are often living beings such as flowers, birds, and crustaceans. The power of life may well include the power of beauty. Thus Nature brings the Ideas of Life and Beauty together from the supersensible to the sensible world. This descent of Ideas is engineered by what Kant calls the technique of Nature, that is, Nature that works like an artist (C_3 390). This is her two-way mediation between phenomena and noumema. She creates living beings in the phenomenal world by bringing down the supersensible Ideas, and some of those living beings have the intelligence to apprehend the noumenal world. Our moral and aesthetic life is only a link in this creative cycle of natural teleology. Kant called this creative cycle the Providence of Mother Nature in his *Idea of a Universal History*.

When Kant wrote the *Groundwork*, he pitted morality against the whole world of Nature. The categorical imperative was conceived as a fierce command for the moral battle against the forces of natural inclination. He proclaimed that there was nothing absolutely good except the morally good will. Even if the good will had the misfortune of getting aborted by the niggardly provision of the stepmotherly Nature, he preached, it would still shine like a jewel (GMM 394). As moral agents, human beings are only the maltreated stepchildren of Mother Nature. So he tried to protect the absolute value of morality against the heartless forces of Nature by enclosing it in the innermost sanctuary of rational beings. He had assumed that the natural world was at best coldly indifferent and at worst cruelly hostile to the supersensible moral ideals. The material forces that are governed by mechanical laws are blind and indifferent to moral values. When they constitute human nature, they produce inclinations that have the perpetual propensity to contravene moral laws. With these ominous forces, the natural world can never allow human beings to feel the assurance of realizing their transcendent aspirations. Hence those aspirations may appear to be the vanity and folly of an unfortunate species that has been born as the most pathetic misfit of the earth. Kant expresses his anxiety over this precarious condition of humanity in the natural world by his talk over the daunting chasm between the sensible and the supersensible worlds. This anxiety has been hanging like a dark cloud over the two great wonders, with whose admiration he concluded the second *Critique* – the starry heaven and the moral law.

For a long time, Kant had revered Newton as the master of natural world and Rousseau as the master of spiritual world. But neither of these two masters could show him how to dispel the darkest cloud in his heart. Thus the two great wonders have turned into his ultimate problem of bridging the enormous chasm between phenomena and noumena. Without solving this problem, his lifelong enterprise would come to naught. He eventually finds the solution for his ultimate problem in Mother Nature by recognizing that she has been the original matrix for realizing the supersensible Ideas in the sensible world even before the birth of humanity and that even the moral and political destiny of humanity has been shaped under the aegis of her eternal providence. He could not see this cosmic truth for a long time because he had been blinded by his mechanistic view of the world. By dispelling his mechanistic view, he gained the vision of Mother Nature as the living force. His new vision is very much like Plato's conception of the natural world in the *Timaeus*, where the Demiurge as the spirit of the natural world (the World-Soul) creates all things in accordance with the eternal Ideas.

Plato began his philosophical career as a spiritual campaign against the amoral forces of nature and the immoral forces of human beings. He installed Socrates in the *Gorgias* to fight against Callicles, the avowed champion of amoral naturalism and immoral humanism. Socrates took the fanatical stand that one could be virtuous even in a totally immoral world and that one's soul could never be harmed by other people's immoral acts. In the *Phaedo* and the *Symposium*, Plato tried to secure a safe haven for the virtuous soul in the intelligible world of Ideas where it could never be affected by the immorality of the phenomenal world. But that could not provide a living community for moral individuals. In the *Republic*, he tried to provide one by constructing his ideal state because he had by then recognized the importance of a moral community for the moral life of individuals. But this was still insufficient because there was little hope of securing a just society in an amoral and irrational world. He recognized this point by the time he constructed the city of Magnesia in the *Laws*. So he wrote the *Timaeus* to lay out his conception of a rational and orderly universe. The opening of this dialogue claims that its cosmological discussion took place in accordance with an agreement made in a previous discussion on political constitution, which seems to refer to the political discussion in the *Republic*. But no such agreement was made at the conclusion of the *Republic*. Hence it has been a controversial topic among Plato scholars. I have interpreted it as Plato's fabrication to indicate his desire to present the *Timaeus* as the cosmological foundation for his ideal state of the *Republic* and for the city of Magnesia proposed in the *Laws*.[14]

In his teleological conception of natural order, Kant is reaffirming the Platonic faith in the rational order of Nature. He is retracing the ancient footprints of Plato's epic journey in search of a suitable natural order for the realization of eternal ideals. In this endeavour, Kant has revived the Platonic conception of Nature as the mother of all creation. This grand conception of Mother Nature became a groundswell for his intellectual heirs. It was fully appropriated by Goethe in his *Faust*, where Nature manifests her inexhaustible creative power as the Earth Spirit, the Eternal Mothers, and the Eternal Feminine. It inspired the supernatural naturalism of most Romantic philosophers and poets such as the Schlegel brothers, Ludwig Feuerbach, and even Richard Wagner and Friedrich Nietzsche.[15] This was one of Kant's precious legacies along with his conception of immanent Ideas.

The teleological nature is the living nature governed by Platonic Ideas. This beautiful and fertile nature is the final destination of our Kantian journey, which we have undertaken by following the transcendental thread from the beginning to the end of this book. But this thread has turned out to be not a simple string. It is woven of two uneven strands. One of them is a formalist strand; the other is a substantive one. The formalist strand is Kant's formalism that pervades his three *Critiques*, but his formalism is not uniform. In the first *Critique*, it is composed of the forms of intuition (space and time) and the forms of understanding (the categories). These two types of form constitute two different versions of formalism. One of them is the formalism of intuition; the other is the formalism of understanding. But the forms of intuition and the forms of understanding are alike in having their own substantive content. How do these two versions of formalism gain their content? This is not a difficult question for the forms of intuition because those forms come with their own content. That is why the forms of intuition do not require a transcendental deduction. But the pure concepts of understanding require a transcendental deduction because those forms are supposed to be purely logical forms without any content. Kant has tried to explain their substantive content by his metaphysical thesis that the substantive categories are generated by the transformation of purely logical categories. But we have seen that the alleged generation is a logically impossible operation. The formalism of the *Groundwork* is truly formal; it is limited to the logical principle of formal consistency. It can be called the logical formalism in distinction from the substantive formalism of the first *Critique*. But Kant transforms his logical formalism into a substantive one in the second *Critique* by surreptitiously employing Platonic Ideas. The formalism of the third *Critique* is different again from the logical and substantive versions. It is the formalism of aesthetic feelings that stands neither on pure concepts nor on a logical principle. Hence it can be called emotive formalism, which sounds like a contradiction in terms because feelings are generally assumed to be the content of experience rather than its form. Although these three versions of Kantian formalism share a common label, they provide altogether different forms of organizing human experience. Hence their difference has been the chief obstacle to unravelling the formalist connection of the three *Critiques*. In spite of their different forms, all three versions of Kant's formalism have turned out to be vacuous and abortive.

The substantive strand of our transcendental thread is spun out largely by Kant's use of Platonic Ideas. But the Platonic connection of the three *Critiques* is even more difficult to detect than their formalist connection because it is largely hidden. It is played out like a deep base tune submerged under the sonorous tune of formalism. In the first *Critique*, Kant even tries to dispense with Platonic Ideas on the ground that they are unnecessary for the knowledge of phenomena. But he introduces them as pure concepts of reason and acknowledges them as the foundation of normative philosophy in the Transcendental Dialectic and the Canon of Pure Reason. In the second *Critique*, Kant's deployment of Platonic Ideas is so deeply hidden beneath the formalist surface that the ideas have never been detected by Kant scholars. But his Platonic theme breaks out into the open in the middle of the third *Critique*, when he finally abandons his faltering formalist program and bravely espouses his revolutionary notion of immanent Ideas. This is the descent of transcendent Ideas from Platonic Heaven to the natural world, which radically changes Kant's conception of Nature. In the first *Critique*, he had conceived Nature as a chaotic world of subjective impressions that could gain a rational order only through the a priori laws imposed by human understanding. In the *Groundwork*, he again struggled with the chaotic natural world by confronting it this time as the world of natural inclinations. This world was supposed to be so unruly that he called it the ultimate source of all radical evil in human nature (R 19). He tried to control the world of natural inclinations by imposing moral laws just as he had imposed a priori natural laws on the world of empirical impressions for its order. But the descent of Platonic Ideas releases Nature from the shackles of humanly imposed moral and natural laws because she can operate with the power of her own immanent Ideas. Now we can see Mother Nature as the Eternal Feminine who has the inexhaustible power to procreate and sustain her countless children. Some of them can even transcend their natural state and create their cultural world by realizing her immanent Ideas. This is Kant's supernatural naturalism, which we have reached at long last in our transcendental journey through his tangled corpus.

REFERENCES

I. THEORETICAL REASON

1 Van Cleve, *Problems from Kant*, 147.
2 Guyer, *Kant and the Claims of Knowledge*, 91, 131.
3 Ameriks, *Interpreting Kant's Critiques*, 52.
4 Allison, *Kant's Transcendental Idealism*, 134–6.
5 Guyer, *Kant and the Claims of Knowledge*, 160.
6 A full discussion of the Paralogisms is given by Karl Ameriks, *Kant's Theory of Mind*.
7 Wood, 'Kant's Compatibilism'.
8 Hudson, *Kant's Compatibilism*.
9 Allison, *Kant's Theory of Freedom*, 5, 28, 34.

2. PRACTICAL REASON

1 Beck, *A Commentary on Kant's Critique of Practical Reason*, 192.
2 Paton, *The Categorical Imperative*, 139.
3 O'Neill, *Constructions of Reason*, 96–101.
4 Aune, *Kant's Theory of Morals*, 47–51, 56–8.
5 Korsgaard, 'Kant's Formula of Universal Law', 24–47.
6 O'Neill, *Constructions of Reason*, 99.
7 Hegel, *Phenomenology of Spirit*, 252–62.
8 Ameriks, *Interpreting Kant's Critiques*, 175.
9 Beck, *A Commentary on Kant's Critique of Practical Reason*, 247.
10 Russell, *Why I Am Not a Christian*, 13.
11 Silber, 'The Moral Good and the Natural Good'.
12 Gregor, *Laws of Freedom*, xii. Bruce Aune holds a similar view in *Kant's Theory of Morals*, 131–201.
13 O'Neill, *Acting on Principle*, 38–9, 72. Sullivan, *Immanuel Kant's Moral Theory*, 247.
14 Gregor, *Laws of Freedom*, 39. Aune endorses this view, *Kant's Theory of Morals*, 137–40.
15 Rawls, *Theory of Justice*, 251.

3. BEYOND THEORY AND PRACTICE

1 Ameriks, 'Kant and the Objectivity of Taste'.
2 Guyer, *Kant and the Claims of Taste*, 280.
3 This point is well stated by Paul Guyer in *Kant and the Claims of Taste*, 263.
4 Allison, *Kant's Theory of Taste*, 288–9.
5 Guyer, *Kant and the Claims of Taste*, 302.
6 Allison, *Kant's Theory of Taste*, 251.
7 Ibid., 250.
8 McLaughlin, *Kant's Critique of Teleology*, 152–80.
9 Ibid., 174–6.
10 Cassirer, *Kant's Life and Thought*, 331.
11 Pluhar, tr. *Critique of Judgement*, cii.
12 Coleman, *The Harmony of Reason*, 163.
13 Allison, *Kant's Theory of Taste*, 260–6.
14 This point is explained in my *Plato Rediscovered*, 269–75.
15 This point is fully discussed in my *Goethe, Nietzsche, and Wagner*.

BIBLIOGRAPHY

Allison, Henry. *Kant's Theory of Freedom*. Cambridge: Cambridge University Press, 1990.

Allison, Henry. *Kant's Theory of Taste*. Cambridge: Cambridge University Press, 2001.

Allison, Henry. *Kant's Transcendental Idealism*. New Haven: Yale University Press, 1983.

Ameriks, Karl. *Interpreting Kant's Critiques*. Oxford: Clarendon Press, 2003.

Ameriks, Karl. 'Kant and the Objectivity of Taste', *British Journal of Aesthetics* 23 (1983): 3–17.

Ameriks, Karl. *Kant's Theory of Mind*. Oxford: Clarendon Press. 1982.

Aune, Bruce. *Kant's Theory of Morals*. Princeton: Princeton University Press, 1979.

Beck, Lewis White. *A Commentary on Kant's Critique of Practical Reason*. Chicago: University of Chicago Press, 1960.

Bennett, Jonathan. *Kant's Analytic*. Cambridge: Cambridge University Press, 1966.

Cassirer, Ernst. *Kant's Life and Thought*. Trans. James Haden. New Haven: Yale University Press. 1981.

Coleman, Francis. *The Harmony of Reason: A Study in Kant's Aesthetics*. Pittsburgh: University of Pittsburgh Press, 1974.

Crawford, Donald. *Kant's Aesthetic Theory*. Madison: The University of Wisconsin Press, 1974.

Goethe. *Faust*. Trans. Stuart Atkins. Princeton: Princeton University Press, 1984.

Gregor, Mary. *Laws of Freedom*. Oxford: Basil Blackwell, 1963.

Guyer, Paul. *Kant and the Claims of Knowledge*. Cambridge: Cambridge University Press, 1987.

Guyer, Paul. *Kant and the Claims of Taste*, 2nd edn. Cambridge: Cambridge University Press, 1997.

Hegel. *Phenomenology of Spirit*. Trans. A. V. Miller. Oxford: Oxford University Press, 1977.

Henrich, Dieter. 'The Proof-Structure of Kant's Transcendental Deduction', *Review of Metaphysics* 22 (1969): 640–59.

Hudson, Hud. *Kant's Compatibilism*. Ithaca: Cornell University Press, 1994.

Korsgaard, Christine. 'Kant's Formula of Universal Law', *Pacific Philosophical Quarterly* 66 (1985): 24–47.

Kuehn, Manfred. *Kant: A Biography*. Cambridge: Cambridge University Press, 2001.

McLaughlin, Peter. *Kant's Critique of Teleology in Biological Explanation: Antinomy and Teleology*. Lewiston, NY: The Edwin Mellon Press, 1990.

Mill, John Stuart. *Utilitarianism*, 2nd edn. Indianapolis: Hackett, 2001.

Newton, Isaac. Optics: *A Treatise of the Reflections, Refractions, Inflections and Colors of Light*. New York: Dover Publications, 1952.

O'Neill, Onora. *Acting on Principle: An Essay on Kantian Ethics*. New York: Columbia University Press, 1975.

O'Neill, Onora. *Constructions of Reason: Explorations of Kant's Practical Philosophy*. Cambridge: Cambridge University Press, 1989.

Paton, H. J. *The Categorical Imperative: A Study in Kant's Moral Philosophy*. London: Hutchinson and Co., 1958.

Plato. *The Republic*. Trans. G. M. A. Grube. Indianapolis: Hackett, 1992.

Rawls, John. *Theory of Justice*. Cambridge, MA: Harvard University Press, 1971.

Russell, Bertrand. *Why I Am Not a Christian*. London: Watts, 1927.

Seung, T. K. *Goethe, Nietzsche, and Wagner: Their Spinozan Epics of Love and Power*. Larham, MD: Lexicon Books. 2006.

Seung, T. K. *Plato Rediscovered: Human Value and Social Order*. Larham, MD: Rowman and Littlefield, 1996.

Silber, John. 'The Moral Good and the Natural Good', *Review of Metaphysics* 36 (1982): 397–437.

Strawson, P. F. *The Bounds of Sense: An Essay on Kant's Critique of Pure Reason*. London: Methuen and Co., 1966.

Sullivan, Roger. *Immanuel Kant's Moral Theory*. Cambridge: Cambridge University Press, 1989.

Van Cleve, James. *Problems from Kant*. Oxford: Oxford University Press, 1999.

Wolff, Robert Paul. *The Autonomy of Reason: A Commentary on Kant's Groundwork of the Metaphysics of Morals*. New York: Harper and Row, 1973.

Wolff, Robert Paul. *Kant's Theory of Mental Activity: A Commentary on the Transcendental Analytic of the Critique of Pure Reason*. Cambridge, MA: Harvard University Press, 1963.

Wood, Allen. 'Kant's Compatibilism', in Allen Wood, ed., *Self and Nature in Kant's Philosophy*. Ithaca: Cornell University Press, 1984.

Wood, Allen. *Kant's Ethical Thought*. Cambridge: Cambridge University Press, 1999.

INDEX